THE LIFE OF BRIGADIER-GENERAL SIR SAMUEL BENTHAM, K.S.G.

M. S. (Maria Sophia) Bentham

www.GeneralBooksClub.com

Publication Data:

Title: The Life of Brigadier-General Sir Samuel Bentham, K.s.g. ;
Author: Bentham, M. S. (Maria Sophia), 1765-1858
Reprinted: 2010, General Books, Memphis, Tennessee, USA
Original Publisher: London : Longman, Green, Longman, and Roberts;
Publication date: 1862;
Subjects: History / General; History / General;
BISAC subject codes: HIS000000, HIS000000,

How We Made This Book for You
We made this book exclusively for you using patented Print on Demand technology.
First we scanned the original rare book using a robot which automatically flipped and photographed each page.
We automated the typing, proof reading and design of this book using Optical Character Recognition (OCR) software on the scanned copy. That let us keep your cost as low as possible.
If a book is very old, worn and the type is faded, this can result in numerous typos or missing text. This is also why our books don't have illustrations; the OCR software can't distinguish between an illustration and a smudge.
We understand how annoying typos, missing text or illustrations, foot notes in the text or an index that doesn't work, can be. That's why we provide a free digital copy of most books exactly as they were originally published. You can also use this PDF edition to read the book on the go. Simply go to our website (www.GeneralBooksClub.com) to check availability. And we provide a free trial membership in our book club so you can get free copies of other editions or related books.
OCR is not a perfect solution but we feel it's more important to make books available for a low price than not at all. So we warn readers on our website and in the descriptions we provide to book sellers that our books don't have illustrations and may have numerous typos or missing text. We also provide excerpts from books to book sellers and on our website so you can preview the quality of the book before buying it.
If you would prefer that we manually type, proof read and design your book so that it's perfect, simply contact us for the cost. Since many of our books only sell one or two copies, we have to split the production costs between those one or two buyers.

Frequently Asked Questions

Why are there so many typos in my paperback?
We created your book using OCR software that includes an automated spell check. Our OCR software is 99 percent accurate if the book is in good condition. Therefore, we try to get several copies of a book to get the best possible accuracy (which is very difficult for rare books more than a hundred years old). However, with up to 3,500 characters per page, even one percent is an annoying number of typos. We would really like to manually proof read and correct the typos. But since many of our books only sell a couple of copies that could add hundreds of dollars to the cover price. And nobody wants to pay that. If you need to see the original text, please check our website for a downloadable copy.

Why is the index and table of contents missing (or not working) from my paperback?
After we re-typeset and designed your book, the page numbers change so the old index and table of contents no longer work. Therefore, we usually remove them. We dislike publishing books without indexes and contents as much as you dislike buying them. But many of our books only sell a couple of copies. So manually creating a new index and table of contents could add more than a hundred dollars to the cover price. And nobody wants to pay that. If you need to see the original index, please check our website for a downloadable copy.

Why are illustrations missing from my paperback?
We created your book using OCR software. Our OCR software can't distinguish between an illustration and a smudge or library stamp so it ignores everything except type. We would really like to manually scan and add the illustrations. But many of our books only sell a couple of copies so that could add more than a hundred dollars to the cover price. And nobody wants to pay that. If you need to see the original illustrations, please check our website for a downloadable copy.

Why is text missing from my paperback?
We created your book using a robot who turned and photographed each page. Our robot is 99 percent accurate. But sometimes two pages stick together. And sometimes a page may even be missing from our copy of the book. We would really like to manually scan each page. But many of our books only sell a couple of copies so that could add more than a hundred dollars to the cover price. And nobody wants to pay that. If you would like to check the original book for the missing text, please check our website for a downloadable copy.

Limit of Liability/Disclaimer of Warranty:
The publisher and author make no representations or warranties with respect to the accuracy or completeness of the book. The advice and strategies in the book may not be suitable for your situation. You should consult with a professional where appropriate. The publisher is not liable for any damages resulting from the book.
Please keep in mind that the book was written long ago; the information is not current. Furthermore, there may be typos, missing text or illustration and explained above.

1

THE LIFE OF BRIGADIER-GENERAL SIR SAMUEL BENTHAM, K.S.G.

0 By fbf I, c (i
PREFACE.

The following Memoirs will give some account of a life of singular activity, attended by great successes, yet not without vexations and disappointments. The latter involved some personal imputations, from which it was necessary to vindicate the memory of Sir Samuel Bentham; while the results of his incessant labours have tended to diminish the burdens, or to add to the resources of the country. To him are to be traced some of the most important changes in Naval Administration; and to him we are indebted for many inventions which have effected an incalculable saving in pubhc expenditure, as weu as for Dockyard and other reforms which closed the sources of many long-continued and most pernicious abuses.

Official opposition, which sought to uphold all vested interests, prevented him from carrying out many things which he had at heart; while, even in what he was enabled to accomplish, he had to struggle with the obstacles furnished by a passive resistance, and sometimes with personal animosity.

A 4

But at this distance of time a plain narrative of his intentions and his acts can cause no pain or injury to those who may have differed from him or opposed him, while they who may personally have known and valued him will not regret that a narrative so fully justifying all his acts, so clearly attesting the wisdom of his conclusions, should be laid before the public. Many things which he first asserted to be abuses have, since that time, been acknowledged to be such; and if others which he strove to check or to suppress still continue, no evil can arise from allowing his protest to be heard.

ISTo full account of his position at the Navy Board, and with reference to the Admiralty, has yet been published. While the following memoir furnishes a complete explanation of all the events which preceded and accompanied the abolition of his office, and of the various motives and influences which animated his opponents, this vindication is the more conclusive, as every statement rests not merely on his own assertions in letters and journals, but can be attested by public and official documents, as well as by his works themselves.

Few men have followed out the object of their lives with such unswerving perseverance; few haw shown greater fertility of invention, a wider range of observation, and a keener insight into the adaptation of means to ends. Few have worked with more unwearied energy against difficulties which to men

PREFACE. VLL of less vigorous mind, and less disinterested integrity, would have been overwhelming.

The task of vindicating his memory from every aspersion has been accomplished by his widow, who has shown in the following narrative a rare comprehension of the most minute details, as well as of the general character of the technical works in which her husband was engaged. If her last years were occupied with that which clearly was to her a labour of love, her full knowledge of mechanical science, and her clear apprehension of the general bearing and results of mechanical designs, show at the same time that she was actuated by no mere feelings of a partial affection. She has defended the acts of her husband, where they appeared to need any defence, on grounds which can be examined by all acquainted with such subjects, and on which they can pronounce their judgment whether of approval or disapprobation.

The manuscript of this work, which had not been corrected throughout at Lady Bentham's death, was intrusted to the care of her youngest daughter, who, much as she desired to carry out her mother's wishes, would have shrunk from the responsibility of publishing the Memoirs in their imperfect state, but for the kind encouragement which she has received from eminent engineers.

NOTE BY LADY BENTHAM.

The materials from which the following Memoirs have been drawn up, consist, previously to the year 1790, of private letters and of parts of a journal kept during travels in Siberia and to the frontiers of China; and, after his return to England, of his patents; and, from the time of his re-eno-a ements in the British Service, of official docu-ments, and a journal of proceedings, in which were noticed transactions with the First Lords of the Admiralty and other members of that Board; as also with other officers in the Naval Department, and with the Speaker of the House of Commons. For a later period many documents have been consulted which may be considered as official since they are on record at the Admiralty; but throughout the whole nothing is stated which cannot be proved to be correct.

Sir Samuel Bentham published the following pamphlets, now out of print; but in addition to those he had distributed, a copy of each was presented by his widow to the Libraries of the Admiralty, the War Office, the Great Seal Patent Office, the United Service Institution, the Kensington Museum, and the Society of Arts:–

"Naval Papers, containing (1) Correspondence on the Subject of various Improvements in His Majesty's Dockyards, and relative to the Institution of the Office of Inspector-General of Naval Works."

" (2) Letters and Papers relative to the Mode of arming Vessels of War."

" (3) A Statement of Services rendered in the Civil Department of the Navy."

" Letters on Certain Experimental Vessels, on Contracts for providing Naval Stores," andc.

"Answers to the Objections of the Comptroller of the Navy."

" Desiderata in a Naval Arsenal, or an Indication of several Particulars in the Formation or Improvement of Naval Arsenals; together with a Plan for the Improvement of the Naval Arsenal at Sheerness."

" Representations on the Causes of Decay in Ships of War, with proposals for effecting the due Seasoning of Timber," andc.

" Services rendered in the Civil Department of the Navy, in investigating Abuses and Imperfections in effecting Improvements in the System of Management, the Formation of Naval Arsenals, the Construction of Vessels of War, andc. andc. andc. 1813."

u Letter to Lord Viscount Melville on the real Causes of the Defeat of the English Flotilla on the Lake Erie. 1814."

" Naval Essays; or Essays on the Management of Public Concerns, as exemplified in the Naval Department, considered as a Branch of the Business of Warfare. 1828."

"Financial Reform Scrutinised, in a Letter to Sir Henry Parnell, Bart., M. P. 1830."

" On the Aim and Exercise of Artillery. 1830." " Notes on the Naval Encounters of the Rus iauri and Turks in 1788, 1829." (United Service Journal.)

" On the Diminution of Expenditure without impairing the Efficiency of the Naval and Military Establishments." (Ibid.)

"Breakwaters.–Sir Samuel Bentham's Plans. 1814." (Mechanic's Magazine.)

XU CONTENTS.

CHAPTER IV

Condition and Treatment of Exiles in Siberia– He descends the Angora from Irkutsk– Letter to his Brother Jeremy Bentham– Fanaticism of Russian Peasants– Appeal on the Murder of a Tonguse– Slave Trade of the Kirgees– Fertility of Siberia– He visits Nijni Novgorod– Returns to St. Petersburg, and presents a Report to the Empress– Declines Lord Shelburne's Offer of a Commissionership of the Navy– Sir James Harris leaves Bentham as Charge daffaires at St. Petersburg– He is appointed a " Conseiller de la Cour," and entrusted-with the Works of the Fontanha Canal– Engagement with the Niece of Prince " Galitzin– Letter of Sir James Harris– The Engagement finally broken off– He is appointed Lieutenant-Colonel in the Russian Army, with the Command of the Southern Part of the Country. Page 57

CHAPTER V.

Journey to the Crimea–He is settled for a Time at Cricheff–Preparations for Shipbuilding– Extent of his Engagements– Military Duties– Manufacture of Steel– Building of the River Yacht Vermicular– Arming of a Flotilla at Cherson–Defeat of the Turkish Fleet, June, 1788– Bentham receives the Military Order of St. George, with the Rank of full Colonel, and other Rewards– Privateering–Appointed to a Cavalry Regiment in Siberia– Excursion in the Country of the Kirgees, 1789– Expedition to the Mouth of the River Ob– Kirgee Ignorance of Fire– Ship-building at Kamschatka for the American Fur Trade– Visits Paris on his Way to England 74

CHAPTER VI.

Journey through the Manufacturing Districts of England, 1791– Classification of Mechanical Works– Death of his Father– Prison Architecture–Mechanical Inventions and Improvements–He is commissioned by the Admiralty to visit the Naval Dockyards– Resigns the Russian Service–Report on Portsmouth Dockyard, 1795– Improvements and Alterations in the Dockyard– He is ordered to build seven Vessels on his own Plans– Changes introduced in their Construction– Appointed Inspector-General of Naval Works– The Appointment sanctioned by the King in Council, March, 1796– Increased Calibre of Guns on Shipboard 97

CHAPTER VII.

Marriage–Prison Architecture– Invention of a Mortar Mill for grinding Cement– Chemical Tests and Experiments on Ship Timber–Means for guarding Dockyards– Dock Buildings and Fittings– Choice of Materials– Supply of Water–Precautions against Fire–Introduction of Steam

CONTEXTS. Xlll

Engines– Copper Sheathing–Coast Defences– Eeport on the Office of Inspector-General ordered by the Select Committee of the House of Commons– Interconvertibility of Ship Stores– Cost of Mast Ponds– Effect of the Report to the Select Committee–Alterations and Improvements in Plymouth Dockyard–Abuse of Chips– Bad Conversion of Timber–Illness– Smuggling Vessels at Hastings. Page 121

CHAPTER VIII.

Dock Entrances at Portsmouth–New South Dock for Ships of the Line– Choice of Stone in building–Mast Ponds–Reservoirs for Clearing Docks– Treatment of his Experimental Vessels– Floating Dam– Steam Engine and Pumps– A Russian Fleet at Spithead– Interviews with the Officers– Daily Occupations– Character of Dockyard Workmen– Steam Dredging Machine–Enlargement of Marine Barracks at Chatham– Artesian Well–Deptford Dockyard–Sheerness–Proposals for a Dockyard at the Isle of Grain– Improved Copper Sheathing– Success of the Experimental Vessels– Principle of Non-recoil in mounting Guns– Engagement between the Millbrook and the French Frigate Bellone, and between the Dart and the Desiree. 146

CHAPTER IX.

Correspondence with Lady Spencer on Reforms in the Civil Management of the Navy– Payment of Dockyard Workmen– Principles of his new System of Management– Report to the King in Council– Objections urged against a Reform–Office of Master-Attendant–Principle of Dockyard Appointments– Wages and Employment of Workmen– Navy Pay Books– Education for the Civil Department of the Navy– Naval Seminaries– Changes in the Accountant's Office– Interest of Money sunk in Public Works– Dockyard Working Regulations– Opposition of the Comptroller of the Navy– Official Tour to Portsmouth, Torbay, and Plymouth– Renewed Acquaintance with the Earl of

St. Vincent–Dockyard Abuses at Plymouth– Designs for a Breakwater– Return to London– Opposition to the Report– The Earl of St. Vincent succeeds Lord Spencer as First Lord of the Admiralty–The Report sanctioned in Council, May, 1801– Suggestions for arming Vessels of War–Greenwich Hospital– Office of Timber-Master in the Royal Dockyard– Efforts on behalf of Convicts– Management of Timber Stores– Report to Lord St. Vincent, February, 1802– Opposition– Commission of Naval Inquiry– Provisional Plan for the Education of Dockyard Apprentices 170

CHAPTER X.

Tour to visit Cordage Manufactories, January 1803–Report, and Adoption of his Proposals–Treatment of Workpeople in Factories– Services of Mr. Brunei in the Introduction of Block Machinery– Method of rewarding Inventors– Advantages of Non-recoil Guns– Abuses in Job Payments– Proposals for a Government Ropery, 1804– Contracts for Timber– Opposition of the Navy Board– Arming of the Mercantile Marine– Timber Coynes– Dockyard Machinery at Portsmouth– Mission to build Ships in Russia, 1805–Arrival at Cronstadt– Difficulties of his Task– Opposition of the Emperor– Illness– His Proposals rejected by the Emperor– Importation of Copper for Sheathing– Detention at St. Petersburg during the Winter– Panopticon of Ochta– Departure from St. Petersburg– Revel– Carlscrona–Return to England– The Office of Inspector-General of Naval Works merged in the Navy Board Page 220

CHAPTER XL

Changes of Administration at the Admiralty– Influences at work during his Absence in Russia– Acceptance of Office in the Navy Board– Letter from General Fanshawe– Compensation to Mr. Brunei for Savings on Blocks– Proposal for a Canal from Portsmouth Harbour to Stokes Bay– Mixture of Copper and Tin– Faulty Method of Shipbuilding– Covered Docks–Modes of Seasoning Timber– Seasoning Houses– Sheerness Dockyard– Northfleet and the Isle of Grain– Breakwater at Plymouth 250

CHAPTER XII.

Designs for Chatham– Improvements in Dredging Machines– Inadequate Assistance in carrying out his Designs– Works at Portsmouth– Plymouth Breakwater– His Office abolished– Remuneration and Compensation– Count er-Claims of the Navy Board– Continued Designs– Sheerness– Employment of Women– Anonymous Charges– Departure for France, 1814– Return of Napoleon from Elba– Removal to Tours and Paris– Death of his Eldest Son, 1816– Journey to Angouleme– Return to England, 1827–Fate of the Experimental Vessels, Arrow, Netley, Eling, andc.– Transport Service– Interest of Money sunk in Public Works– Form of Vessels– Payment of the Navy– Illness and Death. 291

ERRATA.

Page 31, line 1 (and elsewhere), for " Prata-Pope" read " Proto-Pope." 41, 29, for " Listvenishna" read " Ustvenishna." 53, 17 (and elsewhere), for " Naimatchin" read " Maimatchin."

CHAPTEE I.

Birth and Parentage of Samuel Bentham–Education at Westminster School– Apprenticeship under the Master-Shipwright of Woolwich Dockyard–He is removed to Chatham Yard–Proposal to the Navy Board for an improved Chain Pump– Eesidence at Caen– Return to London– Introduction to Sir Hugh Palliser, and Captain Jarvis, afterwards Lord St. Vincent– Offer from Captain Bazely of H3I. S. Nymph declined– Leaves England, August, 1779; visits Rotterdam and the Hague, Amsterdam, Mittau, andc.

Brigadier-General Sir Samuel Bentham, K. S. Gk, was the youngest son of Jeremiah Bentham, Esq., of Queen Square Place, Westminster. His only surviving brother (his senior by ten years) was the celebrated Jeremy Bentham, well known by his works on jurisprudence. Their father and grandfather were both lawyers. One of their ancestors was Thomas Bentham, Bishop of Litchfield and Coventry, who died in 1578.

Samuel was born on the 11th of January, 1757. He was first placed at Mr. Willis's private boarding school, then at Westminster School at the age of six. Their mother having died soon after his birth, their father married again, in October, 1766, the widow of John Abbot, and the mother of two sons, Farr and Charles, the latter so distinguished in after life as Speaker of the House of Commons, and subsequently raised to the peerage by the title of Baron Colchester. From the time of Mr. Bentham's second marriage Charles and Samuel became in affection
LIFE OF IR SAMUEL BEXTHAM.
to each other as real brothers: their treatment in the parental home was the same, their education similar, their recreations alike. Jeremy Bentham, in a letter to his cousin Mulford, said, "It is with pleasure that I can confirm the favourable account you are pleased to say you have heard of my father's choice, and from the best authority, for such in that case is that of a stepson, who is but too often the last person to do it justice. I became acquainted with her soon after my own mother's death, as soon, or I believe a little sooner, than my father. For some years there has been the strictest intimacy between the two families; she always had my esteem in the highest degree, and it cost me but little to improve it. Since their marriage, she has ever behaved to me and my brother in the same manner (making an allowance for the difference of ages) as to her own children, whom she tenderly loves: they form a little triumvirate, in which, very differently from the great cabals distinguished by that name, there reigns the most perfect harmony." This is but a tribute justly due to a lady who has been mentioned in print in less flattering terms, and is moreover a proof that the bias of Samuel, which led him early away from home, did not originate in any discomfort experienced under the parental roof.

The first circumstances which may have led eminent men, to the choice of some particular career, cannot be devoid of interest; but Samuel never indicated what was the origin of his predilection for naval concerns. Possibly it might have been stimulated, by the circumstance of a building in his father's coachyard, being occupied by a carpenter as his workshop: for there he worked in all his spare moments as a carpenter. Doubtless he must have acquired some dexterity; for, in after life, he often spoke with delight of his having witli his own hands manufactured a carriage for his playfellow, the afterwards celebrated Cornelia Knight, whose father, Admiral Knight, was an intimate friend at Queen Square Place. Samuel's progress at Westminster school distinguished him from the generality of boys, so that he was destined for a liberal profession, and was preparing for the University, when an uncontrollable desire to become a naval constructor, induced his father to gratify the inclination, and to procure for him the best education, which the country at that time afforded in the art of ship-building.

This was secured by placing him as an apprentice to the master-shipwright of a royal dockyard, and Mr. Gray of Woolwich was selected as the master. Some months before Samuel attained the legal age of fourteen, he was bound apprentice to that gentleman, and regularly entered His Majesty's service as soon as he had attained his fourteenth year.

At that now distant period, it was conceived that the apprentices to such an officer, being usually of a superior class and education to those of the common shipwright, were training for future officers. The occasional absence, therefore, from the dockside, of lads so circumstanced, was winked at, though the master received from Government the full wao-es for them, as if their work had been unre-mitted. Much abuse arose therefrom, but the practice still continued, till Samuel himself at a future time was the means of its abolition. In his own case, however, it was fully understood that he should be allowed ample time for the acquirement of such knowledge, as might tend to the advancement of naval construction and equipment. He was boarded in the house of Mr. Gray, to whom was paid the then very ample sum of 50 a-year, besides a considerable apprentice fee. A distinguished master of mathematics, Cowley, of Woolwich Warren, was engaged to give Samuel lessons in that science, in which he made such progress as to write during his apprenticeship a treatise, which had the reputation of having exhibited unusual ability. He was removed with Mr. Gray to Chatham Yard, where his ardent thirst for know-

ledge was gratified by intercourse with men distinguished in various branches of science; but at the same time he did not neglect the handicraft branch of his profession. In a note-book, which still exists, is set down the manner in which he allotted different parts of the day to his several occupations: " Geometry before breakfast; working ship-building between breakfast and dinner; Mr. Davis (his tutor) with me at my cabin from dinner till six o'clock, while I am drawing. Music just before dinner, some light reading immediately after." These note-books exhibit the great variety of subjects in which he was acquiring knowledge,– chemistry, electricity, painting, grammar, especially of the French language, and many other subjects, besides those more immediately connected with naval architecture, such as mechanics and shipbuilding, the defects of which, as then practised, he already perceived. He was also alive to the many abuses that existed in the Eoyal Dockyards, and from his unpretending-station as apprentice was allowed an insight into many abuses, which otherwise he might never have been able to ascertain. His residence at Chatham also afforded frequent opportunities of gaining experience in sailing boats and small craft, and he often went out to sea from the Medway, cruising sometimes as far as Portsmouth and round the Isle of Wight.

At the early age of fifteen, by Mr. Gray's advice, he made his first official proposal to the Navy Board of an improved chain pump, and the Navy Board in reply, to use their words, " admit the improvement and commend his ingenuity," but decline it as they had already a contract for pumps. He afterwards learnt that the Board really was convinced of the superiority of his pump, but they had a contractor whom "they did not like to turn off."

In the year 1775, Mr. and Mrs. Bentham took their three sons Farr and Charles Abbot and Samuel Bentham, by permission of the Navy Board, to Caen, for the jmrpose of giving them fluency in the French language, and for effecting this they had previously provided for the reception of the lads in three different French families. The parents left the lads, that nothing might impede their speedy acquirement of the language; and this judicious arrangement was rewarded by success. Samuel particularly spoke and wrote French with purity and taste.

During his apprenticeship, he was the contriver of several improvements relative to naval matters, such as a Cur-vator for measuring crooked timbers, together with seve-ral small alterations in the form or equipment of sailing and rowing boats. The views which he had for his future employment when that apprenticeship should expire, will best be described by quotations from a letter of his, which commences thus:–" On the 2nd of August next I shall have served out my seven years: at the expiration of that time some alteration must take place, I have not as yet determined what. I should not wish to be there (in the yard), if I were not to continue to be as much my own master as I am at present, and this would be almost impossible. I should like much to superintend the building of some one ship under the foreman of the new works, but as this is not practicable, at the expiration of my time I shall apply myself closely to geometry, and finish the fifth book for publication: you know I have some reason to believe that by this means I might acquire interest enough to get master boat-builder. In such an office, I should have very advantageous opportunities of perfecting myself in the knowledge of the business as it is, and should have sufficient leisure to make some experiments, and apply myse f to gain that knowledge of it which would enable me to investigate what it might be. Practice alone may show how work has been done, but practice is insufficient to teach how it ought to be done. To confess to you the truth, had I not thoughts of the possibility of being at the head of my profession, I

B 3 never would have engaged in it. It is a profession I am exceedingly fond of: I prefer it to any: it is one that affords the largest field for the exercise of that kind of knowledge, which I seem to have gotten the clue to. Money, you know, I consider in no other light but as affording the means of satisfying my darling passion. In the King's service, although the profits are not large, yet could I have confidence put in me, could I but have the favour of those in power, although I should not have money, yet I should have that for which alone I should want it– I might have assistance in trying my experiments, in pursuing my researches: what I should have of my own, with the addition of the little I should have as salary, would satisfy me in such circumstances.

" Very little encouragement now would set me alive. I am acting against the advice of all my friends; they want me to engage in a private yard; to spend my whole life, or at least the younger part of it, in the drudgery of buying timber and patching together ships, for which I must court all such folks as masters of colliers, andc. Supposing in that time I may amass 20,000., when those faculties are weakened by which alone I could enjoy the spending it: I should then be living for the sake of living afterwards, and should be doing all the while the contrary of what it would be my greatest ambition to do."

There were, however, no means of enabling him to remain in the King's service, excepting in a very inferior office. His determination therefore was to employ some time in acquiring further knowledge, previously to deciding on what should be his future career. He attended chemical lectures in London, acquired the German language, became a pupil at the Naval Academy at Portsmouth, and spent two more years in improving himself in the practices of the several different Eoyal Dockyards, as also a part of that time on shipboard, as a volunteer in Lord Keppel's fleet. In a letter to his brother, 5th July, 1778, he says, f On Monday last I breakfasted and dined on board the Formidable, with her captain, Barclay, where, on being introduced to Sir Hugh Palliser, that gentleman recollected me. During my stay on board, I projected an alteration in the apparatus for steering, the purpose for which was to make it easier, by only altering the direction of an eye-bolt; when I mentioned this, the master and carpenters began swearing at themselves for not having thought of the same thing." The part was taken to the dockyard to be altered; but instead of this a new one was made under Samuel's direction.

In a subsequent part of the same letter he says, "I went also on board the Foudroyant with a lieutenant of the Formidable, who was desired to introduce me to Captain Jar vis, as a particular friend of Captain Barclay's. Captain Jarvis, you must know, is one of the highest-rate captains. He went all over the ship with me, and we became quite great friends. I mentioned my alteration in the steering apparatus, and he seemed exceedingly pleased with it, offering to have his altered according to the same plan." Thus commenced his acquaintance with the Earl of St. Vincent. It happened that after that year, they never met again till 1800, during his Lordship's command of the fleet then in Torbay, when their friendship was renewed and manifested itself in the utmost cordiality, and in the most flattering and convincing proofs of the high estimation in which he held Bentham's views of improvements in naval concerns.

In the ear 1778, when at sea as a volunteer on board the Bienfaisant, besides his attention to the nautical branch of the profession and the behaviour of ships at sea, Captain Macbride, whose table and cabin he shared, afforded him many particulars of information relative to general management, all of which data were treasured up, and made use of afterwards under the administrations of Lords Spencer and St. Vincent.

B 4

He had already felt the deficiency in point of appropriate education in civil naval service which could be obtained in either public or private establishments, when, happening to meet with Sir William Petty's plan of a system of instruction relative to the marine department, he perceived the many advantages that such a plan would afford in the training of men for the civil naval service; but as Sir William's was little more than a skeleton, Bentham rilled it up with the many branches of knowledge which in his view seemed desirable. In Sir William's plan several essential items were not noticed, for example, mixed mathematics, particularly mechanics, hydrostatics, hydraulics and pneumatics, naval chemistry, naval economy. These and many other additions to Sir William's plan appear in Bentham's, which, though completed in 1779, was only published in his Naval Papers, No. 1. It had, however, been presented to the Lords of the Admiralty in 1795, and formed the groundwork of the plan for naval seminaries intended to be introduced by both Lords Spencer and St. Vincent.

Amongst many offers of employment was one from Captain Bazely, of the Nymph, who was desirous that Bentham should accompany him to the East Indies, "partly to extend his observations, partly from a view (to use Captain Bazely's words) of the benefit the naval service in those parts might upon any emergency receive from his suggestions. The Captain was with me about it," (wrote his brother Jeremy to Mr. Fitzherbert,) " but my father could not be persuaded to consent."

In the summer of that year, Lord Howe, then First Lord of the Admiralty, suggested that, instead of accepting any immediate employment at home, Samuel should spend some time in visiting maritime countries abroad, to study the ship-building and naval economy of foreign powers. His father was at first averse to this also, but soon perceived the advantages which such extensive means of information LETTERS OF INTRODUCTION TO ST. PETERSBURG. 9 would afford to his son, and gave his full consent to and approbation of the journey. Friends were then applied to for letters of introduction, two of which, to Sir James Harris (first Lord Malmesbury), our ambassador at St. Petersburg, afford examples of the general style of the seventy which he obtained. Besides these, Bentham was furnished with others, that were officially addressed, to various ministers and consuls at foreign courts and maritime establishments.

Letter from Sir Gilbert Elliot to Sir James Harris, Ambassador of His B. M. at St. Petersburg, in behalf of Mr. Bentham:–

"London, Uth July, 1779.

" My dear Harris,– I beg leave to introduce to you Mr. Bentham, with whom Mr. Douglas has lately made me acquainted. The profession which he has chosen is that of ship-building, but he proposes to study it in a much more liberal manner than is generally done, and is prepared for it by school education and an attention to science not to be met with, I believe, in any other of his profession, at least of this country. Part of his plan is to see all that is curious in that art abroad, and his visit to Petersburg is in the same view. It is a great triumph for the memory of Peter the Great that an Englishman shoidd go to learn shipbuilding in Russia. This consideration will, I daresay, procure Mr. Bentham the attention of the country he is going to, and his agreeable manners and accomplishments will ensure to him your good offices and friendship.

" Believe me, my dear Harris, your affectionate

". Gilbert Elliot."

From Ed. Poore, Esq., of Lincoln's Inn, to Sir James Harris:– , "Salisbury, 14: th July, 1779. " I have taken the liberty to commend to your notice the bearer, Mr. Samuel Bentham, who is travelling for his improvement in the theory of ship-building, which he is very likely to advance in, as he is very ingenious and assiduous in the studies connected with his occupation. As his object in visiting other countries is merely information, and not any personal emolument, and he has been very much countenanced and recommended by some of our first people here in that light, I have presumed to add my knowledge of him to what other introductions he may have, and am persuaded he will not fall short of any recommendations you may think proper to give him to any of the naval department at St. Petersburgh, to the principal of whom, indeed, he has letters from Lord Shelburne and others, but would be, perhaps, more properly and more forcibly recommended by your patronage of him.

" I take this opportunity of making you my gratulations on the late accession of honours that has happened to you, which I should have done before but that I would not take up your time with mere compliments. My best respects attend Lady Harris and your sister.

"I am, andc. your faithful friend,

"Ed. Poore."

As Mr. Bentham's agreeable manners and accomplishments have been spoken of, it may be added that his intellectual countenance was engaging from the sincerity of the expression, his tall figure graceful, and the hands that at times worked at the dock-side still retained their delicacy. He could bear his part with elegance in the amusements of the first society, and he could hew a piece of timber with correctness. On the Continent he was distinguished in society as " le bel Anglais."

He embarked on the 24th of August, 1779, on board a Dutch eel boat for Helvoetsluys, such a vessel being safer than the packet during that time of war. His accommodations on board were all of them as luxurious as his bed, which was merely a bag of Scotch barley. His voyage was tedious, and it was not till the 31st that he landed at Helvoetsluys; but he thought it an advantage to have had this early proof of his ability to rough it. He visited Rotterdam and the Hague, having letters to our ambassador there, Sir Joseph Yorke. On mentioning his first visit to Sir Joseph, he said: " Never was I so much pleased with the conversation of any man. He gave me the character of the several people I am recommended to at Amsterdam." On dining with the ambassador next day, Bentham received from him two political pamphlets, one of them by Sir James Marriott. " The other Sir Joseph calls a libel, but says at the same time that it is every word of it true. He insists much on the use and almost absolute necessity of libels against libels, professes himself to have been the cause of a yard-full ot them being written, and says, after the King of Prussia, that it is as necessary to write against an enemy as to fight him out."

At Amsterdam he obtained an insight into the details of ship-building in Holland, and of all the business connected with it. The three brothers May especially were most obliging in their confidential communications, and afforded him valuable information as to the means employed for the preservation of timber, a subject which he held to be of vital importance in ship-building, and which he made everywhere a particular subject of inquiry.

His letters to his father and brother describe the country through which he passed, and the habits and manners of the people when differing from those of England. Such particulars, as being either already known or obsolete, may be generally passed over; still it may be worth noting that at Leyden the plants in the botanical garden are shown " by as pretty a Dutch girl as you will see in a hundred," and, " when we came to the natural history another still prettier girl made her appearance, and ran over a score or two of names in her department; I was astonished to see females so well informed in such matters."

During his stay at Amsterdam, he particularly noted the difference of expense at which naval business is car- ried on in England. In that city there was a Board of Admiralty, consisting of seven members. " They do the business of the Lords of the Admiralty, of the Commissioners of the Customs, Commissioners of the Navy and Victualling Boards in England; their salary is 300 a-year, and about 50 perquisites, besides a house, firing, and, I believe, candles. Yet they are rich, not from their places, for they consider them as posts of honour only. The Burgomaster of Amsterdam clears about 60 a-year by his place, but at the same time he has the disposal of all places in the city, one or two of them with perhaps 2000 per annum. They have never been known on account of this power to go snacks with the nominee." So in regard to France; from information to be depended on, he learnt that " there is about as much work done in the dockyard at Toulon as in that of Amsterdam, an equal number of ships built and fitted in a given time. There are employed at Toulon about 4,000 who work with their tools, and upwards of 200 men who keep accounts and direct the works. Here there are about 12,000 men who work with tools, and about twenty who keep accounts and direct the works. A Dutch workman is very slow in his movements, but he never stops; he drinks only the small beer allowed him, of which he may drink as much as he pleases."

Notes of this kind indicate that Bentham's investigations extended to the management under which the business of a naval arsenal is carried on, and the degree of economy with which works in them were executed–a subject in which, as will subsequently appear, he was afterwards much occupied in England, with a view to reforms in the management of the civil branch of the naval department.

One of the above-mentioned brothers May habitually spent the winter in England, and had large dealings with the Navy Board in furnishing ships for the transport service. Some information which Bentham obtaine from

these gentlemen, affords an example of the difficulty with which improvements then, as up to the present time, are introduced in the English naval department. In a letter of September 10th, 1779, he writes: " It is now upwards of twenty years that they (the Mays) have experienced the efficacy of a method they have discovered of preparing the timber at the expense of a very few pounds. Their father, being masterbuilder of the public yard here, applied his method to several ships of war he built about this time. These ships have since had but the most trifling repairs imaginable, and the timbers remain now as sound as at first; whereas before that time a ship had often been so much decayed in the space of five years as to be broken up as unfit for service. These ships of May's have already outlasted seven such ships. The Dutch wished to keep this secret to themselves, but as nothing can escape the notice of Sir Joseph Yorke, our Admiralty were informed of it, at least in part, and it was ordered to be put in practice; however, it shared the fate of all other proposals. It was at first badly conducted, and by a change in the Admiralty entirely neglected. Our ships were left to rot ad libitum, and the Dutch hug themselves and laugh at us. I know a good deal of the manner in which this was communicated, and of the reception it met with; but what is much more to the purpose, I know, pretty nearly at least, the whole of the method itself."

Bentham remained successively at various ports in the Baltic, long enough to obtain such information as could be acquired at them. At Mittau the Grand. Duke of Cour-land honoured him with much distinction, and here it was that his evident stock of information and judgment obtained for him the first offer of place and pecuniary emolument. The Duke offered him very advantageous terms if he could be induced to take a part in the management and disposal of the timber of the country. Many letters and facts indicated that he was already distinguished by the epithet " le savant voyagewr? and that a all who knew him were astonished at the great modesty they discovered in him." It is not surprising therefore that in addition to the valuable letters of introduction which he took from England, many others not less flattering were given to him from the friends which he made wherever he spent some time.

CHAP. II.

Arrival at St. Petersburg– Reception by Sir James Harris, the English Ambassador– He declines the Offer of the Direct or-Generalship of Marine Works– Visit to Cronstadt, Moscow, and Cherson– Return to St. Petersburg– Sets out to visit the great Factories and Mines of Russia, Peb. 1781– Ship-building at Archangel– Catherinaburg– Crosses the Ural Mountains into Siberia– Mines at Verskatouria– Sect of the Raskolniks–Visit to Nishnai Taghil– He constructs a Vehicle to serve both as Boat and Carriage– Invents a Machine for Planing Wood– Raskolnik Marriage Rites– Raskolnik Resistance to Persecution– General Aspect of the Country.

Mr. Bentham arrived at St. Petersburg in March, 1780, when he was for some time confined to the house in consequence of illness brought on by the overturning of the carriage in which he travelled. In a letter written whilst still laid up he says: " Count Tchernicheff has heard of me, and knows a great deal about me, and expresses a wish to see me every day. He makes me offers before he has spoken to me or seen me." Mr. Samborski, the Eussian chaplain attached to the Embassy in London, had before this expressed a strong desire to engage Mr. Bentham in the Eussian service.

Bentham's first visit on his recovery was, of course, to the ambassador. His reception was most flattering. He said himself: " Although I expected, from his character and from the letters I carried with me, to be received with a great deal of politeness, yet the reception I met with exceeded my expectations." Indeed, far from confining his civilities to a first visit, or to such as are usually bestowed on persons recommended, Sir James Harris bestowed on

Mr. Bentham many proofs of friendship. The young man was permitted to consult him on all occasions, and thenceforward took no step without Sir James's advice and concurrence. The ambassador also introduced him to the first society in St. Petersburg, and Mr. Bentham had reason to say that, " it was not by invitations to dinner that I measure his friendship; he gives me other proofs of it."

Shortly afterwards Count Tchernicheff offered Mr. Bentham the Director-Generalship of all the ship-building and mechanical works relating to the Marine. This was declined, as it would have fixed him in Eussia. His wdshes always led him home again, though his acceptance of the office would have enabled him to carry on experiments with a view to improvements in his profession. It appears, too, that he doubted his father's approval of such a step; but when he alleged this to Sir James as one reason for his refusal, the reply was that, " no employ would be proposed to him but under such advantages that even his father could not but approve of it."

In May he visited Cronstadt, furnished with letters from Sir James Harris and from Count Tchernicheff to the Commander-in-chief of that port and arsenal, Admiral Greig. From this double recommendation, Mr. Bentham said, "I got the confidence as well as the civilities of the Admiral." So that he had full opportunity of acquainting himself with all the various naval arrangements of that port, and of all the accommodations in the arsenal there provided for the construction, equipment, and management of everything connected with the outfit of a fleet.

Mr. Bentham then set out on a journey through the interior of Russia, to visit the seaports on the south, making some little stay at places of interest on his way. On his arrival at Moscow the Governor honoured him with an invitation to his table. A young Russian with whom he had already formed a friendship (Serge Plescheff), being also at Moscow, engaged to convey Bentham to the Governor's, and promised to bring him home. After dinner the party adjourned to the theatre. During the performance the house took fire, and the greatest consternation of course arose. Plescheft hurried out his sister; Bentham assisted other ladies, and escorted them safely to their carriages, when they drove off and in the confusion left him alone and helpless in the road. He was in the full dress of the time, with glittering shoe and knee buckles and the cha-peau de bras. The police accosted him. He had not yet learnt Euss, yet he contrived to understand that they asked his place " of residence.! He could not say that Plescheft had engaged it for him, nor could he name the house of his friend. The good-natured police endeavoured in vain to understand his signs, till at length he managed to make them comprehend his wish to be taken to the Governor. The request seemed extraordinar 7. They hesitated, and were taking him to prison, after much dumb-show parley, when Plescheft appeared, who, having seen his sister safely lodged at home, bethought himself of Bentham and returned just in time to explain matters, and to save him from being placed in durance for having presumed to ask for an escort to the Governor.

Further south, in passing through a village of Easkol-niks, he asked for food and a draught of water. Both were cheerfully and abundantly supplied, but payment was positively refused. When the repast was over, he saw every vessel which he had used dashed to pieces on the ground. The Raskolniks are schismatics from the Eussian Church, with which in certain respects they will have no intercourse; and one of the peculiarities of the sect is that they never eat or drink from any vessel that has been used by a person of the orthodox Church.

He visited Cherson, little dreaming of his future occupation there. The town then consisted of no more than 180 houses. In a letter of August 10th, 1780, he says: "The-

are establishing, or attempting to establish, a marine in the Black Sea. This is at present the favourite object of the Court. General Hannibal, of black parents, though born in Kussia, has the entire management of it under Prince Potemkin. He (Hannibal) has the command of building, fortifying, and settling the new town of Cherson, as well as the first command of all the naval department there. He chose the spot not above two or three years ago, when there was not even a hut there. In a few years he expects to see in it a fleet of thirty-two ships. Sheds to cover them are also to grow up with them. He has the favour of the Empress and her ministers, and snaps his fingers at the Admiralty. He gave me a general description of his plan. Timber they get chiefly from Chernobyl in Poland, for there is scarcely a single tree within 200 miles of Cherson."

Bentham returned to Moscow by Chernobyl and Mittau. Many incidents during this tour show the estimation in which he was held; to notice one of them, after staying some days with Count Chadkiovitz he was not allowed to proceed to Mittau, otherwise than in the count's carriage. " In this manner was I brought all through Poland, and not permitted to be at a farthing's expense."

At St. Petersburg, to use his own words, "in a little time I returned to my old hankering," and in October " contrived a new mode of composing masts," perhaps the same that he afterwards introduced in England with complete success. " I hope I shall be able to show," he says, " by the principles of mechanics, the advantage in point of strength, as well as of economy, of this mode over the present practice." The saving which he afterwards effected in England was twenty-five per cent, in workmanship, besides a considerable sum in timber.

In a letter to his father at this time he laments the expenses which he had unavoidably incurred: " A carriage," he said, ((was as necessary as a pair of gloves, more so than a shirt;"–he then related the economical arrangement which he had now made to diminish his expenditure, and avoid altogether much of the cost of a vehicle. " To Sir James Harris's, unless when there is much company in bad weather, I walk, yet contrive to save my reputation, notwithstanding the great aversion every class of people here has to the idea of walking. You tell me, Sir, that I used to make more shifts and undergo more hardships from economy: believe me, never so much then as now, though perhaps never with so good a will and so great a necessity. Coarse bread, black and sour, with sometimes milk, sometimes water, was my food the greatest part of my journey; not because I could not get other, but really because I would not be at the expense of it. In a bed I did not sleep during my journey, except while I was at my friend Count Chadkiovitz's, neither have I since my return. A sofa on which I sit with a great table before me by day, serves me as a bed at night. The same cloak, which served me so well on my journey, serves me now as sheets and blankets. Apples arid bread are my food when I stay at home; indeed I might have princely fare if I would bestow time and trouble to go out for it."

But Bentham was not yet satisfied with the amount already received of what he considered his education. He wished to improve himself still further by witnessing actual practice in mechanical operations as it existed in foreign manufactories, to investigate the art of management where there were great assemblages of working men, and to improve himself in the knowledge of metallurgy. Accordingly, in February 1781, he set out to visit the great factories in the Eussian dominions, and the most important of the mines, those especially in the Ural Mountains, and to the eastward of them. He arrived at Archangel in March. The greater part of the vast extent of country through which he passed is still but little known, and its inhabitants were then, as even now, considered coarse and brutal

C 2 20 LIFE OF SIR SAMUEL BENTHAM.

in manners as in mind: he, on the contrary, found the higher classes possessed of much information and polished manners, and all orders he found good-natured and good-humoured, with a sincere desire to assist and to oblige. The greater part of the journal kept at this time has unfortunately been lost, but letters to his brother and other friends afford much curious and valuable information.

A heavy fall of snow occasioned the driver of his carriage to lose his way at a distance of eight versts from Archangel. He walked into the town, lodged with General W exel, and was everywhere received most flatteringly. He afterwards was received in the house of M. Sereptzova, the judge appointed by Government, from whom he received much information relative to judicial matters.

He learnt that it was a common practice at Archangel to build ships with the money, and on account of English merchants. The vessels were sent to England loaded with Eussian produce, and then were permitted to sail as merchantmen, the greater part of the profit being secured to the English. A vessel built at Archangel cost 10,000 roubles (the rouble about 3s.), made four voyages in two succeeding years, and was then sold to the British Government for 5000?.

Among the few of his notes that remain, he says, "I have used my utmost endeavours to inform myself whether the peasants do not suffer oppression under the government of officers whom it is so difficult for the wisest laws to restrain, but hitherto I have not been able to discover instances of exaction or injustice. Here and there I have found some villages poorer than others, but according to what I have learnt, poverty in those villages arose from over-population, the surrounding land not being sufficient in extent or fertility to furnish food in abundance."

At Archangel he engaged an Englishman to accompany him as interpreter, and as a sort of companion; for although he had already acquired some familiarity with the Russian language, he did not consider himself suffi-ciently master of it to understand the technical terms.

Pallas, with whom Bentham had made acquaintance in the south, and with whom a strict friendship ever after existed, furnished him with a note of places and mines particularly worthy of notice; and in prosecution of this plan so marked out, he left Archangel before the winter roads had broken up. At one town at which he made a halt on the 21st of March, a sort of contest sprung up between the Commandant and a rich merchant, as to which of them should have the privilege of entertaining him. He urged to the merchant that the Commandant's hospitality had been already accepted. The merchant hied him to the Commandant, and obtained permission from him for the transfer of the traveller to himself. They were splendidly lodged and entertained–magnificent counterpanes on their beds, silk dressing-gowns, two valets de chambre to attend on each of them; (l in short," says the interpreter, " everything was noble "–but they lacked the China ware thought indispensable in an English bed-room. At length the valets contrived to pick up one wash-hand basin. This must not be set down to want of cleanliness. In Kussia the bath is the place for ablutions, and a heated one was ready for the guests next morning. The difference from our habits may appear strange; but it must be remembered that this reception took place nearly seventy years ago. Since that time Russia has adopted much from countries to the westward of her; yet she still retains many usages widely differing from ours. Indeed, persons of distinction not many years since, travelling on the main road from the Crimea to St. Petersburg, were attended by a cook carrying his culinary apparatus in his kibitka.

In after life Bentham often related the straits to which he had frequently been put in Russia and Siberia, by the overwhelming quantities of provision with which he had c 3 been presented. An example of this embarrassment occurred at Solikamisoi. The wife of the Commandant of the place, on the morning of his departure, sent what she thought necessary to allay hunger till Bentham and his interpreter should reach their carriage station. The luncheon for the two consisted of a pie composed of fowls and eggs, a cooked ham, two roast geese, two ducks, between four and five pounds of fresh butter, with bread in proportion to the other fare–all this to be stowed away in a simple kibitka. In his notes he says, "It is a custom, I am told, amongstthese hospitable people, the first time aper-son comes to take up his quarters at their house, to make him some kind of present. I at least have found it so invariably. The satisfaction they seem to feel in making their present increases its value immeasurably. They have seemed to consider a present as a kind of duty they owe me, and are only anxious to find what would be most agreeable." Further on he says:–" One cannot but be surprised that crimes of all kinds are not more frequent in this country, where the parties must go perhaps a thousand versts to bring an affair to trial. At Cherkinska the peasant at whose house I slept, observing that my servant was looking out of the window to watch the kibitkas, told me there was no fear they would be disturbed. At present, however, the Empress is giving an entirely new face to her vast dominions; different tribunals are establishing in every town. All economy, domestic and public, is, 'tis true, in a sad condition. The passion for gaming may, in a great measure, be the cause of the neglect of the former." An instance of the mechanical ingenuity of some of the native Russians was seen at Selsty, where a Euss shopkeeper, without education or instruction, made clocks that chimed the hours and quarters. But in Russia, as elsewhere, the aged adhere to old customs. At a place thirty-four versts from Verska-touria, the son of a peasant had cut a road through the woods to that place which shortened the way considerably. The old father never would use it, saying, that " the road which God had made was the best."

26th March.–At Catherinaburg the General immediately ordered Mdme. Turchisen's house to be prepared for his reception, and two gentlemen were deputed to conduct Bentham to his lodgings–" a very palace (as noted by his interpreter), " both in outward appearance and internal arrangements." In less than half an hour the General paid his visit of ceremony to congratulate Mr. Bentham on his arrival. This formal affair accomplished, the General proposed a walk together through the town. The operations at the Tanetskoi Don were particularly noticed, money being there coined with extraordinary expedition. Each piece passed through eleven hands; yet coins to the amount of 12,000 roubles were finished daily. After entertaining him at dinner, the General accompanied the traveller to pay visits of ceremony–in a coach of six, of course, Another house of Turchisen's, at which he apparently resided, was remarkable for its grandeur and for the very fine hothouses in its gardens. Turchisen had a factory where forty workmen were employed in manufacturing beautiful articles of metal solely for his use.

Having crossed the Ural Mountains into Siberia, Bentham arrived at Verskatouria on the 28th of March, and was conducted to the principal proprietor in that neighbourhood, Gregory Pogodaskina. This young man, though only sixteen years of age, had a month or two before been left by his father sole and uncontrolled proprietor of all his wealth, including mines, one of them amongst the richest of the upper mines in Siberia. The youth, attended by the chief persons of the place, came out upon the steps of his house to receive his guests. After coffee, Pogodaskina accompanied them to the commander of the town. Verskatouria is a place of some commerce in furs, such as white bear

skins, sables, and ermines. Two live sables were given to Bentham, so tame that the would
C 4 take raisins or sweetmeats out of a person's hand or mouth.

Bentham then proceeded to the gold mines, fifteen versts from the town; they are three in number, and at a depth of ten Kussian fathoms, seventy English feet. Specimens of this mine he afterwards sent to England to Sir Joseph Banks, together with a large collection of other of the mineral productions of Siberia. What remained of his own collection he received twenty years later in England, but the valuable specimens of gold had disappeared.

The next morning he set out to visit Pogodaskina's iron and copper works at a distance of 130 versts, where he arrived about nine the following morning. Pogodaskina, young as he was, was, it appears, chief manager of his immense concerns, and having indispensable business to transact at home, regretted that he could not accompany the traveller himself, but deputed this duty to another in his stead. At these works 114 poods, that is to say 4560 pounds of copper, are run from the furnace at one time.

"Near the factory of Kashan is the great iron mine of Slagkodat; a new road had been made over a steep hill, from which there is a magnificent prospect. The inhabitants of the village have taste enough in summer time to repair to a summer-house built on the summit of the hill, a distance of eighty versts.

A village, seven versts from Catherinaburg, inhabited by Raskolniks, gave Bentham a favourable opportunity of informing himself of their religious ceremonies. Under the guidance of an officer sent by the Governor, he inquired of several persons, on entering the village, where the chapel was situated? and to this they replied that they did not know. Recourse was then had to a merchant of the place, an acquaintance of the officer's. This merchant, whilst a messenger was sent to learn when the chapel could be visited, showed his guest a small chapel which he had built for the use of his family, and where he himself daily said morning and evening prayers. On entering the Raskolnik chapel, two flat pieces of iron were seen suspended. They are struck with an iron hammer, when the people are assembled; and five large bells, one of them weighing a pood, are then rung. They have no altar, and their saints are without ornament, but are merely painted resemblances. Except St. Nicholas, whom they say they do not honour, they do not acknowledge any of the saints reverenced in the Eussian Church. The women assemble in a separate apartment, that they may not be seen by the men. Each person is provided with a square flat cushion to lay on the ground when he lies down. On being asked whether they were persecuted by the Russians they replied in the negative, but added that they had formerly been so, and were afraid of it even now, as they were determined to adhere to their own religion. Her Imperial Majesty has commanded head money of thirty-five copecs to be paid by Raskolnik women, which is never imposed upon those of the Russian Church, and an addition of seventy-five copecs per man above what a Russian pays–this tax, Bentham subsequently added, is now taken off. They are (in common with Russians) obliged to supply their quota of recruits for the army, but take care to send those that are least attached to their religion. He learnt, on returning to the Governor's, that, while the Raskolniks were persecuted by the Government, they inflicted great cruelties on themselves and on their families, rather than change their religion. The Empress on hearing the tortures which they imposed upon themselves, decreed that twenty years should be allowed them for reflection, and in the meantime, that by means- of persuasion an endeavour should be made to unite them with the Russian Church, but this leniency did not appear to have any good effect.

9th April.– He set off for Nijni Taghil in the Governor's calesh with four post horses, a hussar behind the carriage, and a soldier in advance to order change of horses. Xijni Taghil, an iron factory, the property of Count Demidoft, is 140 versts northward of Catherinaburg. The owner of the works had furnished him letters to the intendant, containing orders to show him everything that he wished to see, to afford him all the information he might require, and moreover to do any works for him that he might have occasion for, as carriages, andc. Bentham had travelled thither in kibitkas on sledges with the winter roads, and now needed a carriage on wheels for summer travelling. The people proposed making him one of the usual description, but considering the journey which he had in view, he said that one of the ordinary construction would not content him. He therefore contrived a vehicle that might suit his purpose as a wheel carriage on land, a boat in water, and a sledge on ice. This carriage was manufactured while the winter roads were broken up, and the summer ones were not yet passable. He had not only to mark out himself every single piece of wood put into it, but was often obliged to work as hard as any of the workmen in executing those parts which could not be explained to them. In a letter to his brother, dated April 25th, from Nijni Taghil, he says, "The inhabitants, with regard to their manners, are very falsely described," and afterwards in speaking of the hospitable reception which travellers in general receive in this country, he says that the proprietor, Mr. Demidoft, was then at Moscow, but that " his house here, his servants, table, equipage, andc, I am at present master of. If you are not engaged some day next week, and will come and take a dinner or supper with me, whichever is most convenient, I shall be very glad to see you. I mention it only lest, hearing that nobody comes to the table here without my express invitation, your bashfulness might deprive me of the pleasure of your company. Besides soups, you will find, every day beef, mutton, pork, dressed each in

RUSSIAN COOKERY.

several different ways, also geese, ducks, and fowls. You need not, however, criticise the etiquette in serving up the poultry, or find fault with the sauces. Don't make it a tea-table talk at your return if you should see one dish contain a goose and a fowl, another a duck and a fowl laid head and tail on, one up on end against the other, all shrunk by the heat of the oven to half their former size, and the dry remains of the flesh ready to drop from the bones at the first touch– dry, I mean only in the inside, for the outside shines from the oily butter in which they almost swim. You love pastry, you will find some of different sorts, or rather in different shapes, and a great abundance of each. AVith such fare, however, by the assistance of champagne and other French wines and English beer, you may be able to exist for a single day. The wines are brought about 2000 versts overland. So much as I have seen of this country of Siberia, I have always found something more than the bare necessaries of life. At Tolchamskaja, a town further to the north, though without the boundaries of Siberia, I saw, besides other hothouse plants, 500 as fine orange and lemon trees as

I ever saw an) r where. By-the-by what an infamous, malicious, lying work that is of the Abbe Chapuis; have you read the antidote to it? It is said to be written by the Princess Dashkoff; her criticisms are in general, as far as I am able to inform myself, exceedingly just, but now and then her partiality for her country carries her too for." In reference to the growing practice in Russia of availing themselves of aid from abroad, he says: " To pretend to say that arts and manufactures are brought to the same degree of perfection here as in other countries, would be to condemn the practice of engaging foreigners; " but turning his thoughts to the unjust accounts that travellers had given of Russia, particularly the eastern parts and Siberia, he adds, "If I were disposed to criticise and condemn (yet from what I have seen there is more done here for the good of the country than there is done at home), I might say that in some places there are too many people here who have more interest in injuring than in benefiting others; but when I have made this remark, I have found that the interest of the superior is rather to protect than to injure those under him. When I have noticed anything that seemed to the prejudice of Government or of those who are disposed to favour it, I proposed questions to the most intelligent people in the country. I propose them in such a way as to get their opinion before I give my own, and it frequently happens from the reasons which they give me that I feel ashamed of having formed such an opinion. I wish the Abbe could have done the like; his book would have been as opposite as possible to what it is."

April 12th.–The design for the amphibious carriage being completed, the work was begun, and it afforded occupation for Bentham a great part of every day, in chalking out upon the floor the form and dimensions of the boat and the disposition and scantlings of its parts. When the carriage was built he described it to his brother as nothing more than a vehicle hung as usual on springs, and when intended for land service suspended on wheels, but the body was of the novel shape of a boat. For water service, easy means were provided for detaching the carriage from the wheels, so that when taken to pieces they might be stowed away in the bottom of the body, serving then as ballast when the vehicle is used as a boat. When it was completed, he set out in it for Perme, where it afforded no small amusement to the inhabitants. Beins: engaged to dine with the Governor, Bentham just before the appointed hour sailed up the river in his amphibious vehicle in full view of the well-filled windows of the Government house; after dinner it presented itself in another form upon wheels and drawn by three horses to the door. It fully answered the purpose for which it was contrived,–rapid. and certain means of conveyance in a country intersected with rivers, but ill provided with bridges.

During the construction of the carriage, Mr. Bentham's observation of the slowness with which workers in wood operated, and of the frequent inaccuracy of their work, led him to think that machinery might be substituted with great advantage for manual labour in the fashioning of that material. In consequence of this opinion he considered various means of realising his ideas; and here it was that the first foundation was laid of his subsequent inventions of machinery. He first caused a working model to be made of a machine which he devised for planing wood. As this model was found to answer its intended purpose, he forthwith had a planing machine made of full size for large works, which did its duty equally well. He afterwards consulted Sir James

Harris as to the bringing his invention forward, and whether there were any probability of his deriving some such advantage from it in Eussia as in England might be derived by patent. Sir James counselled him to " look forward to old England for the first recompense of his ingenuity." Eelating this to his brother, Mr. Bentham observes, " this, however, does not prevent my trying some experiments, although it sets me wavering in regard to some of my inventions."

During a drive round Nijni Taghil on Sunday the 16th of April a number of fine houses were noticed, indicating that the inhabitants were rich and at their ease, the people about all of them lively, smartly dressed, and very clean. In one street a number of girls assembled together were dancing, singing, and running about, while the men were standing round to look at them; others were playing cricket and other games. In this and other streets several hundreds were so assembled and seemed to enjoy themselves greatly.

A great magazine of flour was kept up by Count Demi-doff when flour was to be purchased at a low price, as fourteen copecs a pood, he caused a large quantity to be stored; and when the price rose to twenty-two copecs, the magazine was opened and the flour sold to the poor at its cost price. Some days were spent in examining the manner in which the iron is sent off in barks to St. Petersburg, and in a letter dated April 14th he says: "You may know, perhaps, that there is no communication whatever by water between the European and Asiatic parts of this country. Mr. Demidoff 's fabrics being on the Asiatic side, he has a wharf on the river Chasavry on the European side. By transporting his iron in winter by sledge roads, he can send it from thence entirely by water to St. Petersburg. I went to this place to see the loading and setting off of his barges. He sent this year fifty-four of them, each carrying about 7000 poods of iron, about 111 tons English."

18th.–Bentham contrived a machine to be applied to General Bashkin's carriage to show the number of versts it travelled over. To-day he went to the painters. In the same street lived several Baskolniks, who take all their water for washing or drinking, not from rivers, but from wells, of which they use several in the street. Bentham, who in going along saw one of the poles for drawing up buckets fixed at an unusually great height, tried whether much force was required to immerse and then raise the bucket filled with water. He found it was easily effected, but as he looked to see whether the water was clean, an old Baskolnik, imagining the heretic was about to drink, called out to him to wait till he had brought a glass. Bentham was preparing to throw the water back into the well when the old man ran to prevent him. He afterwards learnt that the Raskolniks, besides considering it a sin to drink after a person not of their own religion, even do not drink out of a vessel that has been used by their wives; and had Bentham thrown the water into the well again, it would have been reconsecrated.

May 5th.–The Prata Pope having sent to say that he was about to marry a couple, Bentham went to the church to witness the ceremony. As the bridegroom had no parent alive, one of the priests stood at his right hand as father, the bride's mother at the left of her daughter. The bride's face was covered with a handkerchief, which was taken off by the mother, as the priest, advancing, put a piece of coarse linen on the ground for the bride and bridegroom to put each of them one foot upon. The bride stood with the air of a criminal, not daring to raise her eyes from the ground.

One of the priests then brought two wax candles to the Prata Pope, who took one of them, and having it in his hand, crossed the bridegroom thrice. The young man then crossed himself, received the candle from the priest, and kissed his hand. A similar ceremony was repeated with the other candle and the bride. The priest read a prayer, after which, turning to the couple he took both their rings, and went behind the altar, another priest reading a prayer the while. At the Prata Pope's return he asked the young couple their names: whether it was from true love they wished to be united, and whether either of them were under promise to another person. These questions having been satisfactorily answered, prayers were again offered up, and incense brought by a priest to incense the images. The Prata Pope then returned the rings to the young couple with the same forms with which he had received them. They change rings, the bridegroom putting his ring upon the bride's finger. A silver cup of wine is then brought to the Prata Pope;–the young couple cross themselves;–the cup is given to them to sip from alternately two or three times, till between them its contents have been sipped up. Two gilt cups with crosses upon them are then brought to the priest which, with the same ceremonies, are put into their hands, which he afterwards joins together. Then taking both their hands so joined, he leads them round the Holy Bible three times, singing to them the whole time. A boy reads the duty of a husband to his wife, and of a wife to a husband; the Pope gives them his blessing and desires them to kiss one another thrice, and thus the ceremony ends. The Prata Pope was invited to dine with Bentham, which he did at half-past twelve o'clock (that, and till one o'clock, being the usual dinner time; from nine to ten supper; breakfast at about seven, tea at all times of the day and upon every visit of ceremony or friendship).

May 12th.–The Prata Pope dined with Bentham. The conversation turning on the Kaskolniks, the Prata Pope said that, rather less than fifteen years since, when they were obliged by the Russian authorities to change their religion, these Raskolniks used to assemble in numbers of from twenty to thirty, to burn themselves alive–they even burnt and murdered their children. They assembled in a house prepared for the occasion, with firewood, hemp, pitch, and whatever combustibles could be obtained, in the midst of which they seated themselves. Some, not considering themselves worthy of God's blessing, or fearful of being able to endure the pain, ordered themselves to be tied; the pile was then set on fire. The priest said he had received information that a party of thirty had assembled for the purpose of burning themselves, though it is seldom that notice is taken of such self-sacrifices till they are accomplished. On that occasion the Prata Pope, with all his priests, set out for the place indicated, but had the misfortune not to arrive till too late. He saw several dead bodies burnt to ashes; his clerk took up bones of the dead, and lingered in the smoke till it had such an effect upon him, together with general excitement, that he would not leave the place, saying that he too should be blessed if he burnt himself also. He was influenced to so great a degree, that the Prata Pope was obliged to keep him under strict guard for four days. The Paskolniks (or Kirgakies, as otherwise called) used to put their children to death in various ways, as by burning, drawing, stifling, andc. Sometimes they burned their bones to ashes, and pounding them very fine, mixed a very little in food and drink.

May 17th.–A small boat was brought to the Factory to be fitted with sails of Bentham's contrivance, which should themselves change their position, and carry the boat on, steering straight, without even a man on board. The weather was so fine as to admit of drinking tea in the open air at the bottom of a hill, and to remain reading and writing till eight o'clock, by the water-side.

May 2Mli.–Bentham made an excursion to the Factory of Kushva, distant forty-five versts, not setting out till three in the afternoon. It was eleven at night before he arrived at Kushva. His visit was unexpected, and the Colonel-Commandant had lately died, so that it rested with the Mayor to do the honours of the place. He assigned the Colonel's house as lodging for the travelling party of four persons, with their attendants. The supper was not on table before twelve o'clock, but it was excellent in kind, and exquisitely cooked and served. Amongst various other things there was fine fresh butter, Parmesan cheese, a delicious fowl soup, with vegetables, a fat capon, beef steaks–all this at an out-of-the-way place on the Ural Mountains.

On the 19th of June Mr. Bentham set out on an excursion to Catherinaburg.

Notes were taken indicating the return of warm weather by the progress of vegetation and otherwise. The first salad that appeared at table was on the 13th of May. On the 19th June the heat was so great, that bed-chamber windows were left open all night; roses, and other wild flowers were gathered in the woods; snipe was shot on the 20th; and hay-making began on the 12th July.

In a letter dated July 11th, Nijni Taghil, speaking of this long excursion of about 2200 versts, he says: " The

country I have been riding through is in general very beautiful; a great part of the way I appeared to be going through an English park. The weather was very fine, the hay perfumed the air, and one can seldom go ten or a dozen miles without seeing a river or rivulet. Birch trees and the several different kinds of firs form a principal part of the roads. The birch-tree is in great abundance, and grows to a large size, but it is a very unprofitable production in this part of the country, though so valuable near Archangel. It is the best of the fir-trees for building ships; but as the woods are used here only to make charcoal for the mines– and this makes the worst of charcoal–it is almost entirely useless. Corn but seldom thoroughly ripens on the ground, so that the cultivation of it is not much followed. It is a good crop that produces tenfold what was sown, whereas in the Government of New Eussia it is said to produce a hundredfold. The puddles were covered with ice for some nights together, near three weeks ago, and the appearance of winter comes on apace." Eavens seem to have abounded, for he sends bundles of quills to his brother, " enough to supply your harpsichord for your lifetime. It is in this country that the happy effects of a reformation in jurisprudence is to be seen daily; parts of the new code which make their appearance from time to time prove the attention that is still given to this subject.

"What think you of a governor who rules over 110,000 people, whose sole object is to avail himself of the power given him only to produce as much happiness as he can? Such a man it is my good fortune to have formed a friendship with. His name is Lamb; he says he is English, or rather of Scotch extraction. An ancestor of his was taken into the service of a Czar before Peter the Great; but in short, this is a matter so little interesting compared to his good qualities that I have forgotten it. To account for delay in the completion of a machine for

COXDI. N OF WORKMEN IN FACTORIES. 3-5 working wood, he says that it had been retarded by "the six weeks' holidays at this season of the year for the men to make their hay,"– an instance of consideration for the workmen in an immense factory rarely to be met with in any country but Eussia.

D 2

CHAP. III.

Perme– Improvements in Mining Pumps– Cavern near Perme–Collection of Minerals– Arrival at Tobolsk, January 1782– Introduction to the Anchree– Population of Siberia– State of Crime– Arrival at Krasnojarsch–Mines at Narchinsk–The Chinese Frontier– Kiachta– Visit to the Chinese Governor–Chinese Temples and Images–Fortune-telling– Intercourse between Russians and Chinese.

He was present at the ceremony of the first opening, in October 1781, of the new Grovernmen; of Perme, but his chief object at this place was to collect information respecting the country between that place and the frontier of China, as what he had already seen in Siberia led him to expect much useful addition to his knowledge by undertaking an extensive tour in that country. The greater part of the Government of Perme is the property of the Strogonoffs, and he had much satisfaction in rendering them some little service. They derive a considerable revenue from the salt mines, which they work on their own account, selling the salt at a fixed price to the Crown. On examining the several operations carried on in raising the salt water, and for crystallising the salt from it, Mr. Bentham found room for great improvements. He suggested means of confining the fire-heat to the boilers instead of losing, perhaps, some tenths of it, as also a manner of employing the heat of steam from the composition for warming a supply of the solution. But perhaps the most advantageous improvement that he devised, was an alteration of the pumps for raising the brine from underground. The pipes through which the brine was pumped up were very small, the operation of boring holes to a great depth being laborious and costly, and the expense and difficulty of it increasing considerably in proportion to an increase of their size. The then existing pumps, though kept constantly going, never exhausted the solution, so that Count Strogonoff had determined on a costly work of two or three years' duration in boring more holes. But Mr. Bentham had noticed that the sucking-pumps in use only voided the fluid intermittingly, so that when the piston was raised, the fluid below was at rest during a time equal to that of the descent of the piston. His simple device, therefore, was to have the upper part of the pipe made double, with two pistons working in the two pipes, these terminating in one pipe at the fixed valve. Thus, by causing the pistons to work alternately, the fluid from the lower pipe rose in a perpetual stream. The double pipe, carried down to a depth of forty-nine feet, was in a part where the ground is always opened to a large diameter for other purposes; it was in the remainder of the total depth of 245 feet that the great saving was effected.

During his stay at Perme, he visited a cavern celebrated for its minerals, and relates his exploring adventures as follows:– "In the evening I set out for the cavern, in which I spent two days and a night, as I found when I came out, for all is darkness there, and I happened not to have my watch with me. The entrance to this cavern might well put me in mind of poor Gil Bias' residence. It is true the one I was in was not covered with a trapdoor, but the hole was so small that such a precaution would have been unnecessary. Although there was snow on the ground, it was necessary to pull off all but my waistcoat not to run the risk of sticking by the way. Thus prepared we crouched on our stomachs for eight or ten fathoms. We then were able to raise ourselves up on our hands and knees, soon afterwards on our feet in a

D 3 stooping position, and in about a hundred fathoms we came to a spacious vault-like opening: it was, as you may imagine, much warmer than above ground. My companions consisted of my interpreter and a servant, with ei ht or nine peasants, some of whom had been several times, and had penetrated as far as their fears would let them. These gave an account of a lake which they had seen, or rather heard something plunge at their approach; but no one had ever attempted to pass that lake. The site or rock in which this cavern is formed, consists of calcareous stone of a greenish colour. The water from above, as it filters through into the cavern, forms crystals of various figures; it is in search of such curiosities that people have, from time to time, been sent here. I went partly with the same views, but more, perhaps, with the expectation of observing something which, in those who had been sent there, might through fear, ignorance, or laziness, have passed unnoticed. We had a provision of a pood, or thirty-six English pounds, of candles with us, so that, supposing they would burn, we were in little danger of wanting light. As our course was up and down precipices, of ten or twenty feet in height, and we had each of us a basket or bottle of provisions of some kind to encumber us, we were not very expeditious. The distance to this lake had been magnified to about twelve English miles, but, however, after turning round and round two or three times to the same place, in about four hours we arrived where this lake ought to have been. Xothii, however, but a puddle, a little over one's ankles, appeared, and in a few fathoms we came to the end, which was no more remarkable than any other part; but by my compass I perceived that in our course we sometimes turned quite round: I cannot conceive the distance to be above three-fourths of a mile. We now began to be hungry and f. itigued, but found it necessary to return about halt way before we found a convenient place to spread our table.

Some fine English cheese, which Sir James Harris had supplied me with at my setting out from St. Petersburg, with some English beer which Baron Shwonoff had ordered to be packed up with a store of other provisions for the occasion, made the most remarkable part of my fare during my subterraneous residence. As nothing was to be had to lie on but stones, in the choice of a bed place the object was to find one stone, or a number of stones nearly in one level, of a sufficient length to stretch ourselves out upon. I had with me a large Spanish cloak, to which I have been under great obligations on such occasions. This I wrapped nearly twice round me, and stretched myself out on one entire stone with a small one, and my great coat upon it for a pillow. The rest did as well as they could; and after seeing that half a dozen candles were fixed up, besides a little fire made up of bits of wood that had been left at other times, I, no doubt, in a few minutes made the cavern echo with my snoring, and slept very sound for four or five hours; when at my waking, to my no small astonishment, all was darkness. My interpreter, who was just by me at the same time, let me know that the last candle was put out by some water that dropped upon it from above, and that he had just time, before that happened, to observe that all the men were gone away. This was enough to alarm me, as without light we neither of us could move a yard without danger of falling down a precipice of eighteen or twenty feet. It was absolutely in vain to have the least thought of making our way out of the cavern without assistance. However, I comforted myself and him with the idea of having provisions within my reach, which would be enough for a week or a fortnight, and that on any supposition whatever, the same, or other men, would come to see what would become of us in that time. We had not, however, the pleasure of making our reflections on tins situation above half an hour when a

D 4 glimmering light appeared towards the way out. In any country but this (not excepting England) I should have been under some anxiety at seeing a light, from the doubt I should have whether it might be friends or foes who brought it. It proved to be two boys, whose business it had been to look after the horses which were left near the mouth of the cavern, and whom the men had sent to us in their stead. We could learn nothing from these boys as to the reason why the men had left us; all that they could tell was that they were laid down to sleep on the outside of the cavern by a good fire. Although I was determined not to quit the place till I had explored all the windings in it, yet I thought the most certain way of getting the men back was to go and fetch them. Therefore, loading ourselves with some of the choicest stores we had collected, we made our way out into the open air time enough to find all the men asleep before a large fire. The reasons they gave for leaving us were simple enough: they were too tired to go through another day's fatigue without sleeping, and they could not sleep in so cold a place. You must understand that Russian peasants are used to sleep in a degree of heat which would be very disagreeable to those who were not accustomed to it. They said they had left six candles burning, and had sent the two boys as soon as they could. I stayed half an hour by the fire, and in the mean time divided my company into three detachments, for the purpose of taking different courses for the better exploring all the parts of the cave. I cut a great number of small pieces of paper of three different figures, of which each detachment took a different figure, so as that by scattering these pieces of paper in the way, one party might know where the other had been. Thus prepared we returned to our subterraneous employment. We were now so well experienced in the scrambling up and down the steep places, that in about seven or eight hours there was not a hole but what some part of the company had been in; after which, collecting together the stones that we had selected from the different parts, we, with no small pains, made our way out with them, and set off on our return. The colour of our clothes, skin, and every thing we had about us, however different they might have been before, were now all alike. After all, in this same cave, I could find no indications of its ever having served for habitation for either man or beast; nothing alive was to be found but bats or winged mice and gnats. The former were in great plenty; the latter, which more likely had taken shelter on the approach of winter, were but in small quantities, and these, though they settled on our hands and faces, had not seemingly strength to bite. All then I got for my pains, besides a good collection of calcareous crystallisations and stalactites, such as had already been procured from this cave, was some specimens of one or two sorts, such as I had not seen in the possession of anybody else. Hitherto everybody had been deterred from penetrating to the end of this subterraneous chasm from fear and impatience of fatigue. It was an affair of three days."

The making a collection of minerals had become an object of no small importance to him. It now remained to have forwarded to St. Petersburg three or four thousand pounds' weight of cojmer and iron ores, specimens of crystals, (fee, " all chosen specimens, even here on the spot," which were afterwards transmitted to England, and distributed to Lord Shelburne, and other friends. These specimens had been collected in the course of the above-mentioned excursions of fourteen or fifteen hundred miles on horseback, during the time that his head-quarters were at Nijni Taghil.

At Perme Mr. Bentham received a circular letter, under a flying seal from Prince Viasemsky, Minister of the Civil Department, requesting the commanders of the several districts through which Bentham might pass, to give him all the aid in their power for the furtherance of his plans.

At the same time an Imperial ukase gave orders that Major Soginofy should accompany Mr. Bentham to the borders of China and other distant places, as he had requested. Prince Viasemsky had also suggested by letter to Sir James Harris that Mr. Bentham on his return should pass by Taganrog, by the newly added Eussian provinces, to visit Cherson. The Prince also furnished him with no less than eighteen private letters of recommendation to different governors and other Bussians of rank, to which were added nine from Prince Potemkin, and about seventy others from various friends to different influential persons.

"It is now January 1st, 1782, O. S.–I believe my birthday according to your heretical way of counting. If you have not forgotten me to-day at Queen Square Place, and have any sympathy in you, you will begin a letter to me this very evening. I am on my way to Tobolsk."

He had dismissed his interpreter at Perme, and was now accompanied by Major Sogiuort, and was attended by a corporal and a grenadier, appointed especially to serve him during the journey. They none of them understood any language but Euss, but by this time Bentham had become master of it.

13fi January.–Having arrived at Tobolsk at about eight in the morning, he found no news of quarters being-prepared for him. The Governor was ill in bed, and the Place Major escorted him to a cold house, on which Bentham says he "took miff," and ordered fresh horses immediately, as he had sent a letter to the Govern or, giving two days' notice of his arrival. He, however, sent Matrei Ivanovitch to the Governor to know whether the letter had been received. Then came apologies in answer, a pressing invitation to stay a longer time, and saying that the letter had not been forwarded. The Place Major took him to a better house and a warmer one; then further invitations to remain longer at Tobolsk were followed by the Governor's chariot and six, with two footmen, also a guard of honour, a serjeant and six soldiers, to learn how and where he would have them placed. He declined them as a guard, but accepted the services of three of them to attend in their turn, one at a time, as sentinel at his door.

After dining with the Governor, Bent-ham took his leave, and called at the Ancliree's (Archbishop), with a letter of introduction from General Kashkin. The Anchree came to meet him at the very door, so that he was taken for a domestic, and not spoken to till Matrei Ivanovitch kissed his hand. They were presently seated in his apartment, the letter read, and conversation commenced. It turned upon the climate and productions of Eussia compared to England–the Anchree had a hot-house, but could not succeed with fruit–talked of China and the Archimandrite there. " His air and conversation showed him to be quite the simple bonhomme that I had heard he was, without the least ecclesiastical importance. From him went to the Vice-Governor; his wife to all appearance French, though really Russ. Three or four were at cards, one of whom addressed me to let me know it was an English game they were playing. He was a man between forty and fifty; forty-six as he afterwards said; very lively in conversation, which he seemed upon some occasions pretty much to engross. The Governor's lady exceedingly sprightly, gay, and pleasing, if not a beaut) 7. Cards, on my account, were soon at an end, and this man placed himself between the lady and me. He spoke a few words of English, said he had known it, but for these dozen years had lost it for want of practice. It so happened we talked of laws and new government, and I of the clemency of the penal laws in particular, compared to those of other nations, not excepting my own. After taking my leave, I was not a little surprised that this facetious engrosser of the conversation was Poushkin, the man banished for forging bank notes."

I4: th.–" In the morning inquired about the fabric of lacquered furniture in the Chinese fashion, but found that there is only one man that does it, and that he has not always work; at present he had none that I could see. So with respect to furs and Chinese commodities, no stock is kept here, the merchants only transport their commodities through the place.

"Went to see Volodinenoff, one of the capital merchants; found him in a nasty saloop (a kind of loose dressing-gown). I asked him if the master of the house was at home. He told me he was the master himself. After presenting brandy, tea-kettle and tea apparatus was brought into the room, with bread and butter, cream in a cream-pot, which was set in an empty basin, serving as slop basin, into which boiling water was poured to heat the cream. He showed me some tiger skins, which the Buchanans bring to the borders; he deals also in other furs from Beresofska, where he had been himself; said much of the honesty of the people there; that they suffer any injury to themselves rather than molest a stranger; that they have no bread; they do not live in large villages, but dispersed about the banks of those rivers which afford them most fish, and in woods where there are most animals for furs. They give furs in exchange for linen for shirts, coarse cloth, tobacco, andc.

"The Governor says the barks made use of are the worst possible for expedition; they are square at both ends, frequently without even oars–sails are never thought of: this is the reason why water transport by the Irtish is not more used, but if they could be brought to build better vessels, it would be much more expeditious.

" At the Governor's to dinner, he still in bed. Poushkin was there. We talked of the manner in which Siberia became peopled: lstly. Permission was given to the nobility to send any of their peasants there, in consideration of which they were excused from giving the like number of soldiers. 2ndly. By those sent for crimes. This may be considered as an artifice by which the required number of soldiers was kept up. 3rdly. By Easkolniks who came to take shelter from the persecution which they suffered in other parts of the empire. 4thly. Individuals purchased by barter from the Kirgees; but these are all Calmucks, or at least go under that name, and do not amount to one hundred in a year; according to the reports of last year there were but twenty.

5thly. Eussians, who, even before consent was given by government, used to come hunting, and returned with what they procured, but by degrees settled themselves. Gthly. A colony of Bucharians, about thirty years ago, settled in the town, but they now are mixed in great part with the Eussians. 7thly. Tartars, ancient inhabitants of Siberia, with several other tribes, who scarcely, and but by slow degrees, mix with the Eussians.

" Murders there have been none, during the three years that the Governor has been here, and only two attempts at robberies; one of them was on a merchant, known to have much money. He was attacked on returning from Irbit fair; he fired a gun and they ran away: in the other case some merchandise was forcibly taken from a merchant, near Tomsk. In the town of Tobolsk, small robberies now and then happen, but are always discovered, as they are committed only by pilferers, who go immediately to the cabacs to get drunk with the profits of their thefts. They talk of thirty-four and thirty-six degrees of cold (Eeaumur)."

" The part of the country called the Baraba desert is not without wood, but it is birch only, and for the most part consisting of old trees, without any appearance of young ones to supply their places. Within 150 versts of Tomsk, the face of the country changes, it becomes hilly about the rivers. The weather warm or scarcely freezing, and the buds on the trees begin to swell.

" T hen we were within two posts of Tomsk, I sent the soldier on with the order from the Governor to the Commander, requesting, at the same time, quarters to be prepared, and the bath to be heated. The quarters assigned me were at the principal merchant's, where, soon after our arrival, came the Commander, a stout jolly subject, Frenchman by birth and family, but had been forty-five ears in the Eussian service. He eno-ao-ed me to take coffee at his house, and was so urgent in his request that I would dine with him next day that I could not refuse; notwithstanding my wish to hasten on to Kiachta, sat with him till ten in the evening, after which a soft bed was not unwelcome."

" On the 26th arrived at Krasnojarsh.". Here a chasm occurs in his journal, but he appears to have passed some little time amongst the Bratski, nomades in the Government of Tobolsk, and to have obtained a good deal of information respecting this people. He says: " The Tonjmses and the Bratski have not the least communication or intercourse with each other, their languages are totally different, and their religion also; although in their manner of living, they so much resemble each other. The Bratski, Mongol, and Don Cossack languages are very nearly the same, as many of the Bratski read and write the Mongol language, which is all the writing they have. Their books are only religious. If they are superstitious, they are neither fanatics nor intolerant. The principal religious injunctions are very moral, and as they are drawn up, they may be made to give sanction to any salutary injunctions whatever. The number of cattle they keep arises from religious sanction. The head Bratski has about seventy camels, which sell for about thirty roubles a piece; he has also from six to fifteen horses. The camel's hair is cut off in the spring, and is used to make thread and small string. Camels have young once in two years: they will carry forty pood; but when loaded with only twenty-five, they will travel with it thirty versts a day."

" One particular Bratski, Fedenka, seemed much to wish to go with me; he is a servant to one of his tribe who serves the post; he receives as wages ten roubles; he is eighteen years of age, no wife or much hope of procuring one, as parents do not give their daughters without a good price in cattle, from six or eight to one hundred head of large cattle, camels, horses,, or oxen. If few have no more than one wife, it is because they are not rich enough to afford more; those who can afford it have two, three, four or five wives. They suffer much from cold and from hunger; they eat but once a day, and that of their dried meat. We treated them with fresh butter, and different meats I had with me. They devoured the feast with great expressions of joy. They are also very fond of bread, although not accustomed to it. Dirty scrapings flung on the floor they gathered up, and never left what a dog or cat would have eaten.

" At about three versts from the village of Nicolai, a view of the sea of Baikal presents itself. It is seen between the mountains where they divide and give an outlet to the Angora; at the same time the prospect between those hills is bounded by the great mountains near 100 versts on the other side of the sea. These mountains are still almost covered with snow, only those prominences the most exposed to the sun being as et thawed. We passed by Mcolai wharf to Listvenishna, ten versts further. The road was dirty on account of the late rains, and two or three rivulets, which we drove across, were not furnished with bridges, though. the water came up nearly over the fore wheels. These rivulets, falling with great velocity from the hills on the left, contributed to the forming some delightful spots. The young birch trees and a variety of flowers added to the general luxuriance of the ground, giving all between the mountains and the river the appearance of those situations most prized in England.

" To add to the repast we were preparing for ourselves at Listvenishna, I sent for wild nettles, of which two sorts were brought. The people were surprised that such things were good to eat, but when I had boiled them, the dish was relished by all the company. For myself I thought them little inferior to spinach.

" On the way to Narchinsk chance presented an instance of the mechanical ingenuity of a peasant. It was a trap for wild animals, in which the bait was attached to the string of a bow in such manner that the elasticity of the bow was such as to occasion the fall of the trap on the slightest motion of the string. On reaching another fabric we made an excursion of half a dozen versts to a spring of Seltzer water. It is in a pleasant vale, surrounded by hills. The spring issues from a hole nearly in the lowest part of the vale. After spreading itself for about twenty yards it runs into the river. At present it is frozen so as not to run, but a hole of a foot diameter is broken through the ice (now six inches thick), and here the water is taken up."

25th February.–At Narchinsk he found a serjeant waiting at the first guard-house to conduct him to the lodgings which had been for a week prepared for him. They belonged to the possessor of the only silver mines that were in private hands. On examining plans of the different mines in the vicinity, there appeared a great w T ant of economy in the manner of their exploitation.

In the smelting of the lead ore containing silver, he says that, " at the instant the last of the lead is drawn off the silver remains. This is taken out, in general, in lumps; but lest small pieces should remain, which might be pilfered, iron grates are put to the aperture, and a chain passing round them is sealed in the presence of an officer." From thence to the laboratory, where the director was proving a mineral which he found to be a rich ore of bismuth; then to that gentleman's lodgings, which were at the school. He had a small collection of minerals, and the beginning: of a cabinet, intended to be appropriated to the Crown. In this collection specimens of every variety of mine are lodged, with marks affixed, referring to like numbers on the plans of the several mines, showing the parts of them from which each specimen is taken. This cabinet when completed, at the same time that it will exhibit the several varieties which this part of the country affords, will give an excellent description of the component parts of each mine, in as far as it has been worked. Such a description of cabinet cannot but assist a judicious mineralogist in his researches as to new mines, and new manners of working them, as well as in continuing to advantage the working of the present mines."

" The river Angora, which forms the boundary to the Chinese frontier, is but ten versts from Narchinsk. The water of the Angora is very good, and deep enough for the largest boats. The country all around, as far as could be seen, exceedingly hilly; scarcely any wood to be seen; what little there was, very small, but at the same time the country is fertile in iron."

" At 9 in the morning on the following day we set out and alighted at a house, the cleanest and most orderly I had seen in any part of the empire. The owner of it was a criminal who, in Eussia, had been both robber and murderer. His wife presently set before us some brunitska berries and white bread. The man had not only become the most orderly possible, but was particularly noted for the good he does."

" We reached the Zavod about 7 o'clock in the morning. The Commander, a German about fifty years of age, was an acquaintance and fellow-student of Dr. Solander. He had taken great pains in the chemical department, and they were not fruitless. A species of mineral which the
others had been throwing away, not knowing its properties, or suspecting its value, he discovered to be a rich ore of mercury. Narishkin was at that time Commander, and in the name of the Empress gratified him with a reward of 1500 roubles for his discovery. He employed the sum in giving a kind of affluence to his menage until the end of Narishkin's command, when the 1500 roubles were required back from him, on the pretence of Narishkin's having lavished the Crown money. The greatest part of this money had been employed, and much of it irrevocably spent; therefore half his salary was kept back till this last year, when the whole of the money had been repaid. This same ingenious and industrious man discovered that another mineral, which had withstood the experiments and researches of other chemists, was a rich ore of zinc. For this he had not even been thanked. He seemed to hint that he knew of tin ore in the neighbourhood, but was not disposed to give himself much trouble in researches, having so much reason to regret those he had pursued. He gave me some ore of mercury and several other rare specimens. He has an excellent cabinet of Japanese as well as Eussian minerals. He had also, as well as several others, received promotion in rank from Narishkin, but was reduced as well as all the rest. Whatever crimes that man (Narishkin) had been guilty of, certainly he had in many cases attended to the reward of merit."

Mr. Bentham, instead of being stopped at the gate of the suburbs of Kiachta, was met by a soldier, who desired the driver to follow him, "and then conducted us to quarters prepared for me. They were at a merchant's, the best house in the town. As soon as dressed, sent for sledges and drove to the Director's. There was something particularly amiable in the appearance of this gentleman, his lady and family, which consisted of eight children, from sixteen years of age downwards. I knew that I could have admittance to Chinese merchants; but as to the Chinese

Commander, it seemed doubtful as to whether I should have permission to visit him. After refusing pressing invitation to stay supper, went out to call on the Commandant. He also doubted whether the Sergetsky would permit me to visit him. At my return to my quarters, found the supper I would not eat at the Director's sent here in readiness for me."

" The next day, having dressed by 9 o'clock, set out, intending to call on the Director, but met him on his way to my quarters."

" A note came from the Commandant, saying that the Sergetsky much wished to have the honour of my visit. This apparent change in his disposition seemed surprising. Immediately after dinner, Matrei Ivanovitch and I drove to Kiachta, and alighted at the Lieutenant's, who is the Commander there. The winter road is on the river Kiachta, and is not more than three versts. After settling the ceremony to be observed, sent to let the Sergetsky know that we were coming. Imagining that more parade would be expected if we went in sledges, than on foot, I proposed that we should walk, the distance not being more than half a verst."

The notes of this first interview appear to have been lost; the next remaining note runs thus:–" As I wished to see the Chinese manner of eating, we went by 11 o'clock to one of the merchants. He had dined, but understanding the purpose of my visit, he prepared a second dinner. This was shortly done, as it consisted of cold dishes, with one exception. This was hashed meat, enclosed in coverings of paste, and boiled–a kind of dumplings, not too large to be taken into the mouth at once. They were served in basins, about a dozen in each of them, one of which was presented to each of the company. Four of us sat crossed-legged to the table. Each person was provided with a saucer, in which was a piece of sugar-candy, and some thick, black, but not ill-tasted vinegar, poured upon it. This served as

E 2 sauce, into which the dumplings were to be dipped when broken in halves, thus to be made two mouthfuls of. Two or three of the other dishes were filled with hashed meat, made into small lumps of different figures. Salt fish formed another dish; a kind of isinglass another. There were fried batter cakes covered with sugar, but all in very small pieces. Different pickles, in still smaller saucers, were placed between the other dishes. The whole had the appearance of what children in their piny call making a feast, when all is in miniature, and seems more to look at than to eat.

" When returned to the Eussian merchant's, came a message from the Commander, to let me know the Sergetsky was at his house, and to ask if I would take that opportunity of seeing him again. I went immediately. The Commander left the Sergetsky to come out to the steps to meet me, and as I came into the room the Sergetsky left his sofa to meet me. We shook hands in the Chinese manner with both hands. He had been seated on the sofa, to which a table had been put, the Commander on a chair by the side, according to the Russian custom. The suite were standing. Whether by accident or design I was placed on the sofa with the Sergetsky, but next to the Commander; so that I was between them. The tea and three glasses of punch, which were successively served, the Commander handed to me first. The Sergetsky seemed the first time piqued at this, and declined accepting. The Commander, however, in the pressing manner of the Russians, took the glass and put it down to him on the table. In conversation, the Sergetsky asked my age; I did the like by him. Upon his answering forty-four, I observed that by his looks I should have imagined him to be much younger. He replied that possibly that appearance had been in consequence of the healthiness of the part of the country he had long lived in– Canton. This not a little surprised me, as he appeared to be so very ignorant of Euro- pean concerns, notwithstanding the trade that is carried on with England at that place. To assure myself of his veracity I inquired if he corresponded with friends there, and if he did, would he favour me so far as to convey a letter from me to my countrymen, to which he readily assented; and after some inquiries as to my object in writing, it was settled that my letter should be forwarded, if closed with a flying seal."

" When we had drunk the stated number of glasses of punch, he took his leave, got into his two-wheeled cart drawn by one horse, two men leading it, and set off: his attendants were some of them on horseback, others on foot: his saddle-horse was led after the carriage."

66 Kiachta, the general mart for all the commerce carried on by the Russians with China, is, properly speaking, two separate towns–one of them, Kiachta, inhabited by Russians–the other, Naimatchin, by Chinese. Naimatchin has three gates towards Kiachta, three towards China, and one gate on each side of the town. There is not any theatre at Naimatchin. On the site of a former one a new temple has been built: the merchants erected it in thanksgiving for the prosperity of their commerce. The principal figure in this temple is a goddess with a golden face, and otherwise richly mounted; on her right hand a smaller figure, its hands in a praying position; on the other side, a girl holding what they said was a cloth, and they added that both figures were servants. The pedestal on which the principal figure's feet rest, as she sits, is supported by two figures. Behind the goddess, and fronting the opposite way, is a rather smaller figure, which is said to be her son: he has a looking-glass at his breast, holds his hands in a praying position, his knees a little bent, and across them a piece of fanza. This, they say, is not according to their religion, but was permitted at the request of a Mogul, the commander of the limits."

" Painted on the walls on each side are nine figures, very much resembling Christian saints: they have all glories round their heads; some hold beads, shorter indeed than the Catholic rosary, and two books. Above these are some little figures, one of them a man on his knees receiving punishment from a whip. A judge sits to see the execution of the sentence. Near this group is a woman, a sister of their gods. Some of the saints on one side were hideously ugly, meagre, and attenuated; on the other side a frightfully fat saint; but all of them had glories."

" All the gods look towards their country, excepting the goddess in the new temple, who looks towards the great pagoda, to which it is near and opposite. The principal god in the great temple has eight or ten dresses: the merchants, when he assists them, make vows to give him a new coat, and as no one is ever taken off, the new dress is put over the old ones. War instruments are kept on each side the platform leading to the pagoda from the portico."

" For fortune-telling there is a vessel about the size of a quart mug full of fortune-telling pieces that have letters on them: any person desirous of learning his future fate takes one of these pieces and searches for a corresponding figure or letter in a book which lies by, and thus ascertains his future. This may be done at any time, but is chiefly performed either on the new year's day or on the man's own happy day. The fortune-seeker puts money through holes in the altar into a sealed drawer. By permission of the Sergetsky, this drawer is opened by twelve men chosen for the management of the affairs of the temple."

" The god of the temple in the G-obirsky desert (which is between this and the great wall) died about five years ago. The great lama was immediately sent to, inquiring whither the soul had passed. The commissioners were informed that it had entered the son of the Mogul who was commander of the lines. This is a boy, at that time not three years old. He was taken immediately to the temple to be taught his duty. It is sometimes asked, why teach a god? The reply is, that the soul, being god, has no need of instruction; but that the body must be instructed. The boy's father must no longer call him son, but worship the child instead of receiving filial duty from him.

" In the traffic between the Eussians and the Chinese, the China merchant always comes to the Russian, but only to his shop or dwelling-house, not to the storehouse. The Chinaman asks the Russian if he has such and such merchandise; if so, and if the meeting be at the house, the Russian either accompanies the customer to his shop, or sends some one thither with him to see the goods. The Chinese merchant returns to the house, and over a cup of tea the price of the goods is settled in roubles: next has to be determined what kind of Chinese merchandise is to be received to that amount, and at what price. On this valuation of Chinese articles, not only species is inquired into, but also from whence they came, where fabricated, and every other circumstance influencing value. These preliminaries arranged, the Russian accompanies the Chinese home, inspects the goods, and, if according to agreement, brings them home with him."

" The Chinese do not make use of sledges, but transport their merchandise either on the backs of camels or in two-wheeled carts drawn by oxen. The wheels of these carts do not turn on the axle, but are fitted on to it so that the whole turns together."

" There is no interpreter provided by the Russian Crown, nor is there any allowance for such an office. That government allows only the insignificant sum of twenty roubles a year for the payment of spies and other political expenses; nor is there anything allotted for shows or entertainments, excepting 30 vedros a year of common Russ brandy. This allowance is made to the major who commands the borders of China; but as he does not himself

E 4 receive the Chinese, he gives six vedros to each of the officers who reside at Kiachta.

"The Sergetsky's duty is confined to the police of Naimatchin, and to the commerce between Russia and China. All matters that have reference to the frontiers are in the department of a Mogul styled Commander of the Frontiers. He is the superior in rank everywhere but at Naimatchin."

"A few anecdotes were obtained indicative of the policy and manners of the two nations in their intercourse with each other; amongst them a remarkable one relative to an endeavour on the part of the Russian Commandant of the Frontier to reconcile Russian law with the treaty existing between that country and China. According to the terms of that treaty, in the case of a man of the one nation passing its boundaries and committing robbery or murder, the punishment should be death; yet, according to the then existing Russian law, capital punishment was abolished. It happened at two different periods, the one three, the other four years ago, that seven Chinese who had been guilty of these crimes were taken, tried by the Chinese, and condemned. Thereupon, the Russian major, fearing that should any Russians be guilty of the same offence the Chinese would require that they should suffer death, gave orders that the punishment of the condemned Chinese should not be required, or at all events that no Russian should witness it. The Chinese, however, to show the exactitude with which they fulfilled the treaty, endeavoured to engage Russians to be present at the execution; but not being able to effect this, the Chinese commander invited the Russian in command to visit him on the day appointed for the execution. The Russian accepted, but on perceiving the object of the invitation, feigned sudden illness, and endeavoured to get home; but the Chinese officer, running after him, retained him as it were by force to see the execution."

CHAP. IV.

Condition and Treatment of Exiles in Siberia– He descends the Angora from Irkutsk– Letter to his Brother Jeremy Bentham– Fanaticism of Russian Peasants– Appeal on the Murder of a Tonguse– Slave Trade of the Kirgees– Fertility of Siberia– He visits Nijni Novgorod– Returns to St. Petersburg, and presents a Report to the Empress– Declines Lord Shelburne's Offer of a Commissionership of the Navy– Sir James Harris leaves Bentham as Charge daffaires at St. Petersburg– He is appointed a " Conseiller de la Cour," and entrusted with the Works of the Fontanha Caual– Engagement with the Niece of Prince Galitzm– Letter of Sir James Harris– The Engagement finally broken off– He is appointed Lieutenant-Colonel in the Russian Army, with the Command of the Southern part of the Country.

On Bentham's return from Kiachta, he interested himself warmly in the fate of culprits exiled to Siberia. He observed: "I have had an advantage which could be obtained at this period only. I have had opportunities of witnessing the injustice which was habitual under the former mode of government, and at the same time the impossibility of committing it under the new. I have been in districts at the time when the old form still remained in sufficient force to judge of its effects, and I have witnessed the advantages of the new form in places where it has been introduced. I have seen proofs of the very mistaken notions that are entertained of the treatment to which exiles are subjected in Siberia. I passed through several villages in my way from Kiachta to Barnaval, which were inhabited entirely by exiles from different parts of Russia, and who had received the knout. There were no guards, nor any other people within the distance of perhaps a hundred versts. These exiles cultivate their land, and enrich themselves in a manner they never would have done in Kussia. The idea of fear never entered my head when amongst them. On setting out from St. Petersburg I had thought it necessary to provide pistols and other arms, but I had never used, seen, or even inquired about them since I entered Siberia. Some of the men employed in the mines do, it is true, occasionally run away, and have in that case no other means of subsistence but that of pilfering in the villages they pass through in the course they take for escape; but as this happens in summer only, they are generally taken before winter sets in. The punishment for such escape was formerly severe, and sure to be inflicted: this made them resolute in self-defence, and consequently blood was frequently shed on both sides; but of late years, by making the punishment for simple desertion light, though still heavy in the case of violence committed, these runagates almost always return of themselves in the course of a few days."

" The number of working days in the year is 270, but those who labour at the furnaces are allowed every third week as holiday. For some descriptions of work in which free people are employed, the pay given for it amounts only to twenty, eighteen, and even so little as fifteen roubles a year."

In a letter to his brother, Bentham says: " I am now descending the Angora from Irkutsk to Jeneseisk in a bark in which merchants are transporting their goods from Kiachta to different parts of Russia. You never in your days beheld such a romantic scene as I have at present before my eyes: mountainous rocks descending into a broad and rapid river, and forming in it little islands, exhibiting to the imagination the ruins of castles and towns of various figures. Farther on delightful meadow ground, with clumps of birch trees, bounded by a thick, deep green wood. A straggling village, with a white church, that has a gilded cross on it; not a cloud to be seen; and to complete the whole, a peasant on the shore, while his cattle are drinking at the river, sits on a willow stump and entertains us as we pass with a charming lively pastoral air on a Scotch bagpipe. I regret the swiftness with which we glide along out of hearing of these pastoral notes."

To his Brothei" Jeremy Bentham.

" Tobolsk, August 28th, 1782, O. S. "At Omsk fortress, on the frontiers of the empire, towards the Kirgisian territories, I learnt, by the Russian Gazette, of Rodney's success in the West Indies. The post, arrived to-day, brings the disagreeable news of the critical situation of Lord Howe, who, with only twenty-two sail of the hue, seems liable to be exposed to and even determined to engage the fleet of the enemy, amounting to forty sail. The same papers give some little hope that our fleet may be reinforced to thirty-five sail; if so (as according to my calculation 35 + Lord Howe's abilities = 40), we shall be a match for them. Such very interesting public news, together with the circumstance of my not having received a single letter from England of a date later than October last, makes me anxious to an extreme degree to reach Petersburg, and almost incapable of supporting the least delay in my journey. The opening the new mode of jurisdiction in this government takes place here the day after to-morrow, and though this is what I wished much to be present at, and had promised to stay for, yet upon the receipt of this last news I lost all patience. I went directly to the Governor-General for the purpose of taking leave. Nothing, however, would he hear about taking leave; vowed he would not let me have post horses till the day after to-morrow, and in short Avill not permit me to set off before that time. In the mean time 'tis true I shall rest myself a little, which upon the whole may not be time lost. From Barnaval here I have not slept but in the carriage, and as the roads are bad at this time of year my sleep could not be very sound. From hence to Petersburg I shall not be disposed to give a single hour to rest. This letter goes by courier who sets off directly, yet I hope to be at Petersburg a few days after him, notwithstanding the preference on the road with which couriers are served.

" How vexatious it is that I cannot know a syllable of what you are about now; at such a time as this you must certainly be otherwise employed than in pursuance of your former works. The reinforcements for Lord Howe not being ready makes me, as it were, ready to jump out of my skin. Were I in authority I should, I believe, never sleep but in my way from one dockyard to another; Messieurs the commissioners of the navy and dockyard officers should have no more rest than I have now on my journey; the fear of such a whip before their eyes as one of my grenadiers puts life into when my postilions are lazy, would make these gentlemen a little more alert–a little Russian discipline would work wonderful changes in such lukewarm dispositions. The master shipwright himself, if he had nothing better to do, should blister his hands in setting an example to the workmen. Not one bit of ornament, or of accommodation for an officer should occasion a moment's delay. Is it possible that carved work and mouldings, planings and polishings, should, at such a time as this,, make part of the employment of dockyard workmen, whose labour is of so great moment? Is an hour in the day, that is half a day in the week, still spent in the cutting up and secreting of chips? Is it by such lying reports as are sent up that the Lords of the Admiralty as well as the Navy Board, and whomsoever else it may concern, that the progress of works in the dock yards is still judged of? They would get better information from the newspapers."

It will subsequently be seen that at a much later period, when Mr. Bentham engaged himself in the British service as Inspector-Greneral of Naval Works, he did effect the cessation of many abuses, that of chips amongst others; but that instead of the application of the whip as thus playfully threatened, all of his official communications exhibited that it was not men but the system of management that was at fault, and that it was the imperfection of accounts that gave rise to and fostered lying reports.

Notes of the ceremony on introducing the new jurispru- dence have not been found, but it appears that he collected a considerable mass of information as to facts illustrating the eccentricities no less than the general habits and opinions of the people. As an instance of the excesses to which mistaken religious enthusiasm sometimes leads, he noted particulars that had actually occurred about the month of May of this year, 1782: " A common servant in the neighbourhood of Tobolsk, a man of a sect dissenting; from the established religion, happened, in reading the Holy Bible, to see that the end of the world was foretold to be near at hand. Struck with the importance of this prophecy, and considering it in some measure as a discovery of his own, and himself as it were the author, he became heated with a sort of sacred fire, and, conceiving that the discovery reflected importance on himself, he set about making his fanatic brethren proselytes to his opinions, and soon found many to embrace them. Preparations for this great event was now the business to which all else must give way. The Eucharist was administered, and the most severe fastings imposed. When the imagination of these visionaries was worked up to a certain height their frenzy rendered them impatient for the coming of the happy day, for which they were so preparing; three of them were already stoned to death, a woman and two children; the rest, to the number of fifty, assembled at a lake, fathers, mothers, and children, and plunged themselves into it. The enthusiast, after plunging a child of his own, on its struggling to get out, rendered ineffectual its endeavours to save itself, and held it under water."

" This man, however, enjoyed too great satisfaction in the sensation of his own importance to thus put an end to his own life, and so prevent him from making more proselytes; but the Government getting notice of his proceedings secured him, and he is now in chains awaiting his trial."

An extraordinary case of appeal to the Grovernor-Greneral had been made in the case of a Tonguse who had been killed in pity to his suffering state: " This man had lost his senses, and though in this condition, so long as he did no harm, he was allowed to follow his whimsies, and was supplied with necessaries by the community. At length, however, his madness took a mischievous turn, so as no longer to be bearable by his companions. They assembled together, therefore, to consult as to what should be done with him: the general decision was that, as he had become unhappy in himself and burthensome to others, he should be killed! This judgment was accordingly carried into execution. The Tonguse, though a people living solely by hunting, and in a part of Asia 3000 versts northward of this place, are tributary to the crown of Russia, and are obliged to report deaths to the nearest seat of Government. The family of this man reported how they had put him to death themselves, and for what reasons. The tribunal to which the report came, knowing that according to the Russian law these people would be prosecuted as murderers, appealed to the Governor-General for directions as to how they were to proceed in this extraordinary case. The Governor-General's answer was that as their motive had been compassion for the unhappy being, attention must be paid to their peculiar way of thinking, and therefore that in this case the letter of the law must be waived! Many are the occasions on which a Governor-General in this land of various tribes is called upon to exercise his judgment and his humanity in the fulfilment of the difficult charge imposed upon him, and for the due execution of which he is individually responsible to his sovereign."

" One source of increase to the population of Siberia arises from the depredations of the Kirgees: they seize people of every description who foil into their hands, consider their captives as lawful property, and when they have no occasion for their services, change them away like other merchandise with Russian merchants; merchants nut being noble, cannot generally possess slaves, but to encourage this mode of acquiring subjects, the empress accords to merchants the privilege of purchasing and possessing as slaves people that they buy from the Kirgees. The heir of a merchant cannot inherit serfs, consequently at the death of the purchaser his slaves become free, and thus a number of additional subjects are obtained every year. These being the only kind of slaves a merchant can possess, competition enhances the price of the commodity; a boy of ten years old will sell even up to 200 roubles. General Kashkin has a boy of seven, and a girl of four, which a merchant let him have at prime cost, 110 roubles for the boy, 50 for the girl. Sometimes the Kirgees, tempted by merchandise of which they are in want, will give their own children in exchange for it."

" In the course of travels over such an extent of country, so circumstanced as is Russian Siberia, any unprejudiced foreigner would of course perceive many instances where the management of it might be amended. Thus the policy seems doubtful of entrusting the eastern confines of it to the protection of the Bratski, a people so little attached to Russia, or to any other country. It would seem that, were Government better acquainted than they are with details as to the habits of the different people in Siberia, with the capabilities of the country, with its actual cultivation and its commerce, a great increase of individual comfort to the inhabitants might result, at the same time that the revenues of the crown might be greatly augmented. It occurred to me that such information might be afforded in the most simple manner by means of charts and tabular printed forms. A chart, for instance, exhibiting the state of cultivation, and the population of the different provinces of the Russian empire, at the period of the close of the reign of Peter the Great; another at that of Elizabeth; and so at the conclusion of successive reigns down to the latest period. Were such charts to accompany the history

G4 LIFE OF SIR SAMUEL BEXTHAM.

of the empire, they would give a much more striking and exact account of what improvements had taken place in these respects under each reign than can be obtained by words."

" It is in this country that human nature may be seen in its greatest varieties, and where the most ample field for its study is afforded. There is an assemblage of tribes of various religions, several of which are intolerant in their belief; yet all these people are politically united under one Government, of which they all agree to be peaceable members."

" Siberia has been thought capable of producing only a small pittance of corn, and that by infinite labour; on the contrary, the peasants, who, in this country, are far more indolent than in other parts of the Kussian empire, without ever dreaming of bestowing manure on their ground, live for the most part in abundance. Were a sea communication formed from the mouths of the Siberian rivers, exportation of corn would be carried to a great extent. One reason why Russians have so long remained ignorant of the state of Siberia, may be that officers sent to it have been interested in representing it as unfruitful, in order to account for the high prices they gave it to be understood must be paid for necessaries. Having come to the country before the whole of it was under the new jurisdiction, I myself have known 1000. English to have been sent to the meeting at where a person was sent to examine into abuses. This sum was as a conditional fee upon his resolving to see all as it should be. In the former mode it is impossible but that means the most inhuman conceivable should sometimes have been employed for the extortion of money by those in power; but such practices are now effectually at an end. True, a degree of favour and countenance from those in power may now, in fault of other recommendations, be to be gained by small presents. And where is it not?"

On the 3rd September he arrived at Catherinaburg, visiting in his way manufactories as well as mines, pursuing his route towards St. Petersburg by Kazan to Nijni Novgorod, where he remained ten days. His halt at Ivan Volesta was at the same house where Peter the Great had dined. The monarch had come into it as a boor, sat down and eat with boors, and it was not till after dinner, when his people came in, that those in the house knew him to be their sovereign. He had worked here himself as a carpenter. " I had observed the good workmanship of the vessels built here, as well as their being of the Dutch fashion: certainly it was Peter who had given them this model, and had engaged them farther to give much attention to the workmanship. At the pressing solicitation of the people here, I ate some bread and salt with them." In a letter to his brother, never completed, written at Nijni Novgorod, he says,–"I have been here now 'tis true a week, but it is with the utmost difficulty I have been able to take time to write, and more than once have been nearly taking resolution to quit the place in despair of writing to you in it. Various have been the obstructions; for the most part over-pressing invitations of people bringing me out in the morning to see one thing or another. After dinner one day, a ball, another, a masquerade, and as the Governor gives these entertainments on my account, it was impossible not to stay them out. This made two late mornings. All the world paid me their visits, three or four of them at least I could not but return. Another plague is that melons and water melons are in great abundance, and finding that I was fond of them, I am crammed with them morning, noon, and night: five times I ate of them yesterday. Worst of all is that I am lodged at the house of a prattling, troublesome, civil, old woman, who has a pretty, good-natured daughter, who, unluckily for me, takes it into her head, notwithstanding all I say to the contrary, that it must be irksome for me to sit at home by myself, and thrusts herself and a little officer upon me."

By way of Novgorod and Moscow he returned to St. Petersburg, where he arrived on the 9th October, 1782.

From the above it appears that he had reached Kiachta as early as February 1782, the utmost extent of his travels at this time, Kiachta being the frontier town in Siberia, where all the Chinese commerce with Eussia is transacted. It may here be mentioned that the Chinese authorities allowed him to enter their territory, received him and communicated with him amicably, and with a good deal of liberality of sentiment and manner. They also made him many small presents of teas and silks, which he afterwards sent to his father and stepmother in England. Altogether there was not evinced at Kiachta that jealousy of other nations which was observed by the Chinese in other frontiers of their dominions.

During this excursion he visited nearly the whole of the mines in Siberia that he had not already explored, collecting specimens, with a view to their economical as well as geological importance. Amongst the copper ores, especially, were several varieties previously unknown, with others of great value, such as transparent crystals of copper, malachites, and powerful natural magnets. Nor was he negligent of other branches of natural history. He sent a collection of seeds to Sir Joseph Banks, amongst which were several species that were new. From a lake in the neighbourhood of Irkutsk, he sent specimens of the alkali which it deposits, and which promised to be of value as an article of commerce.

Prince Potemkin had great estates in the south of Eussia, and many concerns connected with traffic, chiefly about the Black Sea. He farmed the duties on many articles, built ships for the Crown, supplied the army and the Crown with almost all necessaries required in that part of the empire; he had manufactories of various kinds, and was then clearing the waterfalls of the Dnieper at his oayii expense. The Prince expressed an ardent wish, before Mr.

Bentham set out on his Siberian excursion, that he would render assistance in the improvement of those concerns. Bentham declined any such engagement, as also others that had been pressed upon him by the Demidoffs and the Strogonoffs, " because," as he wrote to his brother, " such an employment in this country would not be sufficient for me–a man who is not in service under the Crown, however rich he may be, is but little respected." He had, however, promised that, on his return towards St. Petersburg, he would visit the Prince's estates, and did so in a manner which now enabled him to be of use when consulted by His Highness respecting those possessions, as also concerning marine matters in the Black Sea.

On Mr. Bentham's return to St. Petersburg, Prince Potemkin undertook to present a paper prepared for the Empress, and contrary to his usual well-known dilatori-ness actually gave it to Her Majesty the day after he had received it. In this paper he stated that his " long stay in the Grovernment of Perme, had afforded opportunity of observing such defects of the system of operations in use there, especially in the mines and salt works, that he could no longer suffer himself to regard them with the eye of simple curiosity; that it was impossible for him to perceive imperfections in matters of such importance, without employing his thoughts in search of the means of remedying them; that the table annexed exhibited the methods which appeared to him the best adapted to the operations carried on, and that those suggestions were in part the result of his researches, some of them inventions of his own, some of them belonging to the department of mechanics, others to that of chemistry." The Empress approved of this paper, and desired the Prince to obtain further details of the proposed improvements.

Princess Dashkoff, also in January 1783, presented to the Empress a chart which he had invented; it was contrived to exhibit, at one view, the absolute and compara-

F 2 live state of the population of the whole, or of any part of the empire. te A little thing," he says on mentioning it, " too simple to have much merit." The Empress, however, ordered a chart of one of her provinces to be made on that plan.

The details of Mr. Bentham's proposed improvements in the mines were speedily delivered to the Prince, who with his habitual dilatoriness for some time neglected to present them to Her Majesty, although she had thrice asked for them. This delay prevented Mr. Bentham from obtaining a private audience till the month of March. Her Majesty then expressed herself as obliged by his communications, and permitted him for the future to state through the Princess Dashkofy whatever ideas of improvement he might entertain in regard to those parts of the empire with which he was acquainted. This was peculiarly agreeable on account of the intimacy and friendship already existing between him and the Princess, as also with her son Prince Dashkoff.

Lord Shelburne having become a member of the Administration in England, now offered Mr. Bentham a com-missionership of the navy. But his prospects in Kussia were of a nature which induced him to decline the appointment; although in a letter to his father giving the reasons which influenced him, he says: " A strong attachment to my country in general, a kind of patriotism– arising from a comparison between that and every other country I have seen–a longing desire to return to those so entirely separated from me, and apart from whom I could never long be happy–would not permit me to engage in any plan here without very striking advantages."

His brother at this time had intimated his intention of sending to St. Petersburg certain projects in law reform, from which Samuel dissuaded him on the ground that the heads of the law departments would think it a shame for them with their experience to be beholden to a foreigner for improvements in the details in their business. " Different, however," said he, " was the conduct of Count Orloft when the Empress gave him public thanks for his services in destroying the Turkish fleet. I, says the Count, taking our countryman by the hand, had the sincerest desire possible to serve your Majesty and my country, but it is to Admiral Grreig's advice and abilities your Majesty is indebted. Had I been present at such a speech my sensibility to the generous confession of the Count would even have scarcely let me perceive the merit of the Admiral, to which the words of the Count were intended entirely to direct attention. This expression which, from the character of the Count, seems to have come from his heart, could not certainly, from a man in his circumstances, but gain the hearts of his hearers. But enough of this digression, and of sermonising from your younger brother."

A variety of plans were in agitation for fixing him in the Russian service, when, on the 30th May, after a dinner to which Bentham had been particularly invited, Sir James Harris took him aside, and proposed that he should take charge of the diplomatic business from the time of his (Sir James's) departure till the arrival of the new Ambassador,– in short, that Mr. Bentham should become Charge d Affaires. Sir James had the complaisance to put acceptance on the footing of an obligation to himself, saying that thereby he should be enabled to leave Petersburg earlier than he otherwise could do. Such an honourable post was not to be refused, and Sir James wrote the same day to Mr. Fox, acquainting him with the appointment.

In June Mr. Bentham offered, by letter, to inspect the introduction of the improvements which he had suggested. Her Majesty on reading it immediately expressed, in answer, her desire to engage him in her service, and gave him liberty to choose the place of his intended operations, intimating at the same time that he should himself pro-

F 3 pose the terms and manner of engagement. The importance of the mines in Siberia led his wishes to that country, but this was over-ruled by the preference which the Empress entertained for the improvement of those at Olmutz. Still the appointment seemed to linger, and he found that this delay was occasioned by his having accepted the appointment of Charge daffaires; on learning, therefore, that Sir James's successor was shortly to arrive, Mr. Bentham gave up the post.

It happened, however, that circumstances bordering on romance, with which the Empress was acquainted, determined her to fix Mr. Bentham for a time at St. Petersburg, and appointed him a " Conseiller de la Cour," with the civil rank of Lieutenant-Colonel. The works of the Fontanha Canal were given him in charge. In the course of their execution he invented a new pile-driving machine, such as would put an end to the habitual skulking of the labourers, and by which at the same time the whole weight of the men would act beneficially instead of only employing their muscular force. The machine was a kind of ladder which yielded downwards on every step that the men took, on the same principle as that of the walking wheel; but the kind of ladder which he devised was much less cumbersome than the wheel, and therefore more easily moved from place to place as the work of piling advanced.

During the summer he wrote either to his father or to his brother many particulars which he had not had leisure to note during his travels, among others his observations respecting the descent of bodies floating down a river with the stream, the larger body always arriving at its destination sooner than the smaller one, when both started on their descent at the same time. A practical use was habitually made of this fact by the managers of the works at Nijni Taghil, who always despatched their small boats some time before the large ones, in order that all might simultaneously arrive at Tobolsk. Mr. Bentham gave the rationale of this; but the chief subject of his letters at this time was that which caused the indecision manifested in the transactions of this year. A matrimonial alliance was in agitation with a niece of the Grand Chamberlain, Prince Gralitzin, at whose house he made acquaintance with the young lady, and where he met her twice a week. The match was universally favoured by the society of St Petersburg, the lady's mother only being averse to it. The Empress herself took part in the affair, even to the extent of recommending a private marriage. The mother, however, her daughter being a rich heiress and regarded as the principal person of the family, could not consent to bestow her on a foreigner, though she fully admitted that there could be no personal objection, so that after months of anxiety the match was broken off. The following letter from Sir James Harris to Mr. Bent-ham's father bears flattering testimony to the young man's honourable conduct in this romance:–

" Petersburg, May 21st, 1783. " Sir,– I have had too much pleasure in your son's company, ind have too much good to say of him, to make any apology necessary for addressing myself abruptly to his father, when I have no other motive for so doing than to bear testimony that the whole of hs conduct here has been such as does him the highest honour and redit, and such as must give pleasure to those who, like yourslf? are connected with him by consanguinity, or like me by reg r d and esteem.

1 I k ow he has lately informed you of the probability of his entering n to a very desirable and lucrative matrimonial alliance here– h. i it taken place it would have been so; and had your son enrpload the arts of seduction rather than have acted a fair and uprigh Dar t 5 it probably might have succeeded–but he very laudably pr erred the better method, and though the match has failed, he ha re ceived universal approbation for his behaviour, and even the s teem of those who rejected his connection. He has now turnt hi s thoughts another way, and is, I hope, likely to enter into a y advantageous agreement with the Strogonoff

V 4 family, for the working of their mines in Siberia, for which, as they are men of strictest honour and integrity, he is likely to derive very considerable emolument. In whatever undertaking he engages, he will, I am sure, be no discredit to his country, and you need never be apprehensive of his doing wrong. Common justice alone would induce me to say thus much, and as I am sure it will give you pleasure to hear it, I end as I began, without any apology. " I am, Sir, your most obedient, humble servant,

"James Harris."

From this time he was naturally led to wish for employment away from St. Petersburg, and the Empress on her part was desirous of engaging him in improvements relative to the mines of the Crown. He was in high favour with most of the persons who had influence at Court. In a letter from Csarskoe Zelo, 27th July, 1783, he says, "I dined with General Landskoy, as I had done before, when I came here, and his civilities and attentions to me seem still to increase; every mark of attention he showed me while I was looked upon as a stranger I put all to that account; but the manner he treats me now that I am entering the service is really flattering. What I learn by it is that I enjoy the Empress's good opinion." Th place General Landskoy held in her Majesty's good graces is well known. In continuation, Mr. Bentham adds'– " Mme. Sherbinin who, you will please to remember he-ice-forward, is Princess Dashkofy 's daughter, is translatiig? or rather has been attempting to translate, into Englisrsome Essays on the history of this country, which are nc publishing, little by little, in a kind of monthly irigazine printed at the Academy in Russian language. Tese said essays, you are to know, are written by the Emress herself, and she still from time to time works harat it, and means to bring it down to the reign of th Empress Elizabeth. I have the correcting, or sometimes it might be called re-translating, this; which latter eiployment I prefer, as it improves me in the Russian lan ia ge.

Notw? 711 ls Jling the supposed termination of the affair of which Sir James Harris had spoken, the lady's constancy occasioned its breaking out anew, so that Mr. Bentham remained in a state of anxiety during the rest of the year; but in January 1784 he acquainted his father that there was a final end to all further hopes or fears upon the subject. His conduct in the affair was approved of to the last, but he says: " One consequence, however, is that my plans in this neighbourhood must be abandoned, at least for the present; I must certainly quit Petersburg till the affair is blown over, out of delicacy to her, so f hat it is lucky that an offer of Prince Potemkin's affords me a,. a odportunity. He wishes me to go to Cherson; he makes me Ko,, tenant-Colonel in the army, with a promise of promoting me as BO o as possible. As to employment, I am to do anything I am fit for and choose to do."

for

CHAP. V.

Journey to the Crimea–He is settled for a Time at Cricheff– Preparations for Ship-building– Extent of his Engagements– Military Duties– Manufacture of Steel– Building of the River Yacht Vermicular– Arming of a Flotilla at Cherson–Defeat of the Turkish Fleet, June 1788– Bentham receives the Military Order of St. George, with the Bank of full Colonel, and other Rewards–Privateering– Appointed to a Cavalnr Regiment in Siberia– Excursion in the Country of the Kino 13 1 ' 89– Expedition to the Mouth of the River Ob– Kira ignorance of Fire– Ship-building at Kamschatka for thea rfcah Fur Trade–Visits Paris on his Way to JEngjantu

The appointment that had been given to Mr. Bentham of a lieutenant-colonel in the army, had never before been granted either to foreigner or native until after they had already served in an inferior military rank; the new lieutenant-colonel had also the farther advantage of beinp; independent of any other authority than that of Prince Po-temkin. It may be considered as particularly honourable to so young a man, and to a foreigner, that, besides enjoying the friendship of the two successive English ambassadors, Sir James Harris (Lord Malmesbury) and Mr. Fitzherbert(Lord St. Helens), of the French ambassador, the Count de Segur. afterwards so eminently distinguished by his literary works, he was on equal terms of intimacy and friendship with most of the principal persons who then figured at the Residence. His journey from St. Petersburg was in the same carriage with Prince Potemkin, who treated him more as he would have done a son than even as a friend; it was to visit the Prince's estates and the newly acquired province of the Crimea. After this tour of inspection, Lieutenant-Colonel Bentham settled himself for a time at Cricheff.

This town is part of an estate, the property of the Prince; the whole estate is larger than any English county, its population amounted to above 40,000 males. The country produced the principal articles of naval stores in great abundance, and they were of easy transport to the Black Sea by the river Soje, which ran through the estate.

His friend, Colonel Kibaupierre, who had an estate on the Dnieper, not far from Omsk, being desirous of engaging some. Englishman, to introduce improvements, Lieutenant-Colonel Bentham, on writing to his brother, in hopes of engaging a suitable person, gave many particulars of the present state and capabilities of the property. Although snow remained on the ground five months of winter, the land produced corn, hemp, and flax, and, in general, all the hardy fruits of England. To give an instance of the abundance of labouring hands, he mentioned that whilst he was there his friend ordered a plantation to be made on a spot which he had chosen for a garden, but where there was not a single tree. The person in charge said he would take 1000 of his (Colonel Ribaupierre's) mother's peasants, and 300 of his own, and in one day he should have a plantation of 3000 young trees, taken up with their roots from the adjacent woods.

Bentham's letter on the subject of this estate exhibits an instance of the way in which he could turn his attention to agricultural as well as other matters. He suggested the introduction of potatoes, and the making of hemp and linseed oils, so that besides the profit which these articles would afford, a still more considerable one would be obtained by fattening cattle with the oil cakes. Owing to the deficiency of manure, the returns of grain are poor, and it is miserably small. " Ground is never manured nor seed sown here for hay; what happens to grow is cut; ploughs don't take deeper than about three inches, as you may imagine when I tell you that never more than one horse about the size of an ass is put to draw them." Since that time, there have been in some parts of the empire great improvements in agriculture; but, generally speaking, it is still much in arrear of the cultivation of land in other countries.

On Prince Potemkin's estate he sa T s: " A man will cultivate here six acres of land, besides his garden of cabbages, turnips, carrots, andc. and the cutting of hay, where he can find it growing on waste land, for his horses. He ploughs his land, dungs it, sows it, reaps the corn, and dries it in a kind of oven before he threshes it; he makes all his instruments, and, by the help of his wife, makes his clothes, and supplies all his wants."

"May there not," he asks, "be a chance of obtaining the sugar from some root or fruit so as to come cheaper than what is imported? Water-melons, for example, contain as much as an equal weight of grapes, and they may be had in some parts of the country as cheap as any vegetable substance."

Settled at Cricheff, he says, in a letter to his father, 18th July, 1784: " The natural advantages of the situation of this place, together with the much more important consideration of its being the private property of the Prince, made me choose it for the puttidg in execution some of my ideas of improvement in ship-building. I am to be at liberty to build any kind of ships, vessels, or boats, whether for war, trade, or pleasure; and so little am I confined in the mode of constructing them, that one day, in arguing with the Prince about some alterations in a frigate he proposed building, to make a present of to the Empress, he told me, by way of ending the discussion, that there might be twenty masts and one gun, if I pleased." "Workmen and assistants, I am told to find where I can, and on what terms I can. Ships of above 200 tons cannot be built here; their frames only can be prepared."

"The journey I have been making this spring with the Prince, to me who do not think much of fatigue, has been in every respect highly agreeable. Independent of the flattering manner in which he treated me, and the pleasure which must arise from being witness to the steps taken for the improvement of his Governments, I had not for a long time spent my time so merrily."

" The news of the death of General Landskoy, and the affliction of the Empress on that account, made the Prince set out from Krementchuk with only one servant with him, leaving us all to disperse from thence according to our several destinations;" so that Bentham was left to act entirely according to his own discretion. In the same letter he specifies the description of persons by whose instrumentality he was to build ships. Common carpenters and joiners were the only workers in wood to be found on the estate; of rowers, for row boats, there was not one. He had found at Krementchuk a young man from Stras-burg who had been made teacher of mathematics at the public school: " it is well if ever he has seen a ship building, yet this is the person I have chosen as the best qualified for assisting me in my present business, not for any great knowledge he has of mechanics, but because he seems capable of soon understanding anything, and promises to be much more assiduous than any other person I could find: I have besides two or three Serjeants of the army who draw and write, and who can work enough themselves to be qualified for keeping the workmen to their business; these, with a Danish founder in brass and an English watchmaker, are all I have been able to pick up fit for ship-building." A notable set of dockyard officers and artificers, with whom to complete the frames of 60-gun frigates, in addition to the construction of sea-going ships of 200 tons! " I have taken possession of what is called the Prince's house, though it is more like an old tottering barn with windows in it; what I can find of his I make use of, what else I want I buy with his money; what can be got to eat and drink I have, and I do the honours of the house as well as J can to those who come to fare with me." It happened, on that same da 7, that two ladies of rank did so on their way to visit the nieces of the Prince. His fare was not always of the most luxurious nature, that very day his dinner had been bread and salted cucumbers.

The great disorder in which he found all the Prince's factories at Cricheft, induced him to offer his services for its correction. In a letter to the Prince, he confidently spoke of his ability to restore the whole into complete order, and to raise the factories to a degree of perfection which might most easily be attained.

Prince Potemkin in reply entrusted him with unlimited powers for the execution of his plans, and placed all his officers under his control.

The particular factories thus placed under his management were:– 1. A rope walk, where all the cordage was made for Cherson.

2. A sail-cloth manufactory.

3. A distillery of spirit from corn, to which was annexed a malt-house and beer brewery.

4. A tannery and leather manufactory.

5. Two glass houses, one of them more particularly for window glass.

6. A manufactory for cutting and grinding glass.

7. A pottery, principally for making crucibles.

8. An establishment of smiths, coppersmiths, andc. for making and repairing all the tools and utensils required in the several fabrics.

To the letter giving these details he adds: "Besides directing the above establishment with a view to increasing, as much as possible, the profits to the Prince, I must contrive, as much as may be, to ease the workmen of the oppression they have of late been subject to."

Hitherto he had had the rank and the pay of a Lieutenant-Colonel, but without being attached to any regiment; but in September he was given the command of a battalion.

But at this time his operations were for several weeks at a stand in consequence of severe illness. On taking the command of his battalion he had to consider how, without exhibiting his ignorance of military matters, he might best learn the business of a soldier, and determined to instruct himself by close attention to what had been former practice. In this view, when the major came to him for orders as to the hour of parade, "The same as yesterday" was his cautious reply. " How he chose this or that to be done." es As usual; it is not my intention to make unnecessary innovations;" and this, indeed, was truth. He soon rendered himself master of his military duties, and very soon perceived great need of amendment throughout the battalion, amongst the officers particularly; they were, many of them, overbearing, rapacious, quarrelsome, some of them incorrigibly so. " Morning after morning," he said, "I am taken up chiefly with disputes amongst my officers: however, I am in hopes of getting rid of three or four of the worst of them. Military decision I have not been able to put on so soon as the uniform." But he soon took upon himself the principal direction of the economy of the battalion. He was strict in enforcing discipline, yet by his gentleness and regard for the welfare of all ranks soon made himself universally beloved. Passionately fond of music himself, he wrote to England for a complete set of military musical instruments and for an expert drummer; but at the same time the useful was not neglected,–an experienced farrier was one of his commissions, as he had, for military purposes, above 100 horses. His personal attention to the health and comforts of the men were constant; at a future time, owing to his unusual expedients, he preserved his men in comparative good health during a very sickly season. One of the sanitary precautions that he introduced at that time as a part of military discipline, was that, at the daily parade, the surgeon should pass from man to man, examining individually their tongues. Out tongue! may seem an out of the way word of command, but the first symptom of the prevailing disorder was discoverable by the appearance of that member, and when thus detected by the surgeon the afflicted man was ordered instantly to the hospital, where in this early stage of the disease rapid recovery of the patient was almost general.

In the Prince's manufactories he introduced a great variety of improvements, and of new objects of manufacture, amongst them that of steel. He had already, at the mines in Siberia, made experiments in the production of this article; he now turned them to profit. The only steel to be procured at Cricheff was English, at the price of a rouble, then four shillings, a pound; iron cost there, about three copecks– a penny a pound; the expense of cementation less than twopence; thus obtaining a saving of 1500 per cent. He sent some of the tools made of his steel to England, amongst others a chisel that he begged might be tried by cutting off with it the end of a cold poker, or even some piece of untempered steel. In the glass house he experimented on a variety of different compositions; by one of them, a new one, he made ciwstal glass as bright as the best obtainable heretofore, which could be sold at twelve and a half copecks a pound, just half the former price. By the old process the expenses of the glass house were usually greater than the income from it, and never exceeded 600 roubles a year, whereas by the new one as much was expected to be cleared weekly, the profit being, even at the reduced price, about 400 per cent. Many experiments were made as to the fabrication of Eeaumur's porcelain, with the intention of using this material as crucibles for melting glass.

Some of the specimens of the porcelain he produced were hard enough to strike fire with steel, and brass was melted in vessels of that composition, so well did it bear intense heat; and he suggested the use of this material for culinary vessels.

His chief occupation, however, was that of naval architecture, and the introduction of improvements in it. He contrived and constructed vessels not exceeding 200 tons, the largest that could be floated down the Dnieper; prepared the parts of larger ships, ready for putting together at Cherson; contrived light vessels for river navigation, which in use proved of double the speed of the best of those hitherto constructed, also other vessels for floating down timber.

In March 1785, he spent a week at Moscow, and as general medical directions were much wanted at Crichert, he prevailed on an English physician to accompany him thither. He also added an English gardener (Aiton) and his wife to his colony of emigrants. Before August he had already built boats for exercisidg men in rowing; one of those boats had forty oars, the men being placed in two ranks in a mode of his invention. In a letter to his father he says; " I have now about one hundred rowers pretty well trained. It is really surprising how quickly they arrive at a certain degree of expertness at anything which is required of them. They were all soldiers of my battalion who built the boat, as well as those who navigate it; and I have not one man who has ever been to sea, or worked at anything about ship, vessel, or boat, nor scarcely any who had ever had an axe in their hand but to chop fire-wood; yet it is with these men, without any other assistance than that of one English sailor, whom I have for managing the rigging, that I am in hopes of making-several improvements in the construction of vessels of different kinds. The worst is that my business is so various, and I have so few assistants on whom I can have the least dependence, that I have too little time

to do anything so well as I wish, or as I see it might be done."

In February 1786, he had the great satisfaction of receiving his brother Jeremy Bentham at Cricheff, who had made that long journey for the sole purpose of visiting him. One of the works on which Samuel was now engaged was the construction of a pleasure yacht. Prince Potemkin, knowing how heavy the boats and vessels were, that were preparing at the Admiralty to convey and attend upon the Empress on her intended passage down the Dnieper, induced Bentham to give a plan for a light rowing yacht, which the Prince wished, he said, to be in a new taste, and to outrow all others. He must have accommodations for sleeping, andc, but he left the number of oars and everything else to Bentham.

The vessel constructed in consequence was indeed novel. It was 252 feet long, though its extreme breadth was but 16 feet 9 inches. It was planned so as to pass over shoals, and therefore drew but four inches of water when light, and six inches when loaded and with its 120 rowers on board. That it might accommodate itself to the numerous and sharp windings of Russian rivers, it consisted of six separate boats, but so connected with each other by a peculiar mechanism that no interval was left between boat and boat greater than the diameter of a small iron pin; by this contrivance the vessel could twist itself about as would a worm, and hence obtained the name of the Vermicular. The rowers were placed in two and part of the third of the head links, as also some of them in the sixth: these men were seated, four and four across the vessel, at two different heights, in such manner that the stroke of no man could interfere with that of another. The back part of the third link and the whole of the fourth and fifth links were appropriated to habitation, dining-room, with drawing-room, sleeping apartment for the Empress, accommodations for her attendants, and many contrivances for convenience and comfort by making use of space to the best advantage. The apartments, though of a good walking height within, were kept down to that of the rowers without, in order not to catch wind, and there were many new inventions in the putting together of the vessels with a view to strength, lightness, and cheapness of construction. The third, fourth, and fifth links being taken out, the remaining three formed a princely rowing boat. This Vermicular was completed just in time, it was hoped, to have received the Empress at Krement-chuk, but, unfortunately, Bentham arrived in it at that place, just two hours after her Majesty, tired of her heavy boats, had left it to pursue her journey to the Crimea by land; but he received on board not only the English and the French ambassadors, Mr. Fitzherbert, and the Count de Segur, but also the Emperor Joseph II. Another barge that accompanied the Vermicular on this occasion, as her tender, was intended for navigation in the Black Sea. It was also built of timber, on the same principle, and it consisted of three links, and was provided with twenty-four oars. Many other vessels of the same general construction were built for the convevance of timber and other produce from the interior to Cherson, in some of which vessels the links were connected by a very simple arrangement of a cross cord, but so that they also could yield easily to the windings so frequently encountered.

The mischiefs which resulted in the manufactories over which Bentham presided from want of due inspection, led him to reflect on the means by which it might be more perfectly obtained, especially in establishments where the number of efficient superintendents was so very limited as at Cricheff. The result was the invention of a building so contrived as that the whole of the operations carried on in it should be under observation from its centre. This invention has of late been called the principle of central observation. No allusion whatever has of late years been G 2 made to its inventor. In the " Encyclopaedia Britannica " it is attributed to Jeremy Bentham, though in his letter to his father, published in his works, he (Jeremy) distinctly and repeatedly speaks of it as the invention of his brother. The letter is in the third volume of Jeremy Bentham's works, and in it are specified many uses to which buildings on this principle would be peculiarly applicable.

When he had made shipwrights and sailors of a considerable part of the men of his battalion, it was ordered to the south in the year 1787. He had himself been previously ordered to Cherson to direct the fitting out of a flotilla to oppose the Turks, who had lately commenced hostilities, no preparations for such an event having been made by Eussia. On this occasion Jeremy Bentham was left at Cricheff. His brother, in writing to him from Cherson, in September 1787, says: "I am here at present by an order from Greneral Souvaroft, Commander-in-chief, in consequence of Marduinofps acquainting him that he had need of my assistance at this critical time." The assistance required was that of devising means of creating a flotilla of vessels of war, the materials for which were the pleasure galleys in which the Empress had descended the Dnieper, a few hoys and transports, " the strongest of which, according to professional practice, was not capable of carrying anything larger than a 3-pounder." His intimate friend, Admiral Mardvinofy, was his only superior, and it happened that at the most critical time Prince Potemkin called away the Admiral, leaving Bentham in sole command of the Admiralty department and the entire disposal of the naval force at Cherson.

His inventive genius and his powers of making the most of materials at hand were here put to the test, and they failed him not. In some of the barques he put 36-pounder long guns: the breadth of the vessel not being sufficient for the recoil of such ordnance, if opposite to one another, he placed them so that those on the one side should be opposite the intervals between those on the other; in men-of-war's long boats, and such like, he put in some 48-pounder howitzers, in others 13-inch mortars. Weak as was the miserable craft which he had to operate upon he strengthened it sufficiently by a small addition of support to the decks.

In the spring of 1788, when this flotilla was to be put to sea, he was to have commanded it, but was for a considerable time laid up completely with a severe attack of ague, and a consequent extreme debility. In the commencement of his convalesence, he was wholly incapable of application to any kind of even light reading or any other employment.

When at length his health was restored, and the flotilla about to be put to sea, Prince Nassau came to Cherson, bringing orders that he should be employed where he might distinguish himself as a volunteer. Prince Potemkin accordingly gave him the command in chief of the flotilla, at the same time requesting Lieutenant-Colonel Bentham to be the officer next in command. The Prince wished Bentham to change from the land to the sea-service; this he refused, though an advance in rank was offered him; but he consented, though continuing in the land service, to be employed in the flotilla as long as his services might be deemed necessary.

The flotilla, that had been patched up of every thing at Cherson that could float, was so despicable in the eyes of the enemy, that they deigned only to dispatch their small vessels against it, with orders to destroy it in their way to Otchakoff, the object of their expedition. But in a first engagement, 7th June, 1788, they suffered so much, that they ceased to think how easy it would be to destroy this shabby flotilla, and resolved to attack it with their whole naval force. This they did on the 16th of June, the Turkish fleet then consisting of ninety-six men of war, besides small vessels; the Eussian flotilla not of half the number, o 3 including fifteen or sixteen long boats. Paul Jones had a squadron of ships lying off Otchakoff, in the intervals of which the vessels of the flotilla were ranged in line on the 17th, when one of Paul's armed merchantmen, having been struck by a bomb from Otchakoff, presently sank; on which his squadron one by one came to anchor, and left the flotilla to shift for itself. Two of the enemy's ships were soon seen to have got on shore. The flotilla passed by them to follow after the rest of the Turkish vessels; they retreated as fast as they could out to sea, and got close in under cover of Otchakoff. In the action of the 7th one of the guns on board Bentham's vessel had burst, killing two men, and wounding seven. He was standing

O? O CD behind it at the time to aim it himself, j et, though not a yard from the breech, he escaped with no other injury than singed hair and an eyebrow scorched off. This had made him apprehensive of his own guns, so that on the 17th, he at first fired only out of a 13-inch brass mortar, " till spirited on by success, I approached by degrees, and tried again our guns on the poor unfortunate ships; although forsaken by all the fleet, these two defended themselves till the fire caught in different parts; yet some few obstinate fellows kept firing although the colours were struck, and many prisoners taken out." The vessels were completely destroyed by the fire of the bombs and shells that had been thrown into them, which added not a little to the dismay of the Turks, whilst it encouraged the Russians.

On the 18th, at daybreak, the Turks were again in line, " and our flotilla was below Paul Jones's squadron, which we relied upon no more for assistance." Bent ham, on rising in the morning, perceived that some of the Turkish ships of the line were aground, and communicated the intelligence to Prince Nassau. The signal for enefajrina: was immediately made, but as there was not wind enough to blow out the flag, a boat was sent round to give orders:

ENGAGEMENTS WITH THE TURKISH FLEET. 87

" I, therefore, receiving the orders first, set sail and called to all I came near to follow me. We had about as much discipline in our manoeuvres as a London mob; however, we advanced, as many of us as chose, immediately, and the rest by degrees." Bentham placed himself close on the quarter of the largest of the enemy's ships, and remained in action for two hours, exposed not only to fire from the great guns and musketry of the ships, but also to the still more dangerous fire from the guns of the town. " The bomb-shells and shot from those fell round me in a quantity that surprised me much that they did not hit me; 'tis true they were random shot, and came from a distance." The enemy's ship surrendered; boats were sent to take possession, when the battle re-commenced, till at length they finally submitted. Part of the flotilla was at the same time engaged with other vessels of the enemy. Bentham took fifty-six prisoners on board his own vessel: about 3000 were saved altogether, out of eleven ships taken or destroyed in this and the former engagements; but many more men perished, as three or four of the largest ships were burnt and blown up without a possibility of saving many of the crew. " I kept seven of the officer-prisoners on board my vessel for about a week; during which time the making their situation tolerably comfortable was perhaps as great a pleasure as I ever felt." Prince Potemkin afterwards took them, as well as all the other officers, to head-quarters, where they were well taken care of. Of the Eussians very few men were lost on that day, and no vessel but a rowing boat, which was sunk. The ship which Bentham engaged was saved. She had been built for sixty guns, and was fitted out for Eussian service immediately after she was taken. Seven other ships of the line which the Turks lost on that day were all burnt, and one was sunk. They were not purposely destroyed, but as all the vessels of the Eussian flotilla were furnished with shells like bomb-shells or others filled with

G 4 combustibles to be used instead of shot, there was no avoiding the burning of auy vessel into which they were fired. The remaining vessels of the large Turkish fleet were driven entirely out to sea.

Prince Potemkin, as may be imagined, was trausported with the success of the flotilla; all on board of it were advanced a rank: Bentham received a special reward for each of the three days' engagements–the military order of St. Greorge, advance of rank to that of full colonel, and a gold hilted sword of honour– the regiment to which Bentham was appointed, being one of the best regiments of infantry, and the most complete, consisting of 2,472, including all ranks.

A victory so complete would be thought remarkable under any circumstances, but in this case there were many points that claim particular attention. In the first place this flotilla would never have triumphed had the usual routine of naval armament been adhered to; that is, had 3 or 4-pounders only been placed where Bentham fired pieces of 30 or 40; or had those pieces been fired in the usual manner, instead of many of them in his new modes,– without recoil, or if to recoil that one piece should draw out the other– by both which modes unexampled rapidity of firing was obtained; besides which advantage there was the further one, of his having caused all the ordnance to be supplied with either shells or shot of a kind to produce combustion. "We have next to remark the efficacy of small vessels when opposed to large ones in shallow water. That those of little draught have the power of manoeuvring at will, where deeper ones are liable to take the ground, is obvious; but besides that advantage, there is the further one that a small object, presenting but little surface to the enemy, escapes the aim which would take effect on a larger body. But even these were not the only peculiarities of this successful flotilla, for with the exception of half-a-dozen seamen, it was manned only by soldiers and landsmen, scarcely any of whom had ever fired a gun before the attack on the enemy began. Several of the vessels were even commanded by officers of the land service, who were totally unacquainted with naval affairs. Amongst these was Lieutenant-Colonel Fanshawe, afterwards Governor-(xeneral of the Crimea. In reverting afterwards to the signal success of this flotilla, Bentham said, however " I could not but feel that, in point of fact, the success had resulted far more from the manner in which that flotilla was armed, than from any extraordinary skill or bravery on the part of the combatants."

Among the half-dozen seamen, most of whom were English, there was one in particular (Eichard Upsal) who came to Bentham at Cherson, having heard that (i there was likely to be some fun with the Turks," and begged to be engaged to partake of it– his services were accepted, and very eminent they proved to be. During the last engagement he observed that a firebrand had fallen into the magazine. With the coolness and promptitude of an English blue jacket, he followed the flaming log, brought it up on deck, and quietly threw it into the sea.

While Bentham was engaged in the outfit of the flotilla, inducements were held out by Government in hopes that private persons would fit out privateers, but as none were found willing to embark capital in such a speculation, he joined with his friend Admiral Mardvinoft and two other persons in fitting out a privateer. The command of it was given to one Lambro', always called Major Lambro'. This man proved eminently successful in taking Turkish vessels, becoming master of twenty-two sail. Such as were suitable he armed; thus forming a little squadron, with which he even took fortified islands. In May 1790, his squadron being increased to nine vessels, he attacked a Turkish fleet of eighteen, but the latter being joined by seven Algerine xebecs, they proved too much for Lambro'. On this he burnt his own frigate, and two or three others of his squadron. Though wounded, yet he escaped in a small vessel, which, with two or three others, was all that he saved; so that the subscribers reaped no profit from their venture.

Shortly after the signal defeat of the Turkish fleet, Prince Nassau, partly through ennui, fell ill, and found it more convenient to live on shore in his tent than on board his vessel; on which occasion he issued the following " order:"

" To Lieutenant-Colonel Bentham.–During my absence, I entrust to you, as the senior officer under me, the command of the whole of the flotilla under my orders."

It was contrary to all order, and, indeed, letter of the law, that an officer in the army should command officers of the navy. Still Bentham feared that some pretext or other would be found for continuing him in the sea service, but on the receipt of that order, the white coats made a strong representation of the injury done them by putting them under a green coat; so that the next day there came out an order from Prince Potemkin for all colonels to join their respective regiments. On detailing many of the above particulars to his father, Bentham observed that " fighting for once in a way was well enough, but it is an abominable trade to follow" and that in case of peace he should be much tempted to ask to change his regiment for one of cavalry in Siberia. This desire of his, which he had mentioned to all his acquaintance, came to the ears of Prince Potemkin, who asked if he really desired such a change; Bentham reminded him of the preference which he had, on many former occasions, expressed for that part of the empire, and that now there was no part of it which he would not quit for Siberia, where he had prospects of rendering his services most useful. The Prince immediately acquiesced in his views, gave him a regiment of cavalry on the frontiers, and placed in his regiment several officers who wished to go with him, furnishing money to pay for post horses for their conveyance.

After Bentham's early exploration of Siberia, he had, on his return to St. Petersburg, spoken to Prince Potem-kin of the great capabilities of the River Amoor for navigation, and for the carrying on of an extensive fur trade with China, Kamschatka, and the northern coast of America. The Prince had then wished him to communicate his ideas on the subject to the Empress, and had been dissatisfied that in his audiences a preference had been given to the state of the mines. The Prince now reminded him of this, saying a great deal about Kamschatka and the profits derivable from the fur trade there. Bentham, with a view to trading on the American coast, now obtained permission for four of the English seamen who had served with him in the flotilla, to be placed in his regiment, two of them as ensigns, the two others as second lieutenants.

The Colonel gave up his regiment of Raijsk in due form, then repaired to his new command in Siberia. One of his battalions occupied a line of (so-called) fortresses on the Kirgees' frontier, from Tchernovitch to Simiarsk; his other battalion was on the Chinese frontier, to the south of Lake Baikal; these battalions being about 1200 miles one from the other. He was not of a disposition to take his ease on visiting them, by travelling in the ordinary way along a beaten road, especially when there was beside it a vast extent of country unknown and unexplored. By diversifying his way, he would have to pass many rivers, over which there were no bridges, not to speak of other less essential conveniences, which would be found on the ordinary route. He therefore caused two carriages of the amphibious kind to be constructed, more simple than his former one, and built of the materials which the place afforded.

Besides journeys in the interior of the country on his way from one of his battalions to the other, he, in 1789, made an excursion amongst his neighbours the Kirgees. He had leave from his general at Omsk to go amongst them to the distance of fifty versts, but he extended his journey so as to travel no less than 1200 versts in their country. He described the Kirgees as being at that time peaceable, doing no other mischief than sometimes stealing a few cattle, and now and then a man or two. He spent about five weeks amongst the Kirgees; had regular audience of their Sultan, and was altogether well pleased with their conduct and general disposition. He was the first European of any note who had been amongst them. No map, or chart, or any geographical description of their country then existed, but he drew a map of that part of it through which he passed as accurately as circumstances permitted. On his subsequent return to England that map was inserted by Major Kennel in his delineation of that part of the world. It had not, however, been easy for Bentham to ascertain his route. Measurements on observations made with instruments he had reason to suppose would not be tolerated, but he contrived a projecting knob on one wheel of his carriage, which knob, on passing over ground was pressed inward, and acted on an apparatus for noting the number of revolutions made by the wheel. It had been vaguely reported that silver and gold as well as copper mines existed in the Kirgees' country; to ascertain this was one chief object of this excursion, but the journal which he kept of it, and which he sent to England, is nowhere to be found. Its loss is the more to be regretted as the fulness with which it had been written had prevented his entering into details in letters.

On the many journeys made in the amphibious carriages, the willing obedience of the peasant drivers and their firm reliance on their superiors were remarkable. While travelling with the horses of the country, the carriage was not stopped on coming to broad and even rapid rivers, but the peasant driver was directed to continue his course across them. On such occasions the peasants gave a wondering glance at their temporary master, then one of confidence in his superior knowledge, crossed themselves, drove down the bank and onwards across the stream; the horses swam, the boat-built carriage floated, its inmates guided it, and on the opposite bank the land journey was resumed all safe and dry, the peasant again crossing himself with a slava Boghi! (thank God).

During the summer he sent an expedition to examine the mouth of the River Ob, and a small part of the adjacent coast of the White Sea, with a view to the attempting a passage by sea to Archangel for mercantile purposes. He did not conceive that any doubt could exist of its practicability at certain times. The doubt was as to the degree of danger and delay which might be expected from drifts of ice which, even in summer, were brought by certain winds, so as to intercept navigation on the coast completely. Part of the men returned during the same summer, bringing a chart of the sea and part of the gulf. In consequence of the information thus obtained, the Colonel took to Tobolsk an officer of his regiment and fifty men, that they might build during the winter a seaworthy vessel, to be afterwards sent to the mouth of the Ob for the service of the men who had been left there.

The English sailor (Richard Upsal), who had been taken into the service at Cherson, was also on this service. He had been much better educated than those of his calling usually are, and in every respect was superior to the general run of seamen. He had attained the rank of Major. During the expedition near the mouth of the Ob, the party fell in with a tribe of natives who were wholly unacquainted with fire. At the same place the party found coal lying on the very surface of the ground, with which they made a fire, and thus taught the natives its use, it may be presumed, greatly to their future comfort. Major Upsal, after his return to England, frequently recurred to this discovery, saying that one of the greatest pleasures which he had experienced was that of having afforded these poor, half-frozen people the means of obtaining fire.

The Colonel also, at his own expense, afforded funds to a party of English sailors for building and fitting out some vessels at Kamschatka, from thence to explore the opposite north-west coast of America. He commissioned them, if practicable, to carry on a trade in furs, which promised to be very profitable. This was in conformity with views which he had for many years entertained, and which had particularly attracted Prince Potemkin's attention. Nothing more than vague reports were heard of this expedition till the year 1808. At that time one of the Englishmen returned home, and came to his former colonel to render some account of himself, his companions, and their doings. Unfortunately he was not the most literate of the set, but it was collected from him that the vessels had been built, that they made good their landing in America, constructed a wooden fort on its coast, and carried on from thence a trade in fur, successfully and profitably. No specific dates could be obtained from this man, nor any indication of the precise site of their fort, but it is supposed that this, in point of fact, was the first Eussian establishment on the American continent.

Nor did he neglect the exploring many interesting parts of Siberia, or the trade that might be carried on there. In a letter from the late Chamberlain Clarke to his father, some particulars as to the colonel's health and whereabouts were given, as obtained from Mr. Love, who had commanded one of the vessels of the flotilla, and who had, in February 1790, seen " a Major Newton, who was charged with Sir Samuel's account of his discoveries to the Empress at St. Petersburg. The major had left Sir Samuel in good health, vigorously prosecuting a commercial intercourse between Kussia and

China." And this is all that is here known of those discoveries, as no copy has been found of the account w r hich the Colonel gave of them to the Empress.

Notwithstanding these occupations, he failed not during the whole time of his command to bestow a regular attention on the discipline, well being, and improvement of his regiment. He established a school on the borders of China, for both men and boys of the battalion stationed there, on the principal of mutual instruction. There still exist specimens of writing by boys in that school, w T hich, notwithstanding the short period of instruction, would do credit to pupils of the best organised school in any country. When he had thus set on foot many improvements in the discipline of his regiment, as well as laid the foundation for the better instruction of the men, having explored a great portion of country hitherto scarcely known, and done much towards the establishment of a lucrative trade on a scale more extensive than heretofore with China, and of a new trade with America, his never ceasing longings to revisit home, and those that w 7 ere dear to him at home, made him avail himself of a leave of absence accorded by Prince Potemkin to set out on his return to England.

He had found the remote, and in part uncivilised, Siberia to be a country rich in natural productions; the people in towns (especially at Tobolsk) of highly cultivated minds and manners– a society peculiarly agreeable as being free from the restraints imposed upon it near the seat of Government. The country itself was in many parts picturesque and agreeable; in some of its wildest parts, east of Nijni Taghil, resembling an English gentleman's park, in other parts producing wild fruits in such profusion that his soldiers in the strawberry season were sent out to gather these delicious berries by pailsful. South of Lake Baikal the tenderest European fruits, as apricots, arrive at great perfection, and game of many kinds every- where abound. True, on some wandering excursions food of any kind was scarcely found; but Siberia was ever after in his thought a kind of terrestrial paradise.

He happened to pass through Paris just at the time of the first revolution, when his friends the Duke de Eichelieu, Dumas, the Count de Segur, and many others whom he had known in Eussia, were still allowed to retain their rank and many of their privileges. He was furnished with a billet of entrance to the National Assembly, on the last occasion when Count de Segur had power to give him one, and was with the Duke de Eichelieu in his box at the opera the last time that his Grace enjoyed it.

On his arrival in England he had the happiness to find his father, step-mother, and brother well. His half brother Farr Abbott had married and had purchased a kind of sinecure place. Charles had already began to distinguish himself in that political career in which his legal knowledge and sound judgment led to his well-known future eminence.

CHAP. VI.

Journey through the Manufacturing Districts of England, 1791– Classification of Mechanical Works– Death of his Father– Prison Architecture–Mechanical Inventions and Improvements–He is commissioned by the Admiralty to visit the Naval Dockyards– Resigns the Russian Service–Report on Portsmouth Dockyard, 1795– Improvements and Alterations in the Dockyard– He is ordered to build seven Vessels on his own Plans– Changes introduced in their Construction– Appointed Inspector-

General of Naval Works– The Appointment sanctioned by the King in Council, March, 1796– Increased Calibre of Guns on Shipboard.

A life of idleness could never be one of enjoyment to Bentham. He longed to inform himself of what progress had been made since he left England in manufacturing arts, especially by the introduction of machinery. For this purpose, in the year 1791, he made a tour through the principal manufacturing parts of England. To his surprise he found that little advance had been made towards substituting the invariable accuracy of machinery for the uncertain dexterity of the hand of man. For steam power was then only employed for manufacturing cotton, rolling metals, and for some few other purposes, such as for pumping up of water. For the working of wood, though for ten years back he had written to his friends in England of his invention of planing and other machines, yet, so far as he could learn, no machinery had been introduced beyond the common turning lathe, and also some saws and a few boring tools used in the making of blocks for the navy. Even saws worked by inanimate force for

slitting timber, though in extensive use in foreign countries, were nowhere to be found in Great Britain.

This poverty of the inventive faculty stimulated him to the exertion of his own powers, and he applied himself to the extension and improvement of the wood-working machinery, which he had so many years before contrived in Eussia. The logical turn of his mind led him to a conclusion that the artificial, but common classification of works according to trades or handicrafts, without regard to similarity or dissimilarity of operations, could not but be productive of a variety of inconveniences, even according to usual practice, and that it stood particularly in the way when the object was the contrivance of a good system of machinery. He therefore began by classing the several operations requisite in the shaping and working up of materials of whatever kind, wholly disregarding the customary artificial arrangement according to trades. When the operations had thus been classed, he next proceeded to the contrivance of machines by which they might be performed, and that, independently of the need for skill or manual dexterity in the workman.

His father had lately died, so that his brother Jeremy had come into possession of the house and extensive premises in Queen-square Place, Westminster. Mr. Bentham, fully impressed with the importance of his brother's inventions, gave up his outhouses as workshops where machines of kinds contrived by his brother Samuel might be executed of full size, and was about eno-asfing for a steam engine to give them motion, when a new turn was given to their application. Prison discipline was at that period a subject of general interest, and Grovernment manifested a wish to effect the improvements which might be effectually carried out in a Panopticon building. Jeremy Bentham, who describes the advantages of this construction in his letters, was therefore induced to listen to terms for undertaking the management of a panopticon for the reception of 1000 prisoners (Government wished it to be for 1500). He depended on his brother Samuel for the contrivance of such machines and engines as might be profitably worked by unskilled hands (the intended prisoners). An extension of leave of absence from Russia was obtained for the Colonel, who proceeded not only to devise, but to have executed of full size, working machines for planing, sawing in curved, winding, and transverse directions, including an apparatus for preparing all the parts of a highly finished window sash, another for an ornamented carriage wheel, for none of which operations was either skill or manual dexterity of the workman necessary. Patents were taken for these several machines 26th November 1791, and 3rd April 1793: the specification of the latter is said to be the most complete treatise that has yet appeared on the subject of working wood, metals, and other materials.

In conformity with the views of Government, the contrivance of a panopticon prison of the requisite extent became necessary, and the Colonel undertook the task. In addition to such a central building as that which he had erected at Cricheft, he joined to it long, straight buildings to furnish appropriate accommodation for the prisoners, and for the great extent of space requisite for the machinery for their employment; and a young architect, Mr. Samuel Bunce, was engaged to make drawings of both building and machinery, but the one and the other were so wholly different from former examples, that the contrivance of all the parts rested with the Colonel. The building too he designed to be fire-proof, as far as any structure could be made so. Wood he determined should form no part of it, excepting for floor; brick-work and iron were the only materials. According to drawings which still remain, the basement story was of brick-work arched over each compartment; the walls and divisions of the other stories, generally speaking, of brick-work also; but iron, cast and wrought,

H 2 was introduced wherever wood was usually employed in a building. The window frames and sashes were of cast iron, but so designed that, whilst they afforded security superior to that obtained by the customary prison bars, his windows bore no appearance of restraint. Jeremy Bentham, in his letter of 1786, had spoken of solitary confinement, but Samuel was averse to it, excepting as a harmless means of temporary punishment of the unruly, or, for a longer period, of the refractory. It appeared to his mind that employment under the least possible apparent restraint seemed the most likely mode of reclaiming the less vicious of the felons, as probably those also of a more hardened character. The brothers together had determined on allowing prisoners a proportion of their earnings in hand, a larger portion to be laid up in store as a fund with which to begin the world at the end of their incarceration; also, in cases where the liberated might prefer it, it was intended to give them still employment, though at a somewhat lower rate of pay than the usual one to free labour.

The general design of the panopticon having been fixed on, and the due proportion of its several parts for strength ascertained, a model of the central part was made; this and the machinery at work, became (as Mr. Bentham called it) a raree-show; but it was not opened to the idle or the ignorant. Numberless persons of rank, of science, and of manufacturing intelligence, almost daily obtained an introduction to see the wonders at Queen-square Place. So well satisfied were all of the national advantages that would be derived from the use of that system of machinery, that it became the subject of notice in the House of Commons, where it was generally eulogised, but more particularly by Mr. Dundas, afterwards Lord Melville.

During these first years of his return to England it may well be believed that, with workmen on the spot, he had caused various minor inventions to be introduced at Queen-

MECHANICAL INVENTIONS AND IMPROVEMENTS. IOl square Place; such, for instance, as hollow tubes of metal for articles which had before been made solid.

The fire irons which he thus had made were particularly light and pleasant in use; speaking tubes were fixed in the interior of the house, through which orders to servants might be communicated without calling them from a present employ; but the pursuance of an early idea now received much of his attention. He had conceived, even during the time of his apprenticeship, that many chemical and manufacturing effects might be better produced, and more economically also, in vacuo, than by the usual modes of operation. Much of his time and many of his thoughts were occupied for more than a twelvemonth in directing experiments that were made in a receiver exhausted by a common air-pump, but the receiver and connected apparatus he adapted to the several operations to be performed. The experiments, it is true, were made on a small scale, but they were sufficient to exhibit the soundness of his opinions on the subject, and to enable him to take a patent for the inventions. Amongst the experiments, distillation was carried on with a much less expenditure of heat than usual. Leather was tanned through the substance of the hide in the course of a few hours, the passage of the tanning liquid through it being repeated a sufficient number of times to ensure perfect combination of the tanning principle with the hide. A variety of substances were dyed in grain, leather and wood included. Wood was impregnated through its substance with a variety of salts known to be preservatives of timber, such as the sulphates of copper, iron, and zinc, as also alum and corrosive sublimate. Meat was salted, smoked, dried, and flavoured. Generally speaking, in whatever cases the presence of air impedes or resists the entrance of a liquid, impregnation was effected in vacuo with entire success. After the patent was taken, a friend made the first use of it in a cotton-weaving factory; this was to impregnate the cops of cotton with soapsuds.

H 3

H)2 LIFE OF SIR SAMUEL BENTHAM.

The naval business of the British Government in its civil branch was that for which General Bentham had always entertained the strongest predilection. Communication with the Admiralty with the object of improving that business was therefore willingly acceded to. His representations of the advantages which could not fail to result in the naval arsenals from the introduction of machinery, and from the use of steam engines to give it motion, were convincing to the Lords of the Admiralty, who, in the course of several interviews, expressed their approbation of various other improvements suggested. Early in 1795 they arranged that he should address them officially by a letter, in which should be mentioned several particulars in reference to their intercourse with him, and that in conformity with the desire which they had intimated that he should visit his Majesty's dockyards, he should make an offer to do so. Accordingly, on the 21st April 1795, he addressed such a letter to the Secretary of the Admiralty, in which he mentioned that he had still leave of absence from the Empress of Eussia to the following September. The next day, 22nd April, he received a letter, which authorised him to visit his Majesty's dockyards for the purpose of suggesting improvements in them, and acquainted him that the Lords of the Admiralty had given instructions to the Navy Board "to order the several officers to permit his free admission to the said dockyards," and " to furnish him with such information and assistance as he might stand in need of."

The authority thus given to him, the flattering approval of his ideas in private conversation, the desire repeatedly expressed that it might be possible to retain him in the service of his country, with the prospects that naturally flowed from this state of things (to use his own words), "led to the relinquishing his intentions of returning to Eussia," and he shortly afterwards abandoned the emoluments, the gift of lands, the honours that awaited him in

WORKS IN" PORTSMOUTH DOCKYARD. 103 a foreign country, and devoted himself entirely to the service of his own.

He has been much and repeatedly blamed by his friends for this decision. The rank, the wealth, the honours in possession and in prospect which he thus gave up in Russia, far exceeded the utmost that was promised him in England. His friends affirmed that he abandoned a host of Russian friends ready to do him every service and a society such as could not but render life most pleasurable. This was all strictly true; but he also had friends in England, and above all the improvement of the naval service of his own country had been the object of his ambition from his boyhood. His letters remain to prove that at times of his greatest hopes in Russia, and when he was enjoying the greatest honours there, naval improvement in his own country was still with him the paramount thought.

Brigadier-Greneral Eentham, though still retaining his foreign rank, may from this time be considered as exclusively in the English service and devoted to it heart and mind.

His first visit under the authority of the Admiralty was to Portsmouth dockyard, on which he made his report dated 29th May 1795.

The benefits that have resulted from his intervention can only be appreciated by a survey of his many services. It will consequently be essential, in noticing the most important of them, to enter into details sometimes of a purely technical nature. But so rapidly of late has science advanced, that those technicalities are now likely to be comprehended and even read with that degree of interest which the civil concerns of the navy now excite, where true economy, is the object in view. Throughout the whole of the General's English service, it will be seen that his main endeavour was to produce effects not only more perfectly but at a less cost than before; so that his suggestions of improvement, if brought to the severest

H 4 test of arithmetical calculation, would be seen to involve a lessening of expenditure.

A plan which involved very costly masonry works in Portsmouth dockyard had been ordered to be carried into execution previously to his visit in 1795. In his report he objected to many of those works as being of little use in comparison with their cost. One of them was a double dock, which was necessarily more costly than two single ones, use being taken into account, because a ship in the upper dock must remain there after it was finished, till the work required to the vessel in the lower dock was completed likewise. He objected to the costly repairs that were being carried on in the basin without making any enlargement of it, although by its extension the expense of additional work would be little compared to the increased accommodation which it would afford. He also objected to the jetties as proposed, because as they were planned they would not afford means of docking and undocking the number of ships that might have to be moved in a tide. In place of those works objected to, he proposed an enlargement of the basin, two single docks, an arrangement of the jetties which would afford means of moving the greatest number of ships which would be taken in or out of the enlarged basin in a tide. His proposals were adopted, and the works were subsequently executed according to his plans. Portsmouth dockyard was thus rendered pre-eminently suited (and was universally acknowledged to be so) for the most important business of that port in times of war, namely, the graving of ships of the line; that is, examining their bottoms and executing trifling repairs to them.

The effect of these improvements was not confined to the advantage of enabling a greater number of vessels to be forwarded at one time. That was in fact but a secondary consideration. He had in early life witnessed the gross abuses, the embezzlement of materials, the extra cost and inferiority of all workmanship when repairs of ships were executed afloat as it was termed, that is, when they were lying at moorings in a harbour or at a roadstead. He now saw that the same mischiefs still continued–artificers lost much time in rowing backwards and forwards to their work, and they were frequently paid extra wages under some concealed form. Materials were stolen or embezzled to a large amount in taking them to ships afloat; and want of supervision induced indolence and carelessness in the artificers. To remedy these evils, by enabling repairs to be carried on in a great number of ships at one time within the precincts of the dockyard, was a chief object; and by his proposed arrangements no less than twelve ships of the line, besides smaller vessels, could be repaired, fitted, and stored within the boundary of Portsmouth dockyard at one and the same time.

Various other works that had been projected (some of them already commenced) were in like manner objected to, and other works proposed in their place both in Portsmouth and Plymouth yards. Those to which he objected were discontinued by Admiralty orders; several of those which he proposed were ordered for execution; others remained for longer or shorter times under their Lordships' consideration, but no one of them was finally rejected.

It is not easy to determine the manner in which General Bentham's improvements in our naval establishments can best be represented. They were so numerous, and of such different natures, extending to civil engineering, architectural, mechanical, naval architecture, ordnance, detection of abuses, with the remedies for them, and the general management of the civil business of the department. But the simplest way of giving a clear and comprehensive view of them appears to be by taking them generally in the order of their dates, though occasionally pursuing the same subject at once to its completion.

In noticing the several services in which General

Bentham was from this time engaged by the Admiralty, use will be made of an official register of correspondence, also authenticated copies of that correspondence. In regard to private communications with First Lords of the Admiralty and others in authority, a journal will be consulted which was commenced towards the end of the year 1796: it was written by a person to whom he related matters which he wished to be noted, and he always himself looked over that journal, causing it to be corrected on the few occasions where the statement had not been strictly accurate.

The correspondence first noticed relates to the construction of certain vessels of war. In intercourse with Earl Spencer, Sir Hugh Seymour, and other Lords of the Admiralty, as also with the Comptroller of the Navy, he had given many particulars as to the usual mode of construction in naval architecture, which demonstrated a great want of attention to mechanical principles; that, in consequence, ships were more costly than they ought to be, and, what was of still more importance, they were weak. In consequence of these observations and the facts adduced in support of them, members of the Admiralty Board informed themselves more particularly as to his ideas of naval architecture, and the Board authorised him to have constructed seven small vessels, uncontrolled by any naval board or dockyard officer, upon his own individual responsibility. These vessels were two sloops of war, named the Arrow and the Dart; four war schooners, the Nelly, Eling, Kedbridge, and Millbrook, and a vessel planned to carry water in bulk for the supply of ships at sea; thus precluding the need of coming into port for water, the most frequent cause of the return of large vessels from their stations.

The chief objects he had in view in planning these vessels were their strength, their durability, their efficiency, diminution of first cost and subsequent wear and tear, and they differed materially in exterior form from the universal build. They were much longer than others in proportion to breadth, and much sharper also: similar proportions were first adopted in some of the early fast-going steamers, and since that time very generally in all vessels whether for war or traffic. The experimental vessels raked forward like a Thames wherry: the topsides, instead of retiring inwards at the upper part, were continued outwards to the upper edge. The Great Britain has since been similarly built in this respect. By this new form vessels are better supported when pitching and rolling in a sea, than others where the sides retire inwards above the water-line.

Oak for ship-building was at that time particularly scarce and dear: it therefore became of importance to exhibit the parts of a vessel in which other kinds of wood might be employed without detriment to strength. In the interior, therefore, fir was chosen where strength depended on resistance to tension, and beech or elm for some parts constantly under water.

For ensuring strength, the combination of the parts of the whole structure was contrived on the principles which mechanical science has demonstrated to be the most efficient. Those principles were even then adhered to in the greater number of mechanical machines and structures on shore, but were neglected in naval architecture. The consequence of such unmechanical combination of the parts of vessels was that they always ivorked at sea, and that to so great a degree that the transverse partitions or bulkheads could not be fixed: they were made to rock–that is, they were hung on rockers; but General Bentham, instead of leaving the bulkheads at liberty to work, connected them firmly with the bottoms, sides, and decks of his vessels, so that they became a main source of strength. This innovation has at length come into general practice in the royal and in private dockyards.

The shell of a vessel, being of plank, is fixed to the ribs or timbers, those timbers being of a curved form conformable to the shape intended for the vessel. The timbers were all of them placed in the usual way, perpendicularly to the keel, thus leaving the plank at the ends of the vessel unsupported by the timbers. This deficiency was usually in a manner remedied by the insertion of a great weight of wood at the wooden ends, adding materially to the dead weight of the vessel, and that at a part where it was mischievous. In the experimental vessels the timbers were placed at right angles to the rising line of the deadwood, that is, conformably to the shape of the shell instead of to that of the keel. The timbers themselves were of less breadth than usual, being of not more than half the customary solid content, thus employing trees of about thirty years' growth instead of that of fifty years. The timbers at the ends too were made to cross each other, thus doing away the need for crutches and breasthooks, which, besides their cost and weight, were a frequent source of the rottenness so often found at the ends of ships. The beams of a ship, besides their use as supports to the decks, connect the sides of the vessel together; the connection, in English ships, having been effected by supporting the beam on brackets, or knees, fixed to the ribs. The beams of ships had hitherto been made as broad as they were deep, contrary to the well-known fact, that beyond a certain thickness it is depth that affords strength. The beams in these vessels were of the usual depth, but only of about half the breadth; the number of them was increased, so that they connected the sides together at perhaps twice the usual places, and they were sufficiently near to each other to support the decks without the use of cartings and ledges, that is, intermediate pieces to which to fix the decks. Still more to prevent racking of the vessel, diagonal trusses and braces were introduced; they were included in the structure of the fixed bulkheads, and in other parts of the ship, as between the pillars, they were introduced independently of any partition. The advantage of diagonal trusses or braces in affording strength had been well known, and was in general use in all works of mechanism. excepting that of a ship. This improvement has since been esteemed one of the greatest that has been made in naval architecture, but the merit of it has been universally ascribed to Sir W. Seppings. General Bentham had introduced them in all the seven vessels commenced in 1795, and gave drafts showing them to the Navy Board 25th October and 20th December 1796. The decks of ships in general were hanging, that is, in a curve from end to end, lowest in the mid-length, rising towards the ends. Decks thus formed afforded no tie against the extension of a ship from one end of it to the other; in consequence of which, such an extension, called breaking of the sheer, or hogging, took place in all ships of the usual construction. The decks of the experimental vessels were made straight, thus acting as a string to the bow formed by the midship section of a ship. By straight decks the collateral advantages were also obtained of enabling the midship guns to be carried higher out of water, and of affording more space in that part of the hold of a ship where height is most desirable. This invention, as it may be called, has since been adopted in various instances.

It must be evident, on a moment's reflection, how much the strength of a vessel depends upon its plank. In these vessels its thickness was increased from the usual three inches to six in the lower part of the ship, an improvement which to a certain extent has since been adopted in many cases, but more particularly in ships fitted out for perilous voyages, such as the Antarctic expedition. The plank in the experimental vessels was also, at the ends of the ship, placed very differently from the usual mode: instead of extending forward and aft over the deadwood, the plank was made to terminate against it, as it does in mid- ships against the keelson. The bulkheads have been spoken of as affording strength by being fixed; but besides this a most important improvement in naval architecture was effected by their means: they were contrived so as to divide the vessel into many water-tight compartments. This was no invention of General Bentham's: he has said himself, officially, that it was " practised by the Chinese of the present day, as well as by the ancients;" yet to him is due the merit of having appreciated the advantages of those water-tight compartments, and of having introduced the use of them. Shipwrights, perhaps, may not be familiar with classic lore, but could they all have been ignorant of the expedient so common in Chinese vessels?–and it has lately appeared that Captain Shancks had employed them in one vessel. A late Act of Parliament provides that no iron steamer should be built without them; yet iron steamers only are even now so constructed; those of wood are still deprived of the advantage, although at various times it was often brought to official and public notice, from the time of the Committee on Finance, 1798, to the last of General Bentham's official letters in 1813.

Water-tight compartments were not, however, the only expedients against foundering that were introduced in the experimental vessels. By the increased thickness of the plank, and by its arrangement at the ends of the vessels, the deadwood, the lowest part of the stern-post, and even the keel itself might have been beaten off without letting water into the vessel. The rudder was also so formed that the lower part of it might have been beaten off, and yet there would have been enough left to steer the ship by.

The fastenings used in ship work were most of them unmechanical. The improvement of these, on which the strength and durability of a ship so much depend, was a subject of first importance. The treenails in use were universally imperfect cylinders of wood, and they were forced into holes in the plank and timbers of a ship, those holes being of the same diameter from end to end. He invented a new form of treenail of different diameters at different parts of their length–in steps, as it were. New tools, also of his invention, were used to bore the holes of different diameters, corresponding with the part of the treenail which they were to receive. Hence, instead of injuring the wood, like the common ones, the whole way through which they were driven, these new treenails slipped easily by hand into their holes for a certain length, then requiring only to be driven home for that portion of it, still uninjured, in which they were to take their hold. The new treenails could therefore be thicker than common ones, thus affording a more efficient hold. Both treenail and hole being made by appropriate machines and augers, the holes were filled up along their whole length, so as to prevent the admission of water and consequent decay. These treenails, though the advantages of them were so apparent, have not been brought into general use. The long bolts usually employed being both a costly and an inefficient fastening, short metal screws were in many cases used instead of them in the experimental vessels, especially for fastening the butt ends of the planks. By these contrivances a much better hold than in the usual way was taken of the timbers and planks by both treenails and screws, at the same time that the timbers were less wounded than by the customary fastenings. A considerable saving was effected where the screws were substituted for long bolts; and the perfection of this form of treenails facilitated their substitution for many of the usual copper fastenings. The treenails were used exclusively for laying the decks. The sheathing nails were of a new form, the points wedge shaped, instead of pyra-midical, by which form, the broad edge being drawn across the grain of the wood, firm hold was taken of it. They were of pure copper, instead of being of mixed metal, in order to avoid an injurious mixture of metals when the sheathing should come to be re-melted; and they were less liable to foul than those of mixed metal. Their heads differed from those of ordinary sheathing nails, being made flat and smooth. Sheathing nails of the same metal with the sheathing are in use, and the form of nail seems now by degrees to be coming into use for other purposes than that of ship-building; but neither the step-shaped treenail nor the screw is yet employed in naval architecture, though screws are of such general use in all other works of mechanism.

The Arrow and the Dart had Captain Shancks' sliding keels. The case for them was formed by two longitudinal bulkheads, water-tight. The effect of these several innovations will appear from the services which the vessels performed, from the appearance which they exhibited as to strength, on an official survey, and from the economy of their mode of structure, as it appeared on that survey, and from the very low rate per ton at which a contractor would have engaged to build others of a similar construction.

For the comfort of the crew the height between decks was considerably greater than usual, so that the tallest man could pass upright under the beams, instead of having to stoop perhaps a couple of feet, or even more in some small vessels. A much greater space per man was provided for health and proper ventilation, there having been in a frigate but from fifty to sixty cubic feet per man, whereas in the sloops there were no less than 137 feet to a man. In various parts of the experimental vessels, which in others are dark, thick glass, either flat or convex, was introduced as illuminators. But the invention which beyond all others contributed to the health and comfort of the men was that by which water was preserved sweet at sea. This desideratum, so long vainly sought for, was effected by the invention of metallic tanks for carrying the water, instead of the, till then, universally employed cask. This very great improvement was not confined to points which alone would have stamped it as of first-rate importance, the health and comfort of the men. The form of those tanks enabled nearly a double store of water to be stowed in the space usually filled with casks; and as the want of water was the most frequent cause of a ship's return to port, vessels were thereby enabled to remain much longer on their stations. At that time the metal that could be most economically employed for tanks was copper, tinned for health's sake, and supported by wood for strength; and they were made to the shape of the vessel, so as to lose no space.

Sources of real danger to a vessel of war, as well as of apprehension of it, are explosions of gunpowder, and the incumbrances in the interior of a ship's side which impede or prevent shot holes from being easily got at to be plugged. In these sloops the powder, like the water, was stowed in metallic canisters instead of casks. The canisters were, in like manner, formed of the shape of the magazine, and their casings were part of the vessel. The powder itself was thus preserved from wet or moisture, consequently no injury could result by surrounding the canisters with water. Accordingly, in case of danger from fire, means were provided for letting water into the magazine around and over the canisters. Magazine lights too, in the customary mode, were fraught with danger. They were no other than common candles placed in a space partitioned off with glass from the magazine. Instead of such a light safety-lamps were substituted. The safety was obtained by placing the lamp in the centre of a double glass case; the space between the inner and the outer glass being filled with water in such manner that in case of breakage the water would necessarily extinguish the light. The tubes for the admission of fresh air and the emission of foul were so arranged that no sparks could find their way through them. To facilitate the stopping of shot-holes, the sides of the

vessel above water were unincumbered with store-rooms, instead of which fixed binns above the middle of the vessel were introduced, not higher than tables, leaving a clear space around as well as above them. Besides thus giving easy access to the sides of the vessel, the stores were more easily got at than in the usual store-rooms.

During General Bentham's first visit to Portsmouth dockyard in May 1795, he was met by Sir Hugh Seymour, then the most active naval Lord of the Admiralty. Sir Hugh entered much into the discussions respecting Bentham's proposed improvements; and the reasons given for his innovations induced strong expressions of a desire that he should without further delay accept a permanent engagement in the naval department. On his return to London, Earl Spencer and Sir Charles Middleton, then Comptroller of the Navy, cordially joined in this opinion. Sir Charles had himself, before this period, perceived the incompetency of the existing Civil Naval Boards to deal with the introduction of improvements, and had contemplated the institution of an intermediate Board between the Admiralty and the Navy Boards, and had already drawn up a paper on the subject, which he now communicated to General Bentham. According to that sketch improvements of every description for the construction of ships and their armament, and all the works subservient to the preparation of our fleets, were to form the business of this Board. He said that the members of his proposed Board must be selected with the greatest care; " their abilities and knowledge must be first-rate in mechanics, in ship-building and in professional sea-skill and accomplishments." Apparently from despair of finding these several requisites combined in any one individual, Sir Charles proposed that his Board should consist of three superior members with competent assistants; and he expressed an earnest wish that Bentham should become the President of such a Board. But as he held joint manage-

ments under any form whatever to be an insuperable bar to efficiency in an office of such a nature, he would not accept it. He proposed, however, as one mode in which he might be useful, that he should return for a time to Russia, at the expiration of his leave of absence, to pursue the course of experiments which he had there commenced; and that in the mean time he should enable others, under their Lordships' protection, to carry on several improvements of which he had already exhibited the efficac. This proposal was at first listened to without dissent; but the novelty of it, and the apprehension of the trouble which it would occasion, were alleged as reasons for its rejection. Their Lordships, in order to retain him in the British service, ultimately decided on creating a new office, the constitution of which they adopted conformably to his suggestions.

That constitution was indeed peculiar. It was based on individual and strict responsibility, a feature without example in the civil service of the department, although pervading the military branch, and habitually enforced throughout all grades of the military officers of the navy. This new office, it was determined, should be that of an Inspector-General of Naval Works, and that Brigadier-Greneral Bentham should be the Inspector-General. He was provided with assistants; but he alone was made individually responsible for the whole business of his office. To ensure the observance of that responsibility, and to affix upon him personally any dereliction from his duty, all orders from his superiors (the Board of Admiralty) were conveyed to him in writing by their Secretary. In like manner every opinion of his given to their Lordships, as also all his proposals of improvement, together with the reasons on which such opinions and improvements were grounded, were submitted to them, not verbally, but in ivriting, subscribed by his sole signature. He had no authority of any kind, or over any person whatever, the assistants in his own office excepted. In regard to them he had entire control, as he was himself alone responsible for every business in which these assistants might be employed, though he had no power either of appointment or dismissal.

The assistants suggested as desirable in the office were a mechanician, a civil architect, and a chemist; professions of which not a single individual was at that time engaged i n any branch or department of the naval service. A secretary was also allowed to the office, two draughtsmen or clerks, according as their services in one or the other of these duties might be required, and a messenger. The office itself was under the same roof with the Admiralty.

So much was determined on after much discussion. When Bentham's leave of absence from Eussia expired, he did not return to that country, considering that the Admiralty had not only pledged themselves to employ him at home in the promotion of naval improvement, but that it was with an ardent desire on their part, most flatteringly expressed, that his own country should henceforward reap the benefit of his acquirements and his genius.

Early in this same year the attention of the Duke of York had been attracted to the improvements of various kinds suggested by Bentham, amongst others to a baggage waggon of his invention, which, by order of Prince Potemkin, had been provided for a corps of yagers. Conceiving that such waggons would be very useful in the English army, the Duke of York communicated with Bentham on the subject, and, having examined a small model of such a vehicle, expressed a wish that a similar one of full size should be constructed on his account. It was accordingly completed, and tried satisfactorily on the Thames. These baggage waggons were amphibious, on the same principle with the carriages which he had devised in Siberia. The one now made was calculated for the conveyance of baggage of any description, or of the sick, or of women, or even for artillery. It was in the form of a boat, to which axletrees were fixed carrying a pair of wheels. A cover was adapted to the body of the waggon, which cover when taken off was a boat; both body and cover were provided with means of rowing, and with moveable seats, so that, on coming to a river, the body on being driven into it sufficed for the transport of its contents; and its cover, having been lifted off, was ready as a boat for the conveyance of a considerable number of men. This baggage waggon was made of copper sheets, secured to ribs, and it is believed was the first vessel of any description of which the exterior was formed of metal. Engagements with the Admiralty precluded his attention to this invention; and it still rests in abeyance till some one shall take it up, and have leisure and inclination to bring it into use.

During the discussions relative to the institution of the new office of Inspector-Greneral of Naval Works, 2000. per annum had been spoken of by members of the Admiralty Board as a proper salary for any man possessed of the requisite qualifications. To this Lord Spencer acquiesced. Bentham continued to be employed in naval concerns alone for many months, under the impression that no farther changes would be made respecting the office, when apprehensions were aroused. A variety of obstacles were thrown in the way of the institution of the office altogether, and endeavours were made at all events to diminish its appearance of superiority. Not only was the salary to be reduced, but the title of the office to be changed. The former was reduced to 750. a year, to give it the appearance of inferiority to that of a Commissioner of the Navy (800.); but in consequence of Bentham's remonstrance to Lord Spencer (February 1796) the title of the office was retained unchanged. Emolument had never been his object in leaving the service of Eussia, in which he was assured of far greater advantages than any that could be expected in the English service. In his letter to Earl Spencer he expressed his sincere wish that the salary should be left unfixed, I 3 until the services rendered by the office should be found to warrant the raising of it to the intended pitch. But Lord Spencer was, as it were, compelled by opposition to fix the salary at the 750l., giving as his reason for so doing the despair of finding an adequate successor. In addition, however, to the nominal salary, 500. a year was added in his favour individually. He saw too well the need for improvement throughout the civil concerns of the department to relinquish the hope of effecting it; and, though he was still assured by Eussian authorities of a compliance with all his wishes if he should return to that country, and was strongly urged to do so, yet he consented to accept the proposed place at home.

At length, 23rd March 1796, the institution of the office of Inspector-Greneral of Naval Works was sanctioned by the King in Council, and on the 25th of the same month Bentham was appointed Inspector-General: " Whose duty it should be to consider of all improvements in relation to the building, fitting-out, arming, navigating, and victualling ships of war, and other vessels employed in His Majesty's service, as well as in relation to the Docks, Slips, Basins, Buildings, and other articles appertaining to His Majesty's Naval Establishments."

The chemist to assist the Inspector-Greneral was appointed on the recommendation of Mr. Wyndham, but of all the other assistants the choice was left to the Inspector-Greneral. Mr. Samuel Bunce was the first architect, Mr. Rehe the mechanist; the secretary, Mr. John Peake, had to this time been an officer in the navy; one of the draughtsmen, Mr. Barr, was chosen, not on account of any neatness or proficiency in drawing, but because, having originally served his apprenticeship in a dockyard, he would be eligible for employment in a naval arsenal, and because, as he had been for several years accustomed to working machinery of Bentham's invention, he was well suited to be intrusted with the management of it, when it should be introduced in the dockyards. The other clerk or draughtsman was Mr. Richard Upsall, who had served in the same vessel in which was Bentham himself during the three days' engagement with the Turks.

To carry out his improvement in the mode of arming vessels of war, he submitted a proposal for making certain experiments at Woolwich Warren, to ascertain the best mode of fitting the gun-carriages for the sloops of war building according to his ideas. The principal object of these experiments was to ascertain the degree of strength really necessary, so that no needless weight or expense might be employed. Experiments in consequence were made, but they were altogether useless. Bentham had intended to have employed carriages which prevented recoil of the gun, that is, made on the same principle on which he had mounted ordnance at Cherson, and which had been used with such good effect in actual warfare in the Liman of Otchakoff. He sent to Woolwich carriages made on this principle to be experimented on; but the Ordnance officers, instead of employing them as furnished, made one of their two experiments on a part, it is true, of one of the carriages, but instead of the other part which it was necessary to use they substituted a mere block of wood. The officers reported on their experiments, condemning, as a principle, the prevention of the recoil of a piece of artillery, and, consequently, the mode proposed by the Inspector-G-eneral, although, in fact, it had not been tried. The Report was transmitted to him for his observations. In submitting his remarks upon it, he brought to their Lordships' notice that the principle of non-recoil, as he had introduced it, was nothing more than applying to artillery of medium. sizes the same principle that is in constant use for ordnance of the largest and of the smallest calibres, namely, the mortar and the swivel gun. Farther trials were accordingly made, both ashore and afloat, of guns mounted so as not to recoil; the result of which was, I 4 their sanction of the mode which he had proposed for arming the Arrow and the Dart.

The ordnance which he destined for these vessels, small as they were, were 32-pounders, twenty-eight in number for each vessel. At the present day, guns of this calibre on board such vessels may be thought diminutive pieces of artillery; in 1796 it was considered a most daring innovation. There can hardly be a doubt but that this example, in the first instance, and Bentham's urgent subsequent endeavours, were the means of introducing artillery of much increased power, now so generally in use on shipboard.

CHAP. VII.

Marriage–Prison Architecture– Invention of a Mortar Mill for grinding Cement– Chemical Tests and Experiments on Ship Timber–Means for guarding Dockyards– Dock Buildings and Fittings– Choice of Materials– Supply of Water–Precautions against Fire– Introduction of Steam Engines– Copper Sheathing–Coast Defences– Report on the Office of Inspector-General ordered by the Select Committee of the House of Commons– Intereonvertibility of Ship Stores–Cost of Mast Ponds– Effect of the Report to the Select Committee– Alterations and Improvements in Plymouth Dockyard–Abuse of Chips–Bad Conversion of Timber–Illness– Smuggling Vessels at Hastings.

A mere register of the business carried on in Bentham's office is not the design of these memoirs; it is not necessary therefore to notice the reports made on proposals of various kinds referred to him for an opinion. It may be sufficient to say in respect of them generally, that the reasons on which his opinion was grounded were uniformly stated in writing, affording to the proposer the means of ascertaining how far he had been fairly dealt with. Not a single instance occurred, during the whole existence of the office, that any one had occasion to complain, or did. complain, of injustice done to him by the Inspector-General's report.

In October of this year he married the eldest daughter of Dr. George Fordyce.

In January 1797 it was in the contemplation of Government to provide a prison for 10,000 prisoners of war. A plan for such a prison was before the Admiralty, which they considered as enormously costly. The Inspector-General was requested to state his opinion of that plan, as also whether he supposed that the requisite security could be afforded at a less expense, and with less than 1200 officers and men to guard the prisoners. Certain buildings of wood were in frame, ready to be set up. The Inspector-Greneral determined to arrange these shedlike structures round the circumference of a large circle, their inner ends pointing towards the centre, and leaving a space between building and building as airing ground, and to glaze the ends of them sufficiently to cause a thorough light through them from end to end. The prisoners, their cooking-rooms, hospital, andc, being so provided for, he proposed the erection of a guard-house in the centre, so that, on the principle of the Panopticon, the prisoners might at all times be under central observation and control. Besides the small arms of the guard, there were to be mounted swivel guns, ready to throw such small shot as migdit be most efficacious in case of insurrection. He purposed that all the prisoners should be fully apprised of these powerful means provided for suppressing insubordination, so that no injustice would be done to them, were those means of necessity to be resorted to. By making the exterior wall a duodecagon, and placing a sentinel at each angle outside, every side would be under the command of two men, ready to repress any single attempt at communication with the interior, or to give notice by signal of any impending greater danger from without. By such an arrangement even a hundred men might be made to suffice for a guard to the 10,000 prisoners; while to the prisoners themselves this arrangement would be in the least possible degree annoying, as for their safe keeping there would be no longer need for guards or keepers to go in amongst them. The prison was not, however, erected, the Inspector-General having been informed that sufficient existing accommodation had been found for all prisoners of war.

Specifying dates may at first sight seem useless prolixity, but as many of Bentham's inventions have been claimed by others, it is but justice to hirn to give their exact dates respectively. If, on the other hand, a previous claim might have existed, such dates will afford means of verif T ing any better title to an improvement. On these accounts they will be introduced throughout, and this must be the apology for it.

On the 17th of January he proposed the construction of a mill of his invention, for grinding and mixing calcareous cements–a mortar mill. The prejudices against steam-engines for a dockyard were yet strong, and as he dared not to propose official) 7 the introduction of them for any purpose, this first mortar mill was to be worked by horses. But prejudice was not only agaidst steam-engines, it extended to machinery of every kind. Still, as the works at Portsmouth were lingering in great measure for want of a sufficient supply of mortar, he was induced at his own risk to order a mill to be made according to his plans. The advantages of these mills were soon perceived, and they have been universally adopted by private engineers for all considerable works.

Just previously to this time the Inspector-Greneral was under the necessity of reporting that the chemist was unfit for the duties of his office, which was virtually abolished in consequence of this report. At the same time there could be no doubt of the need of chemical science in regard to a great variety of works for the outfit and maintenance of the fleet. Many particular experiments had been set down amongst the first to be tried, such as those on which the goodness of copper sheathing depended; the influence upon wood, which the natural juices remaining in it might have on its duration; how far those juices might cause the difference in duration between timber felled in spring and autumn; and by what chemical agents the mischievous effects of those juices might be prevented; also a variety of experiments on calcareous cements.

A rooted aversion then existed, and is said yet to prevail in all departments of Government to the making of experiments that may be called exhaustive. Bentham, on the contrary, considered that where experiments were made at all, good economy required that they should be exhaustive. In timber, for instance, he had collected data which proved that under certain chemical circumstances it was rendered very durable, under others subject to rapid decay; that certain chemical agents, as sulphates of copper, of iron, and of alumine, were preservatives: but whether this good effect depended on the destruction chemically of the natural unassimilated juices remaining in the wood, or whether mechanically, on the filling up of its pores so as to exclude air and moisture, was then, and perhaps remains still, unknown. He would have caused experiments to be made to ascertain how the preservative material acted, so as to show which of the materials that were sufficiently efficacious was the easiest applied in practice, and the cheapest.

His principal attention at this time was directed to the details of the masonry works which he had proposed for Portsmouth yard. Whatever the nature of ground to be built upon, it had been an uniform custom to drive piles as a foundation. At Portsmouth the ground was clay, impervious to water for a considerable depth, and capable of bearing any conceivable weight of superstructure; but in parts, where piles of great length had been driven, they had not only broken up the clay, but had pierced down to a stratum containing water, to the great injury of many foundations. This piling he caused to be discontinued, notwithstanding the strong remonstrances of the dockyard officers, seconded by the Navy Board. The stability of his great works there, after more than half a century, has proved the soundness of his judgment; and the consequent saving of expense has been very great. This was no new invention, but the example thus afforded lias given confidence to many an engineer, who otherwise might not have ventured to build heavy walls on a bare foundation of clay. The form till then given to docks was ill suited to its purpose, as not having its parts conformable to the shape of ships, in some parts not leaving sufficient working room, in others giving useless space, which of course admitted of its being filled with water that had afterwards to be pumped out. For his docks he contrived that the altars, or step-like retreats at the sides, should afford ample room for work, and the best shape for supporting the shores with which a vessel is held up, while at the same time there should be no superfluous space.

The bottoms of docks had hitherto been formed of platforms of wood, a material liable to speedy decay, and very costly. For this he substituted inverted arches of masonry. This mode of structure was strongly objected to. The Comptroller of the Navy thought it even worth while to pronounce an opinion against it, supported by that of both the surveyors of the navy; these opinions were said to be based upon the instance of Eamsgate, where Smeaton had attempted to introduce an inverted arch, but had failed. Notwithstanding this weighty authority, the Inspector-General's reasons in support of his plans prevailed. The bottoms of the docks, and also the entrance to the great basin, were made inverted arches of stone. They have stood, like his other works, the test of time, and the example has been so followed by private engineers, that inverts, as they are now called, are in very general use. Little regard was at that time paid in naval works to the comparative fitness of the materials employed, either as to first cost, fitness for specific purposes, or durability. Portland stone was generpdly employed at Portsmouth, costly as it was, and subject to decay, and wood was employed for copings of walls. Instead of this he introduced granite for the copings of docks and basin, and Purbeck stone in place of Portland. Well-chosen Purbeck stone, when laid on its proper bed, is far more durable than Portland, and is so much cheaper, that by this single change of material a saving on each dock was obtained of no less than 15,000?. besides the farther saving of 10,000. on each dock by the other expedients of his introduction. These improvements and these savings are stated on a comparison with the estimated cost by the dockyard officers of plans not only already sanctioned by the Admiralty, but some of them then actually in the course of execution.

Since these works have been brought into full use, it has been thought impossible that they should ever have been opposed. Yet at the time he had to contend not only with remonstrances from the dockyard officers, but with the more formidable opposition of the Navy Board to every one of his proposals. The Admiralty uniformly transmitted such objections to him. In every instance he had to submit in writing the reasons by which he hoped to refute adverse opinions. This consumed much of his time, which probably might have been more profitably employed; yet he did not consider it as altogether lost, since, perhaps for the first time, it brought each work to the test of accurate data, and of specific reasons. On no other grounds was a decision ever given in favour of his proposals; and it so happened that none were ever rejected.

The dockyards generally were ill supplied with fresh water; vessels obtained their sea-store of it by means of boats, which carried it off to them in casks. Nor had any provision been made in any naval arsenal for preventing the ravages of fire, excepting, indeed, that a few small fire engines were kept in store. To remedy these deficiencies he presented in February the outlines of a plan, which he proposed for execution at Portsmouth, but which he represented as desirable for all public establishments at that port and elsewhere. He proposed the attainment of an abundant supply of fresh water at Portsmouth dockyard, by digging deep wells. This expedient, now so extensively adopted in this and other countries, was at that time rare, though not without example where the required supply was but small; but for large supplies water was still only brought from distant rivers at a vast expense. He had informed himself of all particulars respecting Mr. Yulliamy's overflowing well at Kensington, and of that which supplied the great brewery in Tottenham-court Eoad, while in Portsmouth dockyard itself the immense flow of water, so troublesome whenever piles pierced the stratum of clay, gave assurance that abundance might be obtained for all useful purposes.

For raising water to the reservoirs, and for forcing it through the pipes and hose, he proposed a steam-engine.

Now that steam-engines are of such general use in all of the naval establishments, the prejudice entertained at the end of the last century against them can hardly be conceived. The Lords of the Admiralty, convinced by Bentham's arguments in favour of that motive power, had from the first determined that it should be employed for giving motion to his machinery; but as even they could not venture to sanction the introduction of steam-engines openly, they had authorised him to procure one for facilitating the works to the experimental vessels at Eedbridge. It was ordered, but as it was not completed till after the vessels were launched, it was reserved till some favourable occasion should occur for introducing it in a dockyard. The cry had been, and still continued, that steam-engines would set fire to the dockyard; that the artificers would rise, if an attempt were made to introduce machinery; that neither efficiency nor economy could be effected by machinery for naval purposes. These and many other objections known to prevail against steam-engines, required on his part unusual caution. At this time it happened that new pumps were required for pumping the docks at Portsmouth: he seized upon this favourable occasion to propose that the pumps should be worked by a steam-engine; and specified the raising of water to extinguish fire as likely to be thought the least obnoxious use to which such an engine could be put. Still dockyard opinion was, that there was no use in setting up a steam-engine; men and horses all along had done all the pumping work required; what need for innovation? His perseverance and his arguments prevailed, and the result has proved that those objections, one and all, were altogether groundless.

It was in this year too that he commenced his investigations respecting copper sheathing, with a view to reform in the manner of treating and providing this costly article. Mr. Wyatt had proposed the use of tinned sheets, in order to prevent corrosion; the General had in consequence caused one of his small vessels to be sheathed partly by Mr. Wyatt's tinned sheets and partly by the usual copper sheathing, but so mixed upon the bottom of the vessel as to render the experiment a fair one. The result was as might be expected, that the tinned sheets soon became foul with weeds in Portsmouth Harbour. He had observed a very great difference in the duration of copper sheathing, although it could not be accounted for by any known difference in its manufacture. That this fact mi ht be veri-tied and stand on official record, he caused samples to be furnished him of sheathing which had been remarkable for shortness of duration, as also of such as had lasted unusually long. Some had been corroded in a few months, other specimens had lasted eighteen years; yet of these there was no known difference in their manufacture, nor could any be distinguished by inspection. He could only report, therefore, that the great number of experiments requisite, both chemical and mechanical, rendered it impossible yet to give any final opinion on the subject; but that those already made had thrown considerable light on the subject. Still, he observed, there were many instances amongst compound metals, which show that very small portions of impurity materially influence their immediate properties. He further stated that the mechanical experiments which he had already made were of great importance. The 7-had proved that not only the hardness, flexibility, strength, and other obvious properties of the same piece of copper were greatly affected by the mechanical treatment of it, but also the remarkable fact, that its resistance to chemical agents might be increased as much as one third by mechanical means.

At the beginning of the year 1798, the naval administration was under serious apprehension that a descent would be made on our shores by the French, and that our means of coast defence were inadequate to the protection of the country. In his private conferences with Earl Spencer, this had been a prominent subject of discussion, and on the 20th January 1798, "the apparent urgency of the present state of things' induced him to submit a series of " Queries relative to Coast Defence." They were suggestive of the means of making an effective and immediate addition to the mass of our naval force, general and local, and particularly applicable to the defence of the coast.

These queries, and the notes accompanying them, exhibit, perhaps, the most comprehensive view that has ever yet been taken of the real nature of the coast with a view to its defence. He points out a circumstance of fundamental importance, not noticed by any one else even to the present day, namely, that the shallowness of the water on most parts of the coast is such, that " even our sloops of war cannot approach for the purpose of defence," but where " a desperate enemy in small vessels, and with certain winds, would be able to reach it;" " that for the protection of those shallow parts there do not exist any other floating mearjs of defence than the gun-brigs, vessels incapable of working to windward," notoriously unfit

for sailing, and not fitted for rowing; and that the danger of stationing fleets between the great naval ports, rendered it desirable to have a mass of naval force composed of vessels capable of lying in the small harbours.

It is true that in the present advanced state of naval architecture, vessels are not only constructed so that most of them can work to windward and are capable of sailing, but we have a steam navy at command, which is independent of wind for locomotion. Still, so far from shallowness of structure having been regarded as a desirable property, the tendency has rather been to give increased size and deeper draught of water to vessels generally, steamers as well as sailing vessels. That General Bentham's views on the subject are looked upon as correct by men amongst the most competent to judge, is evinced by the evidence given before the Select Committee, 1848, on Navy, Army, and Ordnance Estimates, by Sir Thomas Hastings, who had been president, in 1844, of a commission to inquire into the state of coast defence.

He then proceeded to submit many points of consideration, essential to the efficacy of a naval force, which at that time seemed wholly disregarded; they were stated in the familiar language of private confidence, and in the form of queries; but as they indicate separate items of consideration, they may best be separately stated as assertions.

" The efficacy of a mass of naval force (cceteris paribus) depends partly on the destructiveness of the shot which it is employed to discharge, partly upon the promptitude with which the vessels of which it is composed, can be brought to act upon any part of the coast at pleasure.

" All of our small ports are capable of admitting vessels that could mount carronades, and even mortars, of any calibre.

" Coasting sloops employed in private service might be obtained by government in any number required. All of them are capable of being armed with from eight to twenty-four carronades, 24-pounders.

" The smallest vessels (incapable of bearing the sea) are all of them capable of being armed.

" The substitution of guns of large calibre for those of small calibre on board the existing stock of ships is the prompter and the cheaper mode of making an addition to the mass of existing force.

" To enable existing ordnance to be fired with a doubled rapidity would, in point of efficacy, be doubling the force of that ordnance. The maximum of quickness of firing a gun with a given number of men depends upon the manner in which it is mounted: but the maximum of quickness of firing, as between any two modes, has never been ascertained; nor even has it been so much attended to, as to have caused any regular set of experiments to be made for ascertaining the maximum quickness of firing in any one such mode."

He next stated his mode of mounting ordnance on the principle of non-recoil, saying that the space necessary for recoil operates as a prevention to the mounting of guns on board many vessels; that two men to a 24-pounder car-ronade would be sufficient for working it, if mounted without recoil. But knowing the prejudice against this mode of mounting ordnance, he indicated simple means of ascertaining what recoil was desirable.

Thus, more than half a century ago, were these important improvements proposed, that have since so greatly augmented the force of naval armaments,– ordnance of large calibre instead of small; carcases, shells, and missiles of the same class in addition to solid shot. In the mode of mounting ordnance now, although recoil is not yet prevented, still an approach is being made towards this improvement, by checking the recoil to a certain extent. And the mercantile marine of the country is also looked to by government, as a source of naval military strength, though

K 2 the nation has been put to an expense from which General Bentham's proposal was exempt. At present (under different shapes) a premium is given to shipowners for the preparation of their vessels to fit them for the reception of guns. But he, by very simple, cheap, and expeditious means, contrived that a trader, in a couple of days, might be fitted for guns and armed; made so that no expense need be incurred by the public, until the time the mercantile navy would be actually required for purposes of war.

The Select Committee of the House of Commons on Finance, in the beginning of the year 1798, inquired into the constitution of the office of Inspector-General of Naval Works; what, if any, benefits had resulted from it? and issued their precept, that the Inspector-General should lay before them an account of the works in his department.

In reply to this order the Inspector-General stated that the execution of all works remained, as before his appointment, in the hands of the subordinate boards, but in as far as concerned the business of suggestion no limit whatever existed; that his time had been chiefly employed in preparing and submitting to the Admiralty various proposals for the improvement of different branches of naval business; that those proposals had been referred by the Admiralty to the Navy Board for investigation; that although the opinions obtained in consequence had, it might be said uniformly, been against the proposals, the Admiralty had, in the most important instances, ordered the works in question to be carried into execution; and that in no instance had any of them been finally rejected.

The intercourse which the business of his office had given him with the several boards and establishments under the Lords of the Admiralty, had confirmed the opinion as to management which he had formed in early life. The more he investigated, the stronger was his conviction, that it is of primary importance that some one individual should stand alone responsible for the due performance of every duty.

The more important of the engineering works which were reported on to the Committee, have already been noticed, as also the peculiarities in the hulls of his experimental vessels. But one method which he looked upon as capable of effecting great saving, should not be omitted, namely, that of inter convertibility. This principle is no other, he said, than that, wherever possible, an article intended for one particular purpose should be contrived of such material, size, and shape as might render it applicable to other analogous purposes. That it is a principle of very extensive application there can be no doubt, but as a general regulation it has not to this time been observed in practice. In regard to it he stated: "The accidents to which vessels, particularly vessels of war, are liable, render it impossible but that certain articles should occasionally be renewed; for this purpose a great deal of space on board ship is taken up by the stowage of spare articles of various kinds ready prepared."–" But in and belonging to a ship there are a great many different articles which, without rendering any one of them less fit for its use, might be made perfectly similar to each other; by which means two spare articles in store, applicable to seven or eight different purposes, could, in the event of an accident happening twice to the same subject, form a more valuable supply than if duplicates only had been provided for each of these seven or eight articles."

He had introduced this principle in several instances on board the Arrow. " Of the three lower masts two were made alike, the topmasts were all four alike, for there were two to the mainmast, one above the other; the three top-gallant masts were all alike, several of the yards were alike; studding-sail booms were alike, five of the principal sails were either perfectly alike, or, by a very easy addition or separation, were capable of supplying the

K 3 place of each other." He further stated that by keeping this principle in view, at the time of proportioning the different classes of ships, as well as the different parts and appendages of them, ships at sea might not only be enabled to possess within themselves a much more efficient supply, but a much less expensive stock might suffice for our storehouses at home.

A Eeport upon the different naval works to which he had objected was furnished at the request of the Committee. In place of one of them, a mast-pond in Portsmouth yard, the expense of which was officially estimated at 189,000., he proposed another work, the cost of which, estimated by the same dockyard officer who had made the former estimate, amounted to no more than 17,725. This difference in cost was obtained by the Inspector-General's skill in the arrangement of engineering works; his mast-pond, notwithstanding its lesser cost, provided more abundant and more efficient water store room than would have been obtained by the plan objected to. This work afforded an opportunity of bringing into view two important considerations habitually neglected in the naval department, as indeed in all other departments of government where capital is sunk in permanent works. These considerations were, first, the amount of the annual money value of benefit expected from the use of a work compared to the annual interest of the money sunk for its attainment; and, secondly, the loss by unnecessary delay in the execution of a work, thereby retarding the period when compensation might be expected for the outlay by the use of that work. This mast-pond is one amongst many examples of habitual extravagance in beginning many works at the same time, and carrying them on simultaneously, by little and little, year after year. The mast-pond in question, if continued in the same manner in which it had already been carried on for some years, could not in that mode, by the greatest possible expedition, have been completed in less than thirty-one years. At the end of that period the cost of the work, as it would appear in the books, would have been simply the 195,495.; but during those thirty-one years interest would be paid upon the money yearly sunk upon it. He had caused a good accountant to calculate how much that interest would amount to, taking it at 5 per cent., and adding yearly to the sum previously expended that which had been disbursed during the year. It appeared from the arithmetician's figures that the real cost of the work at the end of the thirty-one years, instead of being the simple 195,495., would, in fact, have amounted to no less than 4:58,5681. But this was not the strongest point of view in which the example could be seen, for the Inspector-Greneral stated that, taking as a standard the rate of progress at which the mast-pond had already been going on, it would not have been completed in less than 176 years; consequently, at the period of its completion, the sums expended on the work, together with the interest and compound interest upon them, would have amounted to the enormous sum of 132 millions sterling. This statement led (on his personal examination, 9th of May) to the question, "Is there any account kept of the interest of money expended on naval works?" He replied, "None in the dockyards, nor yet, I believe, in any of the public offices; and I conceive great loss arises from want of attention to the subject." He further said, "A parallel thus made and habitually kept up between the expense in the way of interest and the amount (though it were but an ideal one) of the benefit in the way of use, would, in my opinion, be productive of very essential advantages to the public service. It would serve as a check to the undertaking of works, of which the annual use should not seem likely to compensate for the annual expense; it would operate as a spur to the execution of each work; it would serve as a memento to make the earliest, as well as the greatest, possible use of the work."

K 4

No apology seems needed for having introduced these extracts, for up to this time no attempt has been made to keep such accounts as those indicated by the Inspector-General; yet, in respect to the finance of the realm, perhaps no other measure would produce so beneficial a result as a general attention to the value of the interest of money. This disregard in public departments of the interest on money sunk is the more remarkable, as it is habitually calculated and referred to by our merchants and manufacturers, and the annual financial value of the benefit expected from the use of a work, is habitually brought to view in all proposals for works to be paid for by public companies. And as to the wasteful mode of applying to parliament for money by driblets, a little for one work, a littl i for another, that never took place in any case, while Bentham had to prepare estimates for engineering works. He yearly learnt from the First Lord what sum he was willing to ask for, and parliament likely to grant; he then selected the works the most required, and ascertained how much could be expended on each of them, with due attention to economy in carrying them on, and inserted in his estimate no other works than those which the specified sum would pay for.

The Inspector-General's report produced extraordinary sensation in the Admiralty. The Committee on Finance, suspecting that much mismanagement had been going on in subordinate boards of the naval department, were desirous of bringing it to light in a manner the least obnoxious to the superior board, yet such as should promise to produce a remedv. The chairman of the Committee, Charles Abbot (early in February), concerted, therefore, with General Bentham the best means of effecting this purpose, and it was arranged between them that the Committee should call upon him for " an account of the works in the department of the Inspector-General of Naval Works," arranged under certain heads, (which, in fact, Bentham furnished to

KEPORT OF THE COMMITTEE ON FINANCE. 137 the chairman,) " with any other observations explanatory of the above matters."

This precept, 26th of February 1798, was communicated to the Admiralty on the 1st of March. The In-spector-Greneral immediately employed himself in preparing the account required, but without neglecting the current business of his office. The amount of time he spent in actual mental labour may be conceived from the journal of the 4th of March. This journal was not written with his own hand, but by one of his family, to whom he related events and conversations; after the journal was written, he daily read it over and corrected it. On this 4th of March it is noted: "At work, both B. and myself, from seven in the morning till near half-past ten at night, with only one hour's intermission, at observations preparing for Committee on Finance; and on general observations on dockyard officers." The month was spent much in the same way. He saw Mr. Abbot occasionally, from whom he learnt, on the 28th, that all of the public offices were afraid of being examined into; and on the 30th, Bentham learnt from Lord Spencer that the " Navy Board and the Admiralty were at daggers drawn." On the 2nd of April "Mr. Abbot called, looked over and corrected letter to the Committee on Finance–thinks the Committee will publish the papers: if they should not, says B. can publish them himself." On the 3rd measures were taken for having fair copies made of the report; and on the 4th " B. went to the Admiralty to see Lady Spencer; but she was engaged, and could not receive him." In the course of the day he saw Lord Spencer, when other business was discussed, but not a syllable passed on the subject of the report; Bentham afterwards saw Mr. Abbot, and read to him the letter to the Committee. On the 5th the letter and the report were sent to the Committee,

By Lady Bentham.– Ed.

and a copy of both officially to the secretary of the Admiralty.

Now came an explosion of wrath. Mr. Nepean on the 6th sent for the Inspector-General: " told him he thought he was reprehensible in sending in the report to the

Committee." Bentham saw Lord Spencer, who desired him to get it back again. He then went to Abbot for the report, but was told that he could not have it returned. Should he go to the secretary for it? "It was as much as his place was worth to give it."–" He went back and told Lord Spencer that he could not get it." Mr. Nepean told him a that he would be reprimanded by the Admiralty Board." He replied that he must bear it; he was responsible for everything he did. Lord Spencer said, " it was well written; that he had been up all night reading it."

But the matter was not allowed to rest. Those members of the Admiralty Board who wished for no change had taken alarm, and on Monday the 8th the Inspector-Greneral received an official order, " not to forward the report to the Committee until you shall have received their further directions." His answer to this was, that having only been directed to furnish a copy of it for their Lordships 1 "information," he had, in obedience to their commands, sent the copy required; but the report having been so long delayed, he had thought it incumbent on him to submit it on the same day to the Committee. However, the unexpected sensation which his report had occasioned, induced him to call on and consult General Koss respecting his conduct. The General approved of it, and informed him that the Board of Ordnance never interfere in any report made by their inferiors. Other persons were also consulted by him, in the presence too of Mr. Nepean. Many of these persons objected to some of the Inspector-General's proceedings, when Mr. Nepean, on being asked what he thought of General Bentham, replied that "he was too much for them all." Indeed, with the exception of this single transaction, Mr. Nepean approved of all the Inspector- General's proceedings. In the present case, it would seem that apprehension on the part of those who had suffered mismanagement to go on unheeded, had for the moment influenced the secretary of the Admiralty; and that the First Lord himself had on this occasion been worried into a persuasion that this said report was fraught with mischief.

The Inspector-General waited again on Lord Spencer, who announced that a reprimand from the Board would be passed. Bentham related what General Eoss had said, and suggested that any endeavour of the Board to get it back would only render its matter of the more importance. His Lordship asked, "Would you like it yourself?"–" No; certainly he should not."–"It was not called for," said his Lordship. " If you had given an account of one work it would have been sufficient; nobody gives a more particular account than they are absolutely obliged to give."

A peep behind the scenes is rarely obtained when reports to committees of inquiry are being prepared; but what passed on this occasion may well indicate the habit of concealment usual in their fabrication. Much vexation and momentary difficulty was incurred by the Inspector-General by his honest independence; but he was shortly afterwards rewarded by the impression for good which his report had made at the Admiralty, and which led to real improvement in civil naval management.

On the 9th he called on Lady Spencer, who said she had been too ill to receive him before; that the blame about the report was that he had brought it forward just when the French were coming. "That was just the time," he said, " for producing a sensation, and having things altered that required it." General Eoss came in, and recommended most urgently forbearance on Lord Spencer's part. Bentham repeated his regret at what

Lord Spencer had suffered, and said that his object in having wished to show it to Lady Spencer was, that if she should think any expressions in it would be offensive, they should be expunged. General Eoss again said that in the Ordnance it was made a point of delicacy, not to interfere even so much as to inquire what the subordinates wrote or said. But Bentham was advised for the present to keep out of Lord Spencer's way.

The excitement soon ceased with regard both to Lord Spencer and Mr. Nepean; but as the Board persisted in their desire to correct the report, the Inspector-General obtained it back again, and on the 30th April enclosed it to the secretary. On the 8th of May it was returned with certain corrections made in it, and their Lordships signified their desire that it should be returned to the Committee as corrected.

The original copy of the report sent on the 5th April to the Committee, has been examined; and the corrections made by the Admiralty are marked in red ink. They are confined to two instances; the one relating to the steam-engine and machinery in Portsmouth dockyard, which had been stated not to have been determined on, but for which their Lordships' orders had just been given, and a correction was made accordingly. The other correction was the expunging two paragraphs, in which observations had been made as to the superfluous expense that was habitually incurred by uneconomical practices in the construction of vessels; but the statement was allowed to remain, of the comparative saving that would result from the mode of construction exemplified in his experimental vessels. It may be observed that it was probably exposure of deficiencies in naval construction that rendered the Navy Board and their supporters so very sore. But in regard to the report itself, the correction of it by the Admiralty rendered what had been before but the opinion of a single man, an official document, and sanctioned its state-

REPORT ON WORKS IN PLYMOUTH DOCKYARD. 141 ments throughout, by the highest naval authority in the realm.

The report so corrected was returned to the Committee, who did not fail to avail themselves on the same day of the high sanction which it had obtained, for the Inspector-General was examined, and the first question put to him was, "Are the reports delivered in by you respecting naval works presented with permission of the Board of Admiralty?—" They are, having been submitted to the Admiralty Board."

By a further precept of the Committee on Finance, Bentham was directed to report on works proposed by him for Plymouth dockyard, and of such others as he might have objected to. Large sums had been expended on that dockyard, but magnificence had, unfortunately, been more considered than utility. His proposals for Plymouth, therefore, were principally confined to rendering those works of increased use, or more appropriate to the service for which they were designed. He objected to the proposed landing-place, as being inadequate to the accommodation of a sufficient number of boats, and because, in common with all the landing-places in Plymouth yard, boats could not approach them at low water, but planned instead, a boat harbour, where boats might always lie afloat, and where landing and embarcation could be effected at all times of tide. Many storehouses had been built for grandeur of appearance, so that each floor was of double the height that could be employed as store room; for these, he proposed the insertion of intermediate floors: thus these houses were made to receive conveniently double the former quantity of stores. These and many other alterations may- appear insignificant, nor would they be mentioned, were it not to show how little attention had been paid to usefulness, as though magnificence were of more importance in a royal dockyard than convenience. It must not be supposed that he disregarded appear- ance; for though he looked on this consideration as secondary to that of use, his subsequent proposals testify his anxiety to avail himself of architectural skill and taste.

By a precept of the 17th of April he was ordered to " state his opinion upon the expediency of abolishing the practice of chips in his Majesty's dockyards, and the orounds of such opinion." This order had originated in a suggestion of the Inspector-General's to the chairman of the Committee. His well-known intimate knowledge of what was the real practice in the management of the civil concerns of the navy, had led to consultation with him as to what would be the least obnoxious mode of bringing abuses and mismanagement to view, and of laying a foundation, on which effectual reform might be instituted by the Admiralty; and it will be seen that that Board availed itself, during two successive administrations, of the preparatory step thus taken. The abuses consequent on the allowance of chips to workmen had been noticed previously to the appointment of this Committee, yet no administration had had the hardihood to abolish the practice–indeed, no means had yet been devised of effecting this desirable reform, so as not to excite the animosity of the workmen. The Inspector-General had ascertained that the abuses arising from this privilege, much exceeded even his worst expectations; and wheu he had, in private with the chairman, informed him of a variety of particulars on the subject, the precept was issued, and he devised a remedy.

Notorious as was this abuse, the Inspector-General would not, however, have hazarded an opinion without the most positive proof. He had, therefore, during a late visit to Portsmouth yard, taken up his abode close to the dockyard gates, where, without its being noticed by the artificers, he could see the bundles of chips brought out, and many of them opened for sale in a kind of market, held below his windows. As it was winter, he professed to like an addition of wood to his coal fire. In this way bundles were frequently obtained, which, on putting the pieces together, showed that a whole deal had been cut up to reduce it to the greatest length allowed, three feet; or, perhaps, even still more valuable oak planks or oak timber had been thus cut up. This practice of allowing chips had its influence on the construction of second-rate houses in Portsea and its vicinity; stairs were just under three feet wide; doors, shutters, cupboards, and so forth, were formed of wood in pieces just under three feet long. He stated to the Committee, "I am very decidedly of opinion that it is highly expedient that the practice of carrying out of the dockyards any article whatsoever, under the denomination of chips, should be abolished." He observed that a superior degree of vigilance on the part of the officers might sometimes check these abuses; but that it was his decided opinion that whilst chips of any description were allowed, no such vigilance could be depended on. It was only mastermen and foremen who had opportunities of judging of the lawfulness of the way in which chips were made; and these officers living amono 1 the artificers dared not enforce regulations which would bring upon them the resentment of hundreds, and instanced the danger to which such officers would be exposed by an example lately afforded. " An officer of this description, who, having an extraordinary degree of zeal for the public service and a superior sense of his duty, was led to check in some degree these abuses, and rendered himself so evidently an object of resentment to the artificers, that it was thought necessary for his personal security, that he should for some time be guarded on his way to and from the dockyard."

From this time the Inspector-General came to be considered not only as the naval architect, the civil engineer, the naval military engineer, but, further, in the still more important light of the reformer of abuses, and the deviser of a new system of management grounded on sure principles; that is, on those principles which have insured success in the great manufacturing and commercial concerns of private men, and which have at the same time contributed so effectually to the enrichment and prosperity of the nation.

It has been seen that the Inspector-General had represented the need of better management of the timber department to the Committee on Finance, and that evidence was officially before the Board of Admiralty. In addition to this he had often represented to Lord Spencer the great improvidence and waste that was habitual in regard to this costly store; but particular facts, such as could be presented to his Lordship, were wanting, till in June 1798 the late Sir Henry Peake, then second assistant in Portsmouth yard, furnished convincing examples of bad conversion. He sent drawings to the Inspector-Greneral of some of the most ruinous instances. These were not confined to the loss, by waste of substance, in cutting up large timber to a small piece, or to waste of money, in cutting up high-priced timber for purposes where less costly pieces were equally appropriate; but it was further most mischievous, because it was the destruction of timber of a size, of a quality, of a form rarely to be obtained, although essential in the construction of large ships.

Extreme application to business in general, increased as it was by the necessity of replying to the continual objections made to all his plans of improvement, brought upon Bentham a severe illness, so that he was under the necessity of retiring for a month from all official duty. This was the only occasion during his service of seventeen years that he ever allowed any illness to withdraw his attention from the business of his office. When unable to leave the house, he worked at home; when confined even to his bed, still he received his assistants. On this occasion he retired to a secluded farmhouse at Fairlight, near Hastings.

The farm happened to be close to a ravine, and to a creek of the sea where much smuggling was habitually carried on. By personal observations made at this time, he convinced himself of the facility with which small vessels came into the creek at their pleasure, landed their cargoes, and went out again, unanno r ed by the armed vessels on the coast. The smugglers drew very little water; the armed vessels employed against them were of deep draught, and consequently could not approach the shore,– an example proving how well grounded was his opinion, that large vessels alone are not to be depended on for service on our shallow coasts.

CHAP. VIII.

Dock Entrances at Portsmouth–New South Dock for Ships of the Line– Choice of Stone in building–Mast Ponds–Reservoirs for Clearing Docks– Treatment of his Experimental Vessels– Floating Dam– Steam Engine and Pumps– A Russian Fleet at

Spithead– Interviews with the Officers–Daily Occupations– Character of Dockyard "Workmen– Steam Dredging Machine–Enlargement of Marine Barracks at Chatham–Artesian Well–Deptford Dockyard–Sheerness–Proposals for a Dockyard at the Isle of Grain– Improved Copper Sheathing– Success of the Experimental Vessels– Principle of Non-recoil in mounting Guns– Engagement between the Millbrook and the French Frigate Bellone, and between the Dart and the Desiree.

When General Bentham returned to duty, the works at Portsmouth called for his first attention. It had been proposed that the entrance to the basin, its apron, gates, andc, should be constructed as those to other basins and docks usually are. But the enormous expense attending such works, and their inconvenience when executed, induced him to propose that the entrance should be of masonry, the lower part in the form of an inverted arch, which, with its sides, should form a groove. By these means he avoided the expense of the immense number of piles usually employed to tie down the apron or bottom when it is made of wood, as all entrances had been hitherto. In closing the entrance, instead of the usual gates, he contrived a holloiv floating dam, which, when across the entrance, should tit, watertight, into the groove in the masonry, the heel, as it might be called, of the dam to press against one or the other of the sides of the groove, according as the water might be to be kept in or out of the basin. The

interior of the dam was provided with valves, so that water for sinking it could be admitted by them, or run out of it at pleasure, without the need of pumping.

LTp to that time docks and basins had prevented traffic across their entrances, excepting for foot passengers. Instead of the slight bridge used for that purpose, he contrived one supported by the floating dam, over which the heaviest loaded carriages might pass; an accommodation particularly desirable in this part of the yard, where weighty loads were frequently required to be conveyed from one side of the basin to the other. This strong bridge formed a part of the dam itself, so as to be floated away and brought back again together; thus, as soon as the dam could be replaced, the communication between the opposite piers would be effected.

The perfect success of this work at Portsmouth furnished a happy example to private engineers; both inverted arch and floating dam were shortly afterwards copied by them, and have become of very general use. The floating dam has indeed been newly named, and called a caissoon, and thus the inventor of it is lost sight of; but this is by no means the only instance in which General Bentham's inventions have been adopted by others, and the credit of them given to his imitators instead of to himself. The original floating dam, or caissoon, at Portsmouth, though of wood, lasted for the long term of forty-four years, having received during the time no repair of any consequence. The inverted arch of masonry still remains perfect, and has completely answered its intended purpose.

His drawings for the new south dock in the basin at Portsmouth were not submitted to the Admiralty till the 9th of August 1799. This delay had been occasioned by his perception of many inconveniences in existing docks, especially in regard to the shoring of ships; that is, the affording them support when in dock, by shores carried from the steps or altars at the sides of the dock. He had

L 2 bestowed much time in investigating the form best adapted for this business. But there was another and a more important novelty in his plan; it was the increasing the depth of the dock sufficiently to admit a ship of the deepest draught of water that could come into the harbour, and the making the dock capable of receiving such a ship with all in.

The taking a ship of the line into dock with all in, that is, with her armament and all her stores (excepting powder) on board, with her masts and rigging also as she came in from sea, was an operation too daring in appearance even for him to propose without previous preparation. He had accordingly, early in the preceding year, obtained an official inquiry from the Admiralty to Captain Grore, as to whether he had ever witnessed such a practice. The Captain stated officially in reply, that he had, at the Caraccas, seen a ship of the line taken into dock with all in. The Inspector-General had in his evidence to the Committee on Finance stated this fact, and that a similar practice in our own dockyards was habitual in regard to frigates.

The importance of such an innovation may not at first sight seem so great as in effect it really was. Ships were, and still often are, taken into dock merely to examine the state of the bottom, sometimes without anything being-found amiss, frequently requiring nothing more than to scrub off weeds and filth, or to replace a sheet or two of sheathing, the work of perhaps only a few hours. But the clearing a ship of the line of her stores to lighten her, as was then the constant practice before taking her into dock, was work for all her crew for perhaps five or six days. If that crew consisted of but 700 men, and their cost in Wages and provisions at no more than two shillings a day, this for five days, and for five more to put the stores on board again, would together amount to no less a sum than 700l. In dismantling a ship, too, the loss on the stores

CHOICE OF STONE IN DOCK-WOEKS. 49 themselves, partly by embezzlement, partly by destruction or deterioration, amounts to a very considerable sum of money– and, above all, in time of war, there is the loss, often an incalculable one, attendaut on keeping a ship from service.

The kind of stone designed for the proposed dock was Purbeck, as being much cheaper than the Portland stone, the only kind till then used; but for the parts of the work most liable to injury, he introduced Scotch granite. This and the rest of his masonry works afforded the first instance where, in this or any other naval arsenal, attention had been paid to the kind of stone employed. By the substitution of Purbeck stone at Portsmouth for that of Portland, the actual saving on each dock amounted to no less a sum than 15,000. So at Plymouth the savings made at his suggestion were very considerable, by employing the marble of the country instead of Purbeck paving, and the granite of the place in lieu of Portland stone. His greatest innovation was his proposal that its bottom " should be formed by masonry alone, in the form of an inverted arch, without the use of any piles or woodwork." In this instance the Navy Board attempted to quash the plan by private means. When these were found unsuccessful, the Navy Board officially objected to the inverted arch, and the Inspector-General was called upon to give his reasons for introducing it. They proved satisfactory, and the work was executed according to his proposal.

He also proposed the converting the north camber and boat-pond in Portsmouth yard into two docks and a basin for frigates. This was also objected to by the Navy Board, but to no purpose. By the increased facilities thus provided, two docks and a basin for frigates were obtained at an expense of less than 10,000. Similar accommodations could not otherwise have been obtained for less than 70,000. or 80,000.

It has already appeared that he had objected to the

L 3 plans of a new mast-pond in progress of construction when lie first visited Portsmouth yard, and that he had proposed by another plan to provide for the storing of the required quantity of mast logs. Objections, as usual, were made to this proposal. In preparing to reply to them, he became convinced that the stowage room intended by the Board was nowise proportioned to the different quantities and lengths of the logs really received. In order to proceed on sure grounds, he obtained quarterly accounts of the receipt and expenditure of mast timber. It was a laborious task to himself and his assistants to anal se and make out in a tabular form the quantities of each description of such timber that had actually been received and consumed each quarter; yet, without knowing the quantity of store to be provided for, it would not have been possible to decide what provision of stowage room might be required.

He had perceived, in regard to what is called the establishment of stores (that is, the quantities to be kept alwa r s in store), that an essential point of consideration had been disregarded, namely the time requisite for obtaining a fresh supply, a point necessary to be taken into account in providing stowage room for the average consumption. The Navy Board, in their remonstrances against his plan, had stated that by theirs ample provision had been made, which would not be the case with his.

In order to ascertain this point, he classed the different sorts of mast timber according to the consumption and to the time required for obtaining a supply in the case of each sort; he then multiplied its annual consumption by the number of years required to obtain the supply, and this he considered as the proper quantity for which stowage room should be provided. This point, it may be observed, is not considered in the establishment for stores in general, or for any species of store in particular. Mast timber is kept in mast-ponds by constructing round an excavation a number of walled partitions, which are themselves divided horizontally by wooden beams of sufficient strength to keep down a range of mast timber below them, the timber being floated in or out from the middle of the excavation when filled with water; and the spaces between the partitions are termed mast-locks, He found, reckoning the stowage room by inches of diameter of wood, that by the Navy Board's ample plan no more than 18,174 inches could be stowed in both the old and the new ponds together, whereas the stock to be provided for, merely the stock on hand in the year 1797, amounted to 76,040 inches, more than four times the quantity which the Board had provided. By his first plan 34,806 inches would have been stowed, nearly double the Navy Board's quantity; but now, in consequence of his examination of documents, he found it necessary to make additions to his locks, so that they might contain 61,284 inches of mast timber.

When, at a visitation of this yard by the Lords of the Admiralty in 1802, the subject of the mast-pond was discussed on the spot, every possible objection to the Inspector-Greneral's plan was brought forward, but the advantages of it were seen to be so prominent, that their Lordships determined on its adoption. For some reason, however, which never came to light, its execution was delayed; but the cause of its non-execution was surmised to be the Resident Commissioner's apprehension that the mastery would approach too near to his splendid official residence; these fears were groundless. But this impediment to useful improvements by the placing of officers' houses within a dockyard, is not the greatest mischief that has arisen from this practice.

The Inspector-General's experimental vessels had now (1802) been some of them between three and four years at sea, so that their qualities in actual service by this time might be judged of. The prejudice and opposition in regard to his engineering works, great as it was,

L 4 was still far exceeded by that shown towards his vessels. The dockyard shipwright officers of Portsmouth yard spoke of them openly to naval officers and seamen with the greatest contempt, and reported on them to the Navy Board most injuriously. These vessels had all along been treated with unprecedented neglect; insomuch that on various occasions their commanders had been compelled to make complaint to the Navy Board. It may be concluded that the Inspector-General could not let such proceedings pass unnoticed. Frequently he was under the necessity of informing Lord Spencer of real circumstances, very different from those adversely represented–sometimes verbally with facts, often by letter, still more frequently by communicating private letters from the several commanders, or from other persons, on the subject of these vessels. At length, 9th August 1798, he found it necessary to state officially the neglect of the first assistant of Portsmouth yard.

This statement was made on the occasion of the return into port of the Eling, on account of leaks. The depreciating manner in which the experimental vessels were spoken of by the dockyard officers had so prejudicial an effect upou the crews, that the appearance of the smallest quantity of water in them, such as would not excite attention in other ships, was sufficient in the case of these to place their commanders under a moral obligation to return into port. This same schooner had on a previous occasion been returned from attendance on the Sans Pareil on account of a leak, a foot above water, and the dockyard officers laid her by as exhibiting signs of weakness in her construction, such as to afford grounds for the condemnation of all the vessels similarly constructed. This opinion was said, in the dockyard report, to be pronounced in consequence of an examination made by the first assistant. An official inquiry was, therefore, made by Admiralty order, when it turned out that neither the first assistant nor any other of the officers usually employed in such surveys had ever been on board the Eling. The report had farther stated that it would be necessary to take her into dock to repair the leak. It was, however, afterwards easily stopped whilst afloat– not by dockyard artificers, but by the carpenter of the Arrow. The schooner then went on a cruise to Marcon. On another occasion, when the Eling was in port to be fitted with carronades, it again became the duty of the first assistant to superintend the fittings. " This superintendence he performed in the same way as the former one– he never went on board her" In doing the work consequent on fitting the carronades, some scuppers forward were observed to be fitting in a manner never permitted in other vessels, and which must evidently occasion leaks. This was pointed out to those who were doing the work, but the admonition was disregarded; the scuppers thus improperly fitted did occasion leaks; and it was on account of a leak so caused, that the Eling had now returned to Spithead.

Leaks on board some of the other vessels were, on examination, found to have been occasioned by circumstances totally irrelevant to their mode of structure, and it was more than suspected that the leaks were purposely caused, to "dish the vessels," as a sailor was heard to declare was his intention, in regard to the cooking apparatus of the Arrow. As to leaks in the Dart, Captain (the late Admiral) Eagget, in November 1798, said in a private letter: "Something like a survey has commenced, and I believe will throw a new light upon the subject. A bolt hole has been discovered open in our bottom, and a treenail one under the filling forward on the starboard side."

These returns to port on account of trifling leaks were particularly vexatious, as they were continually represented as proofs of the weakness of these vessels; and many were the attempts made to influence Lord Spencer, and bring on a condemnation of them. The expense incurred by petty repairs was also much insisted on; it was rendered considerable by the neglect of dockyard officers, for when anything was required for the vessel, the work was left to the workmen uncontrolled, and uninspected by any of the officers. The Inspector-General, convinced of the strength of these vessels and of their other good properties, contented himself for the present with exhibiting to their Lordships from time to time the conduct of the dockyard officers, and to Lord Spencer such well-authenticated particulars as might induce him to employ them in the most exposed and active service, feeling sure from experience that the more severe the trials, the greater would their superiority be found to be.

Lord Spencer, having determined on a reform in the management of the dockyards, and having charged the Inspector-General with the business of preparing fundamental regulations, as to the management of timber in particular, began by requesting, on the 5th of June, to be furnished with accounts of the receipt and expenditure of timber for a year. They were accordingly sent in forthwith. From this time he employed every spare hour in an investigation of the mischiefs and inconveniences of the actual system. He entered into numberless minutiae of practice as existing at the most important of our ports, Portsmouth, and where of all the ports the practice was least objectionable. The labour was the greater as he would not take information upon trust. He repeatedly attended the musters to witness himself how easily now, as when he himself was apprentice at Chatham, the absence of a man might be overlooked, both unwittingly or often wilfully, by the muster clerk. By similar means he convinced himself of actual facts on a great variety of details, before he ventured to devise a remedy.

On the 6th May 1799, he stated that he thought it highly expedient the Lords Commissioners of the Admiralty should witness the effects produced on copper sheathing by the working of a ship at sea, as affording proof of the imperfections, in regard to strength, of the mode of construction now made use of in the structure of ships in general. He therefore had obtained some sheets of copper from the Tamar frigate, which had been taken off with particular care, so as not to increase the rents or puckering: of them. Considerable as these rents and that puckering were in these sheets, they were far from being the worst, many of the sheets on this vessel having been rent to such a degree, that they could only be removed in fragments. He also stated other tokens of weakness of this vessel, and made a deep impression on their Lordships which tended in no small degree to confirm them in the opinion, that a new system of management would be the only effectual remedy for this, as for other existing evils.

In the spring of this year (1799), the steam engine and the pumps worked by it were put to use with all the success which the Inspector-Greneral had anticipated in planning them. On the 7th of June Lord Hugh Seymour accompanied him to witness this novelty. To the surprise of all, the piston rod of the pump broke whilst at work. The millwright who had charge of this machinery found a broken copper nail in the packing of the pump piston, a score in the upper rim of which proved that the nail had passed down into the packing from above; the master blacksmith, a working blacksmith, and all others present, attributed the breaking of the rod to this nail. This was one of those malicious attempts made from time to time, to injure and bring into disrepute the Inspector-Greneral's plans of every kind. It had been said by all, including the Navy Board, and perhaps some members of the Superior Board itself, that the introduction of a steam engine would cause risings of the workmen. A very humble set of them ceased to be employed at the pumps when this steam engine was put to work–the drivers who had hitherto guided the horses when pumping the reservoir. These men considered it an irksome business, and so far from rising, to express their joy on being rid of it, they clubbed together, and had a supper on the day the engine was first put to work. Bentham was in fact never regardless of injury that might be done to any workman by the adoption of his plans; thus on the 19th he found means by which the keeper of the old pumps could be properly compensated for the loss of his extra pay. The treenail mooters and sawyers had expected to suffer from the introduction of machinery, and had lately applied to him respecting their fears, and so well were they satisfied with bis assurance that no one should be a personal sufferer by any of his proposals, that a murmur amongst them was no longer heard. Their entire reliance on his promises was highly gratifying, the more so as it was never by gratuities of any kind that he acquired and preserved the good will of the workmen.

A pleasurable event of another nature occurred this month. A Eussian fleet being at the port, the admiral and other superior officers of it waited on him, in token, they said, of the high estimation in which he was held in their country in remembrance of his naval and other services. He had frequent intercourse with these officers on shore; and when he went on the 9th to return the admiral's visit at Spithead, not only the more usual honour awaited him of blowing trumpets on board ship as soon as a visitor is in sight, but he was received on board with every honour shown to the most distinguished guests– the guard turned out, drums beating, and so forth. He on his side wore the military cross of St. George on the occasion, and his sword of honour given by the Empress for his achievements in the Liman.

Convinced that the imperfections of numberless works had resulted far more from a want of acquaintance with minute details, than from any want of skill in the projector, the Inspector-General thought it incumbent on him to pass much of his time at the naval ports, particularly at Portsmouth, where, during the struggles of war, more real business was done in the outfit and repairs of our fleets, than was perhaps effected in all the other ports together; but with the rare exception of a half-holiday upon such an extraordinary occasion as his visit to the Eussian admiral, his whole time was occupied in business. One or two of his assistants were usually lodged in his house. The early morning's walk was in the Arsenal. From breakfast to rather an early dinner hour, was generally devoted to consideration of his own plans and projects. In respect to each of them his habit was first to note the desiderata, then the various means by which they might be attained, comparing one mode with the other as to their respective advantages and disadvantages, not forgetting first cost, and whether the benefit to be derived would pay a fair interest for the money sunk upon the work. His official letters were also prepared at this time, all of them by himself, as no one in his office could be depended upon for even the commonest note–his secretary, so called, being in fact his assistant in naval construction. As his official communications were all in writing, no small portion of his time was requisite for this business, more especially as, with rare exceptions, he had to answer and refute the objections habitually made to his proposals. During meal times conversation with his assistants turned on the business which was immediately the subject of investigation. A somewhat hasty dinner over, a walk to the dockyard or other naval establishment followed, to obtain information from officers, to search books, or to consult those who were to clear up any doubtful- question,– artificer, labourer, pilot, dredger, admirals, captains, ship carpenter, no matter what description of person, so that their intelligence and truthfulness enabled him to gain from them information that might be depended on. He was usually accompanied in his walk home by some officer, and after tea there was generally an assemblage of some two or three persons to discuss mechanical subjects principally; or in fine weather a walk was often taken, to see the effects of a remarkably high or low tide perhaps, or to take note of the haunts and habits of dockyard men when the day's work was over.

At this time an example is noted of the delays to which ships were so frequently subjected at Portsmouth, and which the works proposed by Bentham, and then in course of execution, were designed to obviate. The Coromandel and the Impregnable, both of them ships of the line, were lying, their works completed, one in the south, the other in the north dock, incapable for want of depth of water of being undocked till the next spring tides, and if they should happen then to be low, these ships might even have had to wait for the spring tides next following.

During his stay at Portsmouth, in the year 1800, he investigated a great variety of subjects respecting which he had improvements in view, and the year was fruitful in proposals, many of which have led to immense results, to the advantage of the public at large, no less than to that of naval arsenals. It was in the early part of this year that he proposed the steam dredging machine, an invention that has been imitated and generally adopted by the public, and which has proved as efficacious and important as he foresaw it would become. His proposal of this apparatus, which was calculated to raise 1000 tons of soil a day, was dated 16th April 1800.

This proposal, with the detailed drawings of the apparatus and an estimate of the cost, having been sent as usual to the Navy Board for their observations, was there canvassed; and at length the machine was ordered to be constructed. It was completed and at work for trial on the 6th March 1802, and at regular work in Portsmouth Harbour on the 3rd April of the same year.

The dates of this invention are particularly specified, because lately the invention of the dredging machine has by some one been attributed to an engineer in private practice, whose eminence in his profession rendered it needless to ascribe to him works not his own; but Sir Samuel's machine was proposed two years before the first mention of such a machine to the Hull Dock Company, in the year 1802, by that engineer, and it was at work in Portsmouth dockyard two years before a steam engine was applied at Hull to an old existing machine of a different construction. It was not till some years afterwards that a dredging machine of nearly similar construction to Sir Samuel's was used in private works; and it is not impossible but that the drawings of his machine might have been seen by that engineer, since copies of them were sent, on the 25th April 1801, to the Chairman of the Committee for the Improvement of the Port of London, who had called on him for his opinion respecting the new bridge.

The machine in question consisted of a chain of iron buckets worked by a steam engine. The boiler of the steam engine was made of wood instead of metal, the fireplace and flues only being of iron, and all of them surrounded with water. This wooden boiler lasted twenty years, having during that period been once new topped. A similar boiler for the second dredging machine lasted only six years, the former one having been made in Portsmouth dockyard, the other by contract.

When one of Sir Samuel's dredging machines, at a later period, was working off Sheerness to depths frequently of twenty-eight feet, he was desirous of ascertaining the exact cost of digging and raising soil. It appeared from the details of daily expenditure, joined to an ample percentage allowed for capital sunk and for wear and tear of the apparatus, that the expense for raising soil was less than one penny per ton.

On the 8th April he submitted a plan for the enlarge- ment of the Marine Barracks at Chatham, which was approved; but when he proposed a draught of form of contract for the works, the Navy Board applied for a statement of the quantities of materials of each description required. This led to a letter from him, in which he observed in the first place that the drawings were such as to afford sufficient information, and stated, as his reason for not giving those particulars, his desire to ascertain by comparison which of the tenders would on the whole be the most advantageous. Amongst the many fraudulent practices in making tenders for works to be done by contract, was that of setting down at low prices those articles of which the quantities required were small, and at high prices those articles of which the quantities required would be great. The practice at the Navy Board was to add the prices together of the several items, without regard to quantity, and to accept the lowest as it appeared by an average thus made. But by this contrivance of contractors, a tender often on the face of it appeared the lowest, although perhaps upon the whole contract that lowest-looking one might in fact be the most exorbitant. His perseverance did effect a salutary reform in this respect as to architectural works; but as to contracts generally, his endeavours to the last were ineffectual to the crushing of this hydra-headed monster.

Impressed with the insufficiency of our naval arsenals on the eastern coast, and with the extravagance of keeping up petty establishments, such as that of the dock ard at Deptford, he, as early as August 1799, suggested to Lord Spencer the giving up of that dockyard, and of providing a new system of naval establishments " somewhere north of the Forelands," and on further consideration of the subject, he addressed a letter to the Admiralty, 19th April 1800, in which he submitted various circumstances showing the expediency of gradually forming a naval arsenal on the Isle of Grain.

The discussions which have of late taken place respecting the abandonment at one time of Deptford yard, and the subsequent re-establishment of a staff of officers there, may render the Inspector-Greneral's letter the more interesting, since it exhibits grounds on which an opinion may be formed respecting our eastern dockyards, more precise than any others which have as yet been brought forward on the subject. He said that: "With regard to the dockyards of Deptford, Woolwich, and Chatham,– considering their great distance from the sea, the unavoidable difficulties and delays attending the navigation of the rivers in which they are situated, the want of a sufficient depth of water for ships of war when in a state fit for sea, and the want of all accommodations for ships to fit within the precincts of either of those dockyards,– it has appeared to me that however preat might be the sum which might be appropriated to their improvement, still the sending a ship from sea in time of war to either of those yards for the purpose of refitting or repair, must occasion a much greater expense for the performing a given quantity of work, than if it could have been done at an outport; and this, independently of the much greater inefficient expense attending the maintenance of the crews and the wear and tear of the ship during the time it would be thus excluded from the possibility of performing any actual service. The consideration of these circumstances, as well as of others of the same tendency, has convinced me that it would be far more economical to increase the present establishments at the outports, or to form some new ones where ships might be refitted with all the despatch that the nature of the work admits of, than to continue to incur the very heavy expense which necessarily attends the employing inland dockyards for the general purposes to which they are at present applied."

In respect to Sheerness, he stated that although the harbour had a sufficient depth of water, and that the situ-
ation was well suited to the supply and repairs of fleets destined for service in the north seas, or for the protection of the metropolis, yet the dockyard laboured under great and some of them irremediable disadvantages; such as that " the confined plan, on which that yard was first established, has occasioned an arrangement of the docks and buildings very ill adapted to coincide with any regular system of accommodations on a more extensive scale."

He then stated that a situation having been long ago pointed out to him as eligible for a dockyard on the Isle of Grain, he made it his particular business to examine the island itself, and to acquire all the information respecting it which it was in his power to obtain at Sheerness.

The superior advantages which a naval establishment in such a situation would have over the dockyards of Chatham, Woolwich, and Deptford, rendered it advisable, he said, that no more money should be spent on those dockyards except with a view to the particular services to which they would be in future appropriated; namely, the building of new ships, and giving thorough repairs to old ones, with the exception, however, of small vessels, cutters, schooners, andc. In regard to Deptford, the least inconvenient of any yard, he thought it might be expedient to give a part of it for affording additional accommodation to the victualling establishment adjoining.

Although it might hereafter, he said, be found expedient to increase the new naval establishment to perhaps a greater extent than that of any of those already formed, it did not seem necessary to begin on all the points of so extensive a plan at once. He would rather propose the completing first for use, so as to accord with the general plan, a single dock capable of receiving the largest ship at the greatest depth of water, looking upon this establishment as an appendage to Sheerness; but as that port, already much out of repair, became less and less fit for use, the works in Grain might be extended until it should eventually supersede the port of Sheerness. Earl Spencer, with whom the need of a naval arsenal north of the Forelands had been discussed in the preceding year, remained but a few months in office after this proposal was made. The Earl of St. Vincent, who succeeded him as First Lord of the Admiralty, considered it as highly desirable, and in his visitation of the naval arsenals in 1802, he himself examined with great attention the part of the Isle of Grain which had been pointed out.

Sir Samuel, in consequence, received orders to have the ground examined. It turned out that the ground, though on a good subsoil, was soft to a considerable depth. This rendered it advisable that the first work should be a part of the proposed canal, and that the basin should be formed. The expense to be thus incurred was greater than his lordship was disposed to encounter, at that moment of war and financial pressure. But what in fact operated the most powerfully against the immediate adoption of the plan, was the unfortunate loss of a valuable officer, Mr. Bunce, architect in the Inspector-G-eneraps office. This gentleman, already worn out with fatigue from his excessive labours during the visitation of the dockyards, had, in the excess of his zeal, undertaken the surveys and borings of the Isle of Grain, aud was seized with fever and died. This sad event threw a damp on the proceedings, and was held up by adversaries as proof of the unhealthiness of the island, which, though marshy, is certainly not so objectionable as Sheerness.

In addition to these difficulties Sir Samuel Bentham continued to suffer much vexation from the prejudice against his experimental vessels, but by degrees their good qualities had manifested themselves as regarded their strength of structure, their properties as sea boats, and their efficiency in armament. Their form has been in many respects copied by subsequent naval architects, as also have many of the modes of structure with a

M 2 view to strength, but the prejudice against their peculiar mode of armament still remains. An extract from a letter of Earl Spencer on the subject of the Dart, may be acceptable to the general reader as an example of the interest which he took in the result of this shipbuilding experiment, and of the intimate knowledge of details which he acquired in the service over which he presided.

" Admiralty, 2 th November 1790. " Dear Sir,–The Report of the state of the Dart is very satisfactory, more especially as she ran foul of two ships on her way home, and in running foul of the Vestal frigate the shock was so great that the people on board the Vestal (not seeing anything of the Dart afterwards) concluded she must have gone down; one of the Dart's men got on board the Vestal at the time.

" Yours very sincerely,

" Spencer."

The glorious victory that had been obtained in the Liman of Otchakoft by the flotilla of small vessels which Sir Samuel had fitted out, naturally led him to wish that his English experimental vessels might be armed in a similar manner; but he was aware that the heavy ordnance which he had put on board the Russian barks would not be tolerated in small vessels in this country. He had applied to (xeneral Ross for howitzers for his schooner ships, but none could be spared; he therefore confined himself to 32-pounder carronades, and to the Sadler's experimental guns. With these guns be had been desirous of employing shells and other explosive missiles of great power; but from this he was dissuaded by the observation of (reneral Ross, that as the enemy had not such in use, it would not be well to show them the destructive powers of such missiles. At the first arming of all the six vessels, it may be said that very few excepting the commanders of them could admit the expediency of fixing guns so as to ck the recoil; but by degrees experience of this mode in actual warfare, soon diminished the aversion to it in those who had had opportunities of seeing it in use. In the expedition against Holland, some of the experimental vessels had distinguished themselves in the Texel; and General Bentham, wishing that the Admiralty should be officially informed of the real effects of non-recoil mounting, requested Lord Spencer to obtain a statement of it from the Commander. His Lordship replied:

"Admiralty, 16th September 1799. " Dear Sir,–I have, in consequence of your letter, directed the officers commanding your vessels who were employed in the expedition to be called on for an official report on the effect produced by firing on the non-recoil principle; and if it is favourable it will be of use in counteracting the strong prejudices which continue to be entertained on this subject.

" Want of men has been the sole cause of the Millbrock's detention, but I hope we shall soon be able to put her into activity.

" Yours very sincerely,
" Spencer."

The Inspector-G-eneral had defined what he meant by the principle of non-recoil as follows:–" The mounting a piece of ordnance in such manner as that it shall have no other recoil than that wdiich takes place in consequence of the elasticity of the materials employed to hold it; to which may be added in sea service the yielding of the whole vessel." " It is on this principle that mortars (the largest pieces of ordnance), and swivel guns (the smallest), have always been mounted; and it is in conformity to this principle that every one holds a musket or a fowling-piece to his shoulder."

The most prominent advantages of this mode of mounting ordnance are, shortly, that vessels too small or frail, or being in some parts too weak to bear ordnance when mounted so as to recoil, are sufficiently strong to bear heavy ordnance if mounted on the principle of non-recoil. Half the usual number of men suffice to work ordnance so mounted. Each gun so fixed may be fired at least twice for

M 3 once if mounted as usual. The use of the gun is not prevented by any weather, however bad. The gun can be used however much the vessel may heel; it is in constant readiness for action; it does not jump on quick firing; it can be left without lashing it; it does not require for working it half the room necessary for the recoil of a gun; the expense of the carriage is diminished by half; the weight of the carriage is but a third of the usual weight; it is much less likely to be injured in action than a carriage that admits of recoil, and even if damaged, the gun might in most cases be refixed notwithstanding. Advantages such as these are sufficiently important to justify some detail in exhibiting their reality. The official reports which Lord Spencer had caused to be called for from the commander of the Dart, stated that (the Dart, on the side of the forecastle towards the enemy, fired eighty ixmnds, without even the breeching being at all chafed, nor the ship in the least affected by it." The commander of the Eling reported " that the carronades fitted on the non-recoil principle, in his Majesty's schooner under my command, stood the firing on the 27th August perfectly well. As to the effect the cannonading had on the vessel that day, it was nothing; for it did not even crack the pitch in the seams, neither was there a square of glass broken in any part of the vessel."

The Netley schooner, during the twent T months she was stationed off the coast of Portugal, took no less than forty-five vessels, of which eight were privateers–one of them a man-of-war; and it was only in two instances that any other English vessel had been in sight. In fact the Netley alone had taken "more of the enemy's vessels than were taken during the same time by all the other vessels of war on the station. One of the prizes, a packet, had on boa I'd, as officially stated, " a valuable cargo and 10,000. in cash;" there were also valuables in gold, andc., in addition to the cash and general cargo. It was gratifying that the commander (then Lieutenant), the late Admiral Bond, received honourable promotion and considerable prize money. It was said that his share of it from this vessel alone amounted to 20,000. The full complement of fifty men on board the Netley, including officers, was less than half the number that would have been required in the ordinary mode to work sixteen 18-pounders and two smaller guns; besides which many of the crew were at times necessarily absent in prizes: for instance, the commander says, in a letter, 20th November 1799:–"At this moment I have not any one to take charge of a watch. I have no midshipman; and the master, the only person of responsibility, is in the privateer."

The very small number of men required for the non-recoil method of mounting artillery was fully exemplified in the Millbrook when she engaged the Bellone. It is generally known that the greater part of the men necessary for the service of a gun on shipboard, are required solely for the mere labour of drawing back the piece to the port after its recoil on firing. The Millbrook, armed with sixteen 18-pounders and two 12-pounder carronades, would in the usual mode have been allowed six men to a gun, which together with those required for manoeuvring the vessel would, including officers, have made a crew of at least 100 men; but the crew of the schooner on this occasion amounted to no more than fortv-seven. Her opponent, the French frigate privateer the Bellone, was armed with thirty-six guns, most of them, if not all, long guns, and 350 men. To quote a recorded narrative of this brilliant action of the Millbrook, "By the time the Bellone had fired her third broadside, the Millbrook had discharged eleven broadsides; and the Millbrook's carronades were seemingly fired with as much precision as quickness, for the Bellone from broadsides fell to single guns, and showed by her sails and rigging how much she had been cut up by the schooner's shots. At about ten

M 4 the ship's colours came down." The Bellone had twenty men killed, forty-five wounded; whilst on board the Mill-brook, though nine men were very slightly wounded, and three more severely, not a single man ivas hilled. Here then was positive proof of some of the most important advantages of this mode of mounting, namely, its efficiency in action– the small number of men required to work the guns–the rapidity with which non-recoil guns can be fired–and besides these advantages, the great objection that has been made to it, danger to the men, was by this action proved to be fallacious; not a single man was killed in the Millbrook, although she had killed no less than twenty of her opponent's crew. The commander was rewarded for this glorious action by the thanks of the Committee of Merchants at Oporto for the protection which he had afforded to their convoy under his charge, and these thanks were accompanied by a handsome piece of plate. The Admiralty immediately promoted him, considering his own gallantry not less remarkable than the superior qualities of the Millbrook.

Another of the experimental vessels, the Dart, had also during the same year an opportunity of exhibiting her superior properties, the efficiency of non-recoil, and the skill and gallantry of her commander, Lieutenant Campbell. He took her into Dunkirk Eoads, attacked a French 36-gun frigate, the Desiree, in the presence and vicinity of four other French frigates, carried her off, a new vessel, and brought her home to an English port, to be taken into the British service as a 40-mm frigate. Lord St. Vincent expressed himself as considering this as even the most brilliant of the many glorious achievements of the time. Lieutenant Campbell was immediately promoted to post rank.

Another quality which the Inspector-General looked
James's "Naval History," Nov. 13th, 1800.
SUCCESS OF THE EXPEEIMEXTAL VESSELS. 169 upon as an important one for service, but which he represented as too generally neglected– shallow draught of water–was exemplified in these sloops, and which contributed to Captain Campbell's success in Dunkirk Eoads. Small draught had been found a most desirable property of the Dart and Arrow in the passage up the Texel in the expedition of 1799. All other vessels of the squadron of any considerable force were necessarily left behind, whilst these sloops worked from the Fluter to the Middlebank because they drew only thirteen feet water. The extraordinary strength of these vessels was at the same time put to the test. The carpenter of the Dart, in his report, states: " Our ship's draught was thirteen feet: for some miles we had but ten or eleven feet, never more than eighteen feet at the most; so we were on the ground two-thirds of the way." The bottom must necessarily have been soft, but it may be asked what other vessels would have borne to be pushed on for miles where the water was two or three feet less than her draught?

CHAP. IX.

Correspondence with Lady Spencer on Reforms in the Civil Management of the Navy–Payment of Dockyard Workmen–Principles of his new System of Management–Report to the King in Council– Objections urged against a Reform–Office of Master Attendant–Principle of Dockyard Appointments–Wages and Employment of Workmen–Nat Pay Books– Education for the Civil Department of the Navy–Naval Seminaries–Changes in the Accountant's Office–Interest of Money sunk in Public Works–Dockyard Working Regulations– Opposition of the Comptroller of the Nary– Official Tour to Portsmouth, Torbay, and Plymouth–Renewed Acquaintance with the Earl of St. Vincent–Dockyard Abuses at Plymouth– Designs for a Breakwater–Return to London– Opposition to the Report–The Earl of St, Vincent succeeds Lord Spencer as First Lord of the Admiralty–The Report sanctioned in Council, May 1801–Suggestions for arming Vessels of War– Greenwich Hospital– Office of Timber-Master in the Royal Dockyard– Efforts on behalf of Convicts– Management of Timber Stores– Report to Lord St. Vincent, February 1802–Opposition–Commission of Naval Inquiry–Provisional Plan for the Education of Dockyard Apprentices.

Although the services enumerated in the preceding five years might appear to have afforded sufficient occupation for any man's time and thoughts, they had been in fact but subordinate to the one great end which Sir Samuel Bent-ham had in view, that of improving the management of civil naval concerns, which, since the year 1798, he had been directed by Lord Spencer to consider as the most pressing and the most important of the several businesses in which he was concerned. The need of such improvement was first pointed out by the Inspector-General; he felt that it was a hazardous undertaking, and hardly knew how he could best break ground. His intimacy with Lady Spencer induced him, in the year 1796, to venture on the subject with her. Lady Spencer could not be accused of interference in political decisions, nor of meddling with her husband's department; yet many matters proceeded the more smoothly and more beneficially for the public service by her tact in indicating what would be agreeable, or at least tolerated, by those with whom Lord Spencer had to act. The Inspector-Grenerafs letter to her in the year 1796 will best give the first indications of his attempts to improve management. It runs thus:

" Your Ladyship has not forgotten our conversation, the clay before you left town, on the subject of certain principles of naval economy, which, notwithstanding their importance, appear to have been entirely neglected–a neglect which never could have existed but from a deficiency in the mode of keeping accounts, and which a change in that mode might effectually jrovide against. The interest you seemed to take in those ideas of mine, and the severe injunction you laid me under respecting them, increased my hopes with respect to certain important effects which may one day or other be expected from them, and thereby induced me to address myself to you now on a subject bearing some relation to those ideas. Were I to address myself directly to Lord Spencer I might appear, not without reason, to expose myself to the imputation of meddling with matters beyond my province.

" The case is simply this: I feel myself persuaded that I shall, in the course of a short time, be able to make it appear most clearly and decidedly to Lord Spencer, and to every other zealous and intelligent well-wisher to his Majesty's service, that the accounts and mode of management with respect to the expenditure will require to undergo certain alterations.

" Before you accuse me of the rao; e of fancy in sr nobody knows anything but myself, you will have the charity to consider in what respects, and to what a degree, my situation differs from that of anybody else. Having all sources of information laid open to me, and leisure for the investigation of the reasons on which any given practice can be supposed to be founded, I have nothing to do but to suggest improvements; and to a man in my situation, common sense must be wanting if he had not improvements to suggest.

" In excuse for my troubling you with such a letter, let me once more observe that your Ladyship is the only person to whom I dare address myself on such a subject."

It has been seen that the Insnector-Greneral had com-municated instances to Lord Spencer of enormous waste of timber by extravagant conversion–that he had exhibited to the Committee on Finance a variety of cases in which want of economy was habitual in the dockyards. Lord Spencer, though at the first moment he felt that exposure of such bad management might occasion dissensions with the Navy Board, yet was himself perfectly convinced of the need for reform–a "radical reform," as he himself expressed it in a letter to the Inspector-Greneral. In a few days after the first excitement caused by the Inspector-G-eneral's report to the Committee on Finance, his Lordship often discussed generally the means by which reform might be effected, and not long afterwards directed him to devote himself exclusively to this business– an injunction which could not however be complied with literally, while he had also to prosecute the vast engineering works which he had suggested, to introduce machinery, besides the ordinary duties of reporting on all proposal referred to him, and to attend more or less even to trifling details in the architectural and mechanical departments of his office, under the ever present sense of his individual responsibility.

The works which he had proposed were no small calls upon his time and attention, even after they were ordered, since the dockyard officers, so far from forwarding them with good will, threw numberless petty obstacles in the way of their execution. Lord Spencer, well aware of this, and also of the impediments to the speedy and economical refit of vessels of war coming into Ports-mouth for repair, had determined on the first occasion of a vacancy to appoint Mr. Henry Peake to the important post of principal shipwright officer in that yard; but the Navy Board circulated a report that the consequent appointment and change of officers in the several yards would not be according to their wishes. The Inspector-General, feeling generally how greatly the service would thus suffer, being then at Portsmouth, wrote to Lady Spencer in a doleful strain. Her Ladyship's answer does honour to her lord and to herself, no less than to General Bentham. To his letter, 11th July 1799, she replied:

" Wimbledon, 13th July 1799.

" I am much mortified to find that all my persevering, hearty, eloquent scolds, have been entirely thrown away upon you,– and that you are as bad as ever, fretting, plaguing, worrying yourself to death, about what?– about nothing. You are incorrigible, I fear, and therefore I will not lecture you any more– rather a fortunate resolution for me to have adopted just now in your favour,– since I am here, perfectly idle, having nothing to call me away, and having plenty of paper, pens, and ink to make use of– had I not resolved not to scold, how all these circumstances would have acted against you!

"I don't know which is the worst,–you, or your man Peake,–not an ounce of patience falls to either of your shares–but what vou want in this quality, you make up in a superabundant quantity of imagination, and you create bugbears of every kind with a fertility truly surprising. All this long circumstantial detail of dockyard arrangements is an instance in point;– not one word of it is founded in fact, but is a mess of your own cooking, for the sole purpose of disturbing your own peace and tranquillity, and of calling one away from Italy and the Mediterranean, where I am all day long fighting by land and sea, and gaining incredible victories. When I am so well employed, vou really have done harm by calling me away to settle such pitiful and inferior business as the broils of a dockyard are in comparison. All that you wish will happen in due time, if (and mind, I am serious) you will permit it to be put into execution,–but if you begin to work, and to set people on their guard, you will render the accomplishment of your wishes an impossible task to him who is firmly resolved, if youll let him, to do all you want. Now, be quiet, and don't let Peake, or allow yourself to, open your lips on this subject from henceforward, and everything will be right, not else.–Adieu."

This letter was gratefully thus acknowledged on the loth:

" Many, many thanks for your consolatory scoldings– but with respect to the quantity of patience you are pleased to prescribe, there was certainly a little slip of the pen– for ounce you meant Tox.

" At such a time as this, I envy you exceedingly your occupation of fighting over your battles in the Mediterranean and elsewhere. I think you have some obligation to us Russians.

" Unluckily for me, it was in that country I got the habit of thinking all things possible– for I am apt to forget that this can only be true where there is power to persevere.

" I am at the fortieth page of a letter calculated to be more than usually interesting to the Navy Board."

In framing a new system of management for the dockyards, he felt it to be but an act of justice, no less than of humanity, towards the workmen, to keep constantly in view and provide for their well-being, in as far as was not incompatible with the interest of the public. If by taking away their chips, the means were withdrawn from them of constructing cheap houses and furniture, it seemed requisite that a reasonable compensation for them should be granted. On the other hand, some practices on the part of Grovernment diminished their nominal emoluments without corresponding benefit to the public; such, for instance, as delaying the pay of working men till the end of three months. Hence the workmen were forced to have recourse to money lenders, giving them as security a power to draw their pay at the quarter's end. The loss to the men was not confined to the interest in money required by the " dealers," as the lenders were called, but the loss was greatly increased when the loan was furnished in goods instead of cash; a lot of shoes, or of bread,–the shoes not fitting either the man or any of his family, and my more than were required for their wear,–the new bread, besides its superabundance, becoming stale and mouldy if kept, so that the poor dockyard people sometimes were thus receiving little more in value to them than perhaps half their pay. The details of information on this and many other points which the Inspector-Oreneral considered essential to ascertain before he could venture to suggest a change, occasioned much delay in drawing up new regulations; but early in the year 1800, after two years of patient labour, he had made up his mind as to the general principles on which they should be founded, and had made great progress in the details of the system which he had to propose.

The general principles on which he grounded his new regulations were– 1st. Individual responsibility throughout all the subordinate departments.

2nd. Choice of subordinates left as much as possible to the superior of each branch of business.

3rd. Total separation of the controlling or accountant from the operative duties.

4th. Employment of each individual to be registered.

5th. Immediate transmission to the Navy Board of the minutes of all transactions which are to form the data on which bills are to be made out or wages paid.

6th. *Z7)icertainty* as to what particular man would be the witness employed as a check on certain transactions, namely, all those in which personal interest can be supposed to stand in opposition to duty.

The Admiralty the authority that is to order everything-.

The superior operative officer at each port the instrument by which everything is to be done.

The Commissioner of a dockyard the eye by which the superior Board is to see whether things be done well or ill.

The Navy Board the check upon all expenditure. The Clerk of the Cheque their instrument by whom they are to be informed of all expenses incurred, and to be assured of the reality of appropriation to use of goods or money.

These principles were widely different from those on which the business of the dockyards was. then, or indeed is still, conducted. There was not then, nor is there now, any one individual really responsible for any transaction, operative or accountant. The superior of a dock-ard had no choice amongst his subordinate officers as to whom he should assign any specific duty. The minutes of all transactions remained in the dockyards, to be concocted so as to exhibit a fair face, before accounts of them were transmitted to the Navy Board. There was no register showing how each man was employed. The clerks emplo ed as witnesses of transactions, such as the musters of the men, were always one and the same for each transaction of the same nature.

The above short statement of principles indicates that a future great change of the Navy Board was projected, particularly that it should be no longer implicated in the direction of works, so that they might neither feel, nor be supposed to feel, a bias in favour of any particular operation, but become really free and impartial investigators of that important branch of service (the accountant), including the exposition of the means by which any effect had been produced, and a comparison of the cost at which any given effect had been obtained under different circumstances and different managements.

The Admiralty being at this period much pressed by members of the late Committee on Finance, as also by the House of Commons, to make their report on the dockyards in conformity to the order of 1792, the Inspector-General's sketch of a new system of management took the form of a report to the King in Council. The Secretary of the Admiralty had at first been charged with the business of drawing up a report in obedience to that order, but he had had little leisure to bestow upon it, and latterly, moreover, became so well convinced of the Inspector-General's more intimate knowledge of the real business of a dockyard, that he now was happy to transfer this duty to him. They acted, however, as coadjutors, General Bentham as he proceeded taking his papers to Mr. Nepeau, and reading over the articles which he had prepared; comments upon them were jointly made as seemed desirable. A copy of this report still remains in MS. in which insertions by Mr. Nepean are made wherever he thought it desirable to change either the matter or the expression. That MS. proves how very rarely he conceived any alteration necessary. The sketch was then put into the hands of the First Lord, who, after considering it, approved of the whole. The next step, at the particular request of the Inspector-General, was to have the sketch printed, and a copy distributed to each of the members of the Navy Board, the Eesident Commissioners of the dockyards, and to other persons believed either to have an interest in the projected regulations, or to be able to give valuable opinions respecting the proposed measures. Those several persons were requested to make observations as to the several items, whether for their alteration, improvement, or omission.

Amongst the returns of these sketches was a long statement written by the Comptroller of the Navy, in which he objected to almost every change proposed. This paper, comprising all the objections that had been made from every other quarter, was given by Lord Spencer to the Inspector-General, with directions to make his observations on it. He did so, of course, and drew up an answer to the Comptroller's objections, which, in some instances, exhibited such a want of information (on the part of the Comptroller) as to the real mode of carrying on the business of the dockyards, that the Inspector-General felt averse to allow particulars to fall into the hands of clerks. He therefore caused the fair copy of his answer, some

eighty pages, to be made by one of his own family, who could be depended on for secresy. He was subsequently directed by the First Lord to make this paper official, which was accordingly done by letter to the Secretary of the Admiralty, 15th July 1800.

The particulars of the Comptroller's objections, together with the answer to them, are mostly of too little general interest for insertion here; yet some of the principal items seem worth extracting. The economical and efficient management of a naval arsenal is a subject of great importance to the nation at large. Perhaps the difference between good and bad management might amount to the expenditure of even millions more or less in the year, and this may be considered a far more important reason for giving some account of this paper, than that it redounds to the Inspector-General's credit as evincing his intimate knowledge of dockyard concerns.

The Comptroller, in his introductory remarks, gave it as his opinion that no change in the system of management was necessanr, and adduces, in support of that opinion, the Report of the Commissioners of Inquiry, 1784, the opinion of Sir Charles Middleton, and the Select Committee on Finance, 1798. In refutation of this view of that testimony the Inspector-General quotes the Report of those Commissioners, who in the conclusion of it say, "When the frauds and abuses to which we have adverted are combined with the immense amount of expenditure for naval services, we do not hesitate to declare that a neiv system is indispensably necessary." In regard to Sir Charles Middleton, the Inspector-General refers to a paper written by him, which had contributed to the institution of the Inspector-General's office, and which indicates that its author was strongly impressed with a conviction that some very great changes were indispensable. As to the Committee on Finance, the evidence of Lord Keith and of the Inspector-General was decidedly

OBJECTIONS OF THE COMPTROLLER OF THE NAVY. 179 in favour of reform, and the Committee themselves expressed their opinion that that evidence was deserving of the attention of the Admiralty.

The Comptroller and the Inspector-Greneral differed materially as to the duties of the Eesident Commissioner. By Bentham's plan the Commissioner was to be relieved from many duties, such as interference in operative and manufacturing business, for which he could not be supposed to be competent; but, on the other hand, he was to become strictly responsible for many other duties capable of being executed by any man of sound judgment and nautical experience, at the same time receiving authority to interfere in every transaction whenever he might feel assured that his interposition was desirable; but he must be willing to take upon himself responsibility by giving his orders not verbally but in writing, and by transmitting to town on the same day information that he had so interfered. He instanced cases requiring knowledge in naval construction, such as a commissioner could not be expected to possess; for instance, which of two defective ships could in time of need be sooner got ready for service; whether necessary repairs to a ship could best be effected at moorings, at a jetty, or whether the ship must necessarily be brought into dock; whether the hold must be cleared or not– matters, like very many others, evidently requiring the practical knowledge of a shipwright.

The Inspector-Greneral further observed that the Commissioner, though not responsible " for the due execution of orders, may nevertheless be considered as an instrument by whom, in the hands of the Admiralty, the existence of any abuse may be brought to light, and the correction of abuse be much facilitated; whereas, were the Commissioner himself to be charged with the continual direction of the business, he would necessarily be himself implicated in any mismanagement or abuse, and consequently, instead of being an efficient check upon those to whom the direc-

N 2 tion of the business is intrusted, he would become himself interested in the concealment and palliation of any errors to which, in the first instance, he may have been led unawares to give his sanction."

Of late years this powerful argument seems to have been lost sight of, since the officer holding the place of the Commissioner under the title of Superintendent, has been by degrees more and more charged with interference in the current operative and accountant business of a dockyard; so that, although he is supposed to be the Admiralty's instrument whereby they may discover errors, he has become really nothing more nor less than the principal operative officer, as also the chief accountant officer, instead of being alone the Admiralty's " eye."

By the proposed new system it was the Master Shipwright, under the title of Surveyor, who was made responsible for shipbuilding and repairing, and for all the other manufacturing works, and who was to have under his orders and control the whole of the officers and workmen of the dockyard, excepting only the officers and other persons employed in the accountant branch, which was to be entirely separated from, and act as a check upon, the operative branch.

The Comptroller objected to the placing this whole business under any one man. A shipwright officer, is, however, a man who, from his education and previous employments, could not but be acquainted with the most important parts of the business of a dockyard, in contradistinction to assigning the same duty to the Commissioner, who neither from education nor experience can be conversant with any part of the operative business of a dockyard; but the real ground of objection, there can hardly be a doubt, was that it interfered with the Masters-Attendant of dockyards.

Favour to Masters-Attendant has always greatly influenced the Admiralty and the superiors of other depart- ments under them. They are always selected from Masters in the nav, and this is the only promotion to which officers of that class can look forward as the reward for eminent services on shipboard. In the navigation of a ship, especially in its pilotage, the skill of the Master is often of pre-eminent importance; yet the Admiralty have nothing on board ship to bestow as promotion or reward to this description of, it may be said, scientific officer beyond the change from a small vessel to a larger one. A Master in the navy remains always a Master; he has no command to look forward to, like the mere boy midshipman; neither pennant nor flag flutters in his eye, and on retirement his half-pay is not commensurate with the importance of his duties afloat. Considerations of this nature have excited a laudable desire to reward this class of officers by honourable employments on shore. The place of Master-Attendant in a dockyard is the only one suited to their former occupations; and as there are but few such places to bestow, the desire has always prevailed amongst the naval members of the Admiralty and other Boards to make these few pre-eminent in emolument as well as rank. The Inspector-Greneral, impressed as he was with the value of a Master's services at sea, could not assent to granting them promotion and reward, andc, at the expense of interference with a proper arrangement of the business of a dockyard. But he was induced to enter very fully into the details of that officer's duty, perhaps with a minuteness that can only be accounted for by the disposition which he knew to exist of rendering the Master-Attendant superior in rank and in emolument to all other officers of a dockyard. He showed that the business of this officer is in fact subservient to that of the Master Shipwright; that most frequently the Master-Attendant had actually to receive instructions for his guidance

N 3 from the shipwright. Whilst these subordinate duties were assigned to him in a dockyard, the most important of those which he performed on board ship, pilotage, was withdrawn from him when he became a Master-Attendant, so that his knowledge of coasts and harbours, so essential at sea, could no longer be of use on shore, where his constant presence was the better insured by giving him a house within the yard. In those dockyards where there is more than one Master-Attendant, the Inspector-General further stated that the business of their department " is carried on with much more disorder and much worse management than the business of any other department;" "they change duties, according to their owm division of it, every week," so that " it often happens that they do and undo alternately what the other had done the week before." As to what seemed the most important article of a Master-Attendant's duty (the examination of the sails, rigging, and other boatswain's stores on a ship's coming in from sea), new officers had, in 1795, been appointed to do this duty, namely, the Surveying-Masters, who were placed, not under the Masters-Attendant, but under the Commissioner; and although the appointment of these Masters had been to prevent waste, it was shown how ill-suited the arrangement was to effect the desired purpose.

The Comptroller further objected to the change proposed, because for the Master-Attendant's business "no shipwright officer could be qualified." How is it then that the surveyors at the Navy Office were considered competent to direct, and did direct, the Masters-Attendant at all the dockyards? " Yet, if the surveyors at the Navy Office had not been qualified for this branch of duty while they were master shipwrights on the spot where the duty is carried on, I should not suppose that the mere circumstance of their removal straight from the situation of a master shipwright in a dockyard to the superior situation of surveyor at the Navy Office, could at once inspire them with the requisite knowledge."

The Comptroller concludes the subj ect by observing that " the dockyards do not at present produce persons in the shipwright line capable of conducting so extensive a plan." Yet, although the Comptroller looked upon the shipwright officers as not competent to conduct the business of any one dockyard, these very persons were the only ones who ever became surveyors of the navy, in which situation they had the superior direction of the operative business, not only of one, but of all the six dockyards, and moreover of the whole navy. The Inspector-Greneral observed, however, that "as any superiority of talents in the management under the new svstem would become immediately efficacious and apparent, greater discrimination of talent would in consequence appear necessary in the selection and appointment of dockyard officers. It might very well happen also, that some of those who have been advanced to the higher classes before such dis-crimination was requisite, may now be deemed unfit to remain in them, and that some officers of this description might, perhaps, on the introduction of individual responsibility, feel their own incapacity and shrink from so arduous a duty: whereas now, the tit and the unfit are equally anxious to undertake any charge, because they must have reason to suppose that any degree of unfitness in point of intelligence under the present system may remain unnoticed."

Amongst the masters (Art. 19) there was introduced " an additional officer, who may be styled a master engine-maker, who should be a man conversant in the principles of mechanics as well as in the business of a millwright, so as to be capable of assisting the surveyor on all mechanical subjects." The Comptroller observed that the propriety of this " must depend upon the extent to which the new system of mechanics is intended to be introduced

N 4 into the dockyards." The Inspector-General leniently supposes that the word mechanics had by mistake been used instead of machinery, then introduced at his proposal into Portsmouth yard. On this, he observed, "I do not see how the propriety of introducing into the dockyards an officer skilled in general mechanical knowledge should at all depend on the introduction of this, or any other new system of machinery; since, independently of the practical knowledge necessary for the management of any article of machinery, no well-grounded judgment can be formed respecting the need there may be for improvement in the shape, in the mode of putting together, or in the fastening of any of the component parts of that very complicated machine, a ship, without a perfect knowledge of the principles of mechanics? He then observes that seamen and shipwrights did all of them acquire some ideas of mechanical causes and effects; yet that "the study of mechanics as a science, does not necessarily constitute any part of the education of any of the persons who are concerned in the direction of the business of a dockyard."

At this day it may be difficult to conceive that a knowledge of the principles of mechanics should, so late as the end of the last century, have been esteemed altogether unnecessary in a dockyard. But so it was–there were doubtless some rare examples, amongst the officers, of men who might have acquired some knowledge of those principles; but it has not been till after the exertions of General Bentham, that a knowledge of mathematics and of the principles of mechanics has come to be regarded as essential to the naval architect.

Article 29 of the sketch related to the working men. " In order that such encouragement be held out to them, as shall afford sufficient inducement to every individual to exert himself continually in the performance of his work in the best manner he is able, according to the directions of his superiors, and that this may be effected at the least

REGULATIONS RELATING TO THE WORKMEN. 18.5 expense to the public, we propose " principally " that the artificers be arranged under as few denominations as possible;" "that the artificers of each denomination be divided into not less than two, and generally into three classes, according to their degrees of ability, diligence, and good behaviour;" "that the pay allotted to each of these classes be different;" " that the classification be made anew every year;" "that the pay be proportioned to the number of working hours, winter and summer;" "that ten hours of work be considered as a day's work, excepting only in winter with regard to such work as cannot be done by candlelight;" "that the artificers or others, when wages are reckoned by the day, be paid at the end of every week, and that the payment be made clear of all deductions and fees."

In reference to these articles, the Comptroller observes: "I do not see that any alteration in the present mode would have much use. The work is carried on chiefly by task and job, and performed by men in companies."

The subterfuges and falsifications habitually employed in order to produce an apparent conformity to regulations as to the pay of artificers, afford abundant proof of the great need which existed of a reform of the system of management; and the Comptroller's assertion as to the manner in which work was carried on, is a glaring instance of his ignorance as to the real transactions of a dockyard, and of the regulations and orders by which superior officers are habitually restrained.

A part of the work was, it is true, done by task, that is paid by the piece, but so small a proportion that, taking Portsmouth yard as an example, only four companies of shipwrights out of " the forty-three employed there were task companies. These companies were allowed peculiar privileges; they had a right to exclude from amongst them all men whom they conceived to be inferior workmen, idlers, or too old to do a hard day's work, so that the task companies consisted of prime men alone. Their work was almost exclusively building new ships, or making such great repairs of old ones as admitted of accurate delinea-ment of the work to be done. Their privilege of rejecting men could not but have a prejudicial moral influence on the thirty-nine other companies, but otherwise it might be considered as highly advantageous.

The thirty-nine companies which were employed in the repairs and fittings of vessels, which constitutes the greater part of the work in times of war, were paid by what was called the job–or, as falsely supposed by the Comptroller, in proportion to the work done by them at prices paid by the surveyors of the Navy. In point of fact they were paid, not according to the quantity of work executed, but at the paid rate of 4s. 2cz. for a day's work. Accounts of work done by job were regularly sent up to the surveyor's office, and there the prices for it were corrected; but as " there is a standing order of the Navy Board which forbids the Clerk of the Cheque to set down

the earnings of any man employed in job work as greater than a certain established daily allowance" (4s. 2d.) "this extent of earnings to which it has been thought fit to limit the most industrious, has become the exact uniform greatest allowance which every man employed in job work is allowed to receive." By falsifications of various descriptions, the most laborious, the best skilled, the idle, the infirm, those employed on regular work at the dock side, or those buffeted about half their time in going out to Spithead, all were made to appear in the books to have done work of the same value, 4s. 2d., neither more nor less. Thus, " by falsification continually connived at, such an uniformity is given to this mode of payment by the piece, as may, on a hasty view of the subject, appear to be the result of the utmost perfection in management."
" In justice, however, to the good disposition and willing industry of many of the artificers themselves, as well as to the zealous alacrity of some of the officers, it seems proper I should state that in several instances which have come within my knowledge, a company, or more, of shipwrights have in cases of emergency been induced by their officers to exert themselves in so extraordinary a degree, that, reckoning the value of the work done at the allowed rates, the real earnings have amounted for some days successively, to ten, twelve, or fifteen shillings a day for each man; yet these industrious men received no more than the exact stipulated rate of payment, and consequently no more than what is allowed to the most idle." He then stated that, on some occasions, falsification of the job notes not only made the quantity of work appear greater than it really was, but that sometimes the shipwright officers thought it prudent to suppress altogether mention of some articles of work that had actually been done. The Inspector-Greneral's intimate knowledge of what really took place in the dockyards enabled him to state many other mischievous effects that had resulted from this mode of payment.

The observations on the Comptroller's objections were, at Lord Spencer's desire, furnished to him piecemeal, as they were written. The statements respecting job work appeared so extraordinary both to Lord Spencer and to Mr. Nepean, that as an unusual favour they obtained for the latter from the Navy Office the loan of a pay book for each dockyard, and in confidence they were intrusted to the Inspector-General for examination. These books were kept secret and sacred at the Navy Office, and well they might be, for although the Inspector-Greneral in the course of his investigations had been led to suspect that the pay books were not altogether so satisfactory as they had been represented to him,- yet " On my first inspection of these books, I must confess, that notwithstanding all I had already witnessed in regard to the keeping of dockyard books, my astonishment was very great, for never before; had I seen the existence of such scaring instances of inac- curacy and inefficiency." He noted and extracted for his Lordship's information the general dissimilarity in the manner of keeping these books in the different yards, and " the glaring incorrectness, falsifications, and abuses that present themselves on a bare inspection of the books." " As to the falsification and abuse of the setting down pay for a far greater time than had been worked, nay, even to the amount of double what could possibly be worked, I found it regularly and officially tolerated–I might say, authorised." Artificers in a dockyard, when quite worn out, or discharged after long service, have usually a superannuation allowance granted them; but not a fixed one either as to amount or to the time of its commencement.

His views on the subject were the giving a fixed but low annuity commencing at a rather early age, increasing the amount of it every five years, till at last it should be sufficient really to provide for the wants of an old man. As the small annuity in earlier years could not suffice for entire maintenance, he would have forbidden the recipient from the moment of its acceptance to work at day pay, but would have allowed and encouraged him to continue his labours at any of the works which could fairly be paid for by the piece. As any such measure would, at that time, have been regarded as visionary, he confined himself to proposing a fixed superannuation. The making this allowance adequate to a man's maintenance, he said, would, in fact, be a saving to the public, who " would no longer suffer, as at present, in consequence of the retention, from motives of humanity, of infirm men in the service after they have ceased to be able to earn their pay; but who, if discharged according to the present system, would be left destitute of the means of subsistence." Many such infirm men are still retained in the service at day pay, receiving from 60. to 70. a year.

Art. 45 to 51 proposed naval seminaries at each of the four principal dockyards, to which the Comptroller objected altogether.

During the Inspector-General's own apprenticeship to the master shipwright at Woolwich, and afterwards at Chatham dockyard, he had felt severely that the means which Government employed for the education of young men who were being trained for the civil department of the navy, were altogether inadequate; nor were the deficiencies of dockyard instruction compensated in the Naval Academy at Portsmouth, where he had become a pupil after his apprenticeship, so that all along, in his own instance, instruction was necessarily obtained by the means of masters and men of science in no wise connected with government establishments. The time, too, requisite for study was stolen; for many an hour and many a day which appeared in the books as if he had been at shipwright's work, he had been really at his studies, and even absent from the yard. He was driven to seek in foreign countries the further information in naval architecture and the subservient sciences that was not obtainable at home. On his return to this country he found the same deficiency in naval education, which w 7 as the more extraordinary, as during his absence very great advances had been made in the application of science to the improvement of private manufacturing concerns. The establishment of naval seminaries had, therefore, been amongst the first measures of improvement that he had suggested to Lord Spencer, and with his approbation he arranged the outlines of a plan of them.

The plan embraced both manual and scientific instruction in every art and science subservient to the creation, maintenance, and efficiency of his Majesty's vessels of war, exclusive only of strictly military matters, and military knowledge in naval warfare.

The pupils were divided into three distinct classes in point of rank, the education in each class being suited to the station in life which the pupils were afterwards likely to fill. The first class was to consist principally of sons of superior military and civil officers; the second class principally of sons of warrant officers, of master workmen, of clerks, and others who in general estimation might be considered of the same rank in society at large; the third class of sons of workmen, or of boys to be reared as workmen or as seamen.

General arrangements conducive to health, strength, and cleanliness, as also general fundamental instruction in religion and morality, were to be pr vided for all classes alike.

Means of acquiring all the information, and even accomplishments, usual in a liberal education, were to be provided for the first class, and to a certain extent for the second, including, of course, classical education.

To do away with the feeling of thraldom so unfortunately frequent in all apprenticeships, it was intended that in each class the friends of a pupil might redeem him at any time on payment of a fixed sum, sufficient to reimburse to Grovernment the expense incurred yearly on his account.

Considering that in the naval civil service the highest officers, the surve 7 ors, had first served their time as working shipwrights, and had risen from that inferior grade through many different ranks of dockyard officers– that in private life, many amongst the most distinguished in liberal professions, as well as in manufacturing concerns, had risen by their talents from very inferior stations to wealth, honours, and high rank in society– means were proposed by which in these seminaries some few of the lower classes might, by superior acquirements, attain the first-steps to similar eminence; so that at examinations at fixed periods the most distinguished pupil of the third class should be raised to the second, and so on, provided that

he should also have satisfactory testimonials of general good behaviour.

On calculation of what had hitherto been paid in the dockyards for wages to apprentices, and of the value of work to be expected from younger boys in light works– as peg-making, line-spinning, boat-building, andc.–it appeared that the expenses of the second and third classes would be more than repaid by the value of their labour. The first class was intended to afford an almost gratuitous education to the small number of pupils of which it was to consist, and was considered as placing in the hands of the Admiralty means of assisting meritorious officers of the higher ranks, when they happened to have large families. Indeed, in specific cases, it was intended that sons of officers should be admitted to the seminary as a matter of course– such as those of officers killed in action. Details of this nature the Inspector-General did not presume to decide; he merely considered this part of his proposal as the broad outline of assistance that might be thus afforded at little cost to meritorious servants of the public. But however much the liberality of Government might be extended, he felt assured that the third class would more than repay its own expenses. Whether in the higher classes pupils should be admitted or not, on paying the actual expenses incurred on their account, was a point of secondary consideration.

A peculiarity of these seminaries as proposed, was that of giving, particularly to the third class, two different callings by which a livelihood might be earned. Generally speaking, seamanship was intended as the secondary means. For this, and many other important reasons, it was intended that the greater part of the pupils should pass a portion of their time on shipboard, in the navigation of vessels used exclusively for dockyard service more particularly, in which, whilst they might acquire sea legs and somewhat of a seaman's skill, attention to their moral conduct and industry might be provided for by a judicious choice of the masters of those vessels.

To these seminaries the Comptroller vaguely objected the necessity of " keeping down " the expenses of a dockyard, and that by increasing the number of men competent to perform the work carried on in it, the artificers would "become more refractory and difficult to be kept in order." As to the latter objection, it is well known that an increase of the number of workpeople in any business is the most effectual bar to combinations. The seminaries were intended to rear a greater number of shipwrights than were ever likely to be required for the dockyards; no engagement was intended that employment should be found for them when out of their time; therefore the idea that because they were shipwrights each individual of them was of importance to the State would no longer exist; and as to the then present stock of these artificers, the prospect of so great a number coming on to supply their place, w T ould not fail of rendering them much more orderly and tractable.

Although this plan was in the year 1800 in preparation to be acted upon, it has never been more than partially carried into effect. A limited establishment of superior apprentices was a few years afterwards formed in Portsmouth yard, and exhibited in practice several of the peculiarities which the Inspector-General had proposed. Several of the young men so educated have since been distinguished for their superior attainments; but in the successive changes of administration this establishment was abolished. The consequence of the continued want of appropriate and scientific instruction has been that the Naval Department have felt themselves obliged to call in -istance from the Department of Military Engineers, many of whose officers fill several important scientific institutions in our naval establishments. Of late some schools of a secondary nature have been established for shipwright apprentices in the dockyards, and annually the best pupil from each yard is promoted to an establishment at Portsmouth where scientific instruction is afforded. Still the education afforded never can produce the superiority which was expected to result from the naval seminary–that is, it never can do so without subterfuge; for the bovs must have served four years as working apprentices before they can be received at Portsmouth– a boy working as an artificer the whole day cannot possibly have time for study, so that, unless his absence from the dock side be winked at, perhaps encouraged, by the officers, it is next to impossible that at the age of eighteen a lad should have acquired scientific knowledge in either mechanics, mathematics, chemistry, or in any other of the sciences subservient to the business of a dockyard.

New arrangements for the accountant business of a dockyard were proposed. The Comptroller said, in regard to them, "It changes the manner in which the accounts have ever been kept in the dockyards and at the Navy Office." In reply to this, the Inspector-General stated that he looked upon a change in the manner of keeping the accounts as " next in importance to the introduction of individual responsibility." In support of this opinion he brought to view particulars in proof that " in the general system of accounts, the most important purposes to which accounts of mercantile and manufacturing operations, such as those of a dockyard, should be directed, have been altogether overlooked," or that they did not afford the means of ascertaining, still less for exhibiting at one view, either the real or the whole expense of any work, and consequently did not admit of a comparison of the expense of any two works; that so many were the books to be referred to, that it would occupy a clerk's time for weeks to ascertain to which of several works, various articles of expense properly belonged; yet so uncertain were the results of such examinations, that the expense of one work of which he had

had occasion to learn the cost, had been put down at different times at the very different sums of 98,929., 87,525Z., and 102,058.; and this without any intention to make the cost of the work appear greater or less than its real amount. In some cases this inaccuracy, in others the falsification of accounts, amongst other mischief, precluded the possibility of coming to any well-grounded conclusion of the expediency of any permanent work of improvement, so that instead of calculations of savings to be effected by it, decisions were usually based on such expressions as that it was a necessary work, or a national work, or some other such vague term of recommendation.

Unfortunately, to this day, the thousands and hundreds of thousands of public money that are sunk on permanent works, still continue to be expended without considering the amount of savings or benefits that would result from them. The facility with which such estimates may be made, was proved in the instance of every permanent work of the Inspector-General's introduction, for before proposing any of them, he had entered into particulars of the annual money value of them, and discarded many that had presented themselves to him in an advantageous light whenever he found on investigation that a rent of eight per cent, at least on the capital sunk was not likely to be obtained by their use.

Another example of the insufficiency of accounts was the facility which they afforded of lessening the apparent expense of a favourite work, and heaping it on some such work as repairs. The Inspector-General had himself witnessed falsification of accounts in this respect. Indeed it was still practised in the year 1830; for in one of the best conducted dockyards which he then visited, he saw an artificer employed in a business not authorised by the Navy Board, and learnt that he was so employed all the year round. It was a useful business, indeed a necessary one; but that man's time must necessarily have been set down to some work to which he had never done a stroke; and the evidence to the Select Committee, 1848, indicates that the practice still continues of lessening the apparent amount of favourite works.

He stated also that the accounts of the receipt and expenditure of stores were as ill calculated to detect fraud and mismanagement, as in the case of those relating to workmanship. Improvements in these accounts have since been made; but the total want of responsibility in the storekeeper that the stock actually in hand should tally with the receipts and expenditure, necessarily implies that the agreement in quantities exists only on paper. The stock actually existing in the storehouses was never verified.

In regard to the accounts of expenditure of money, he said that disregard of the value of interest upon it, led to immense losses, such as certainly never could have been suffered bad the accounts exhibited this item. One instance he noticed of an unperceived expense that had been incurred, where a work stated to have cost but 591,891. had really amounted to the sum of 830,031., consequent on the interest of the capital before the work was brought into use.

For five-and-thirty years Sir Samuel Bentham continued to bring to notice the losses incurred from a disregard of interest on money, upon every possible occasion, and in a great variety of forms, from the time of the Committee on Finance, 1798, to that in

1828, and to the Admiralty again in 1831–yet it has not attracted the attention of the House of Commons. It is not only in the Naval Department that this item is neglected, but it may be said that interest of money is disregarded in all the departments of government. It is true that very lately the cavillers against manufacturing articles on Government account, have brought forward the non-attention to interest on capital sunk, as an objection to such measures, and it is possible that the outcry of the interested and discontented may o 2 produce improvement in this respect, although Bentham's strenuous endeavours for so long a series of years could not effect it, and this though he had shown the practicability and facility of bringing interest to account in the manufacturing concerns under his direction, in which he had had the disbursement uncontrolled, but not un-watched, of about a million of money.

The measures to which the Comptroller objected were, that the accountant branch should be committed to a distinct set of officers; that the accounts of all works performed should be so framed as to show the expense incurred for each separate part of the work, so that it might be compared with previous estimates for similar works under different management, and with the supposed value of expected benefit; that the books kept in the dockyards should exhibit all facts; but that all comparisons should be made at the Navy Office in town. The Inspector-General concluded his observations respecting accounts by saying that, for the reasons which he had adduced, "I cannot, on my part, but look upon a gradual alteration of the mode of keeping accounts, as well in the Navy Office as in the dockyards, as essential to an improved system of management."

That the Inspector-General's strong assertions of abuses and mismanagement were founded on fact, there cannot be a doubt. No denial of them was ever attempted by either the Comptroller, the Navy Board, or the dockyard officers, although all of these officers had shown themselves adverse to his plans of improvement, and for the most part still continued willing and ready to object to his proposals, and to deny their utility. The answer to the Comptroller's objections, as soon as it was made official, became very generally known amongst the officers whose duties it concerned, so that had it been possible to invalidate his assertions, there can be no doubt that they would have been contradicted and their falsehood prominently brought out.

OPPOSITION OF THE COMPTROLLER OF THE NAVY. 197

But it was not only in the written paper that the Comptroller made objections to the proposed plan. On the 18 th March 1800, Lord Spencer related to the Inspector-General several particulars of a conversation which he had had with the Comptroller. He had stated that " General Bentham had set out with saying that the Resident Commissioner was to be invested with more power, but that when he came to read the plan he found that he could give no order whatever but by writing it" " Well, said I" (Lord Spencer), " then we shall know what orders he does give." Sir Andrew: " No Commissioner would submit to giving a written order; in fact, it was taking the whole power out of his hands." Lord Spencer: " Not at all, if a Commissioner had any proper orders to give." Lord Spencer then said to the Inspector-General, "What the Comptroller has told me of the plan (by way of finding fault with it) I think very good."

The Comptroller had thus insisted on the particular point, which to this moment, as it then was, is a complete obstacle to good management, that is, the putting into the superior officer's hands a power to interfere and give his orders without record of them, or any means of bringing them to light.

It has been urged of late that the expenses of our civil naval department exceed the value of its products, but no efficient remedy for the evil has been suggested. Whenever the attention of Government may be seriously turned to new arrangements of the operative and mercantile business of a naval arsenal, even now, after the lapse of half a century, probably nowhere would such ample and correct data be found as in the Inspector-General's papers.

In July, on taking leave of Lord Spencer before setting out upon an official tour, he was requested to make an abstract of the proposed new regulations in order that it might be shown to Mr. Pitt. This journey was to Portsmouth, and along the south coast from thence to Plymouth.

On visiting Torbay he formed a new arrangement of necessary works, which was approved of and carried into execution. They had not required new inventions or any superior engineering skill, but simply an inquiry into the real wants of the service, so seldom taken into account. Thus, instead of the pier that had been proposed, at which only five boats could lie to water (the supply of which only amounted to a sufficiency for that number of boats), his plan provided a pier at which twenty-nine boats could at once fill their casks from suitable cocks delivering water from a large main. The pier that had been proposed was so situated as to afford no protection to the boats in certain winds, but by his plan perfect protection was afforded whatever way the wind blew. To this work he added a storehouse sufficient to contain a month's sea store of provisions for a fleet of thirty sail of the line; in recommending which he observed that it could not be considered as an extra expense, since it would supersede the construction of a storehouse of the same extent then intended to be built at Plymouth.

In September of this year (1800) he had the gratification of renewing his intimacy with Admiral the Earl of St. Vincent, to whom, while Captain Jarvis, Bentham had been introduced while studying at Portsmouth, who, with the fleet under his command, was lying in Torbay. During the week that the Inspector-General remained at Brixham, the greater part of his time was passed with his Lordship. The proposed new management of the dockyards was discussed, and Lord St. Vincent approved altogether of the regulations devised; indeed, so thoroughly was he convinced of their expediency, that he proposed to get some member of the House of Commons to speak of them in the House, so as to insure their introduction, and undertook to manage the whole business himself if Bentham would but consent.

This was an interesting week. Besides the weighty
RENEWED INTIMACY WITH LORD ST. VINCEXT. 199 matters discussed, Lord St. Vincent's habit of prompt decision exhibited itself on many an occasion. He wanted a guard-house to be fitted up on the instant; the Inspector-General undertook to do the business, but he happened to say that he wanted the assistance of a marine officer. His Lordship instantly called for his principal officer of that corps. On his entering- the cabin: " There, Colonel, that is General Bentham; I appoint you his aid-de-camp; you will do everything he wishes." One day it happened, whilst the

Inspector-General was on the wharf at Brixham, that some accident happened to a man which rendered bleeding necessary, but the ship's surgeon, who was there on the spot, had no lancet. At dinner, the same day, the Inspector-General gave a hint of the occurrence, observing: at the same time that it would not be amiss if surgeons were obliged to carry about their instruments, as officers did their swords. The order was instantly given, that rt all surgeons should have their instruments always in their pockets." In " Lord St. Vincent's Life," by the son of his secretary, Benjamin Tucker, this anecdote is related, with the sole difference that the origin of the order is not mentioned, and that the word " pocket" was changed to " about their persons," as doubtless Mr. Tucker worded the order when he wrote it out officially.

Different plans had been proposed for some time back for the forming a breakwater in Plymouth Sound, to which the General's attention had been called no less by the Lords of the Admiralty, than by the persons who had devised those plans. It had been one subject of discussion when he was with Lord St. Vincent in Torbay, whose only reason in favour of any work of the kind was that the rocky bottom of parts of the Sound was apt to injure a ship's cables. Eough sketches of his plans still exist, by one of which it appears that by forming a breakwater off Causand Bay (one of the plans that had been proposed) security might be afforded to a large fleet, at what might be called a small expense. Another one was for damming up Catwater, and forming a breakwater on that side of the Sound. But would the use of such a work compensate for its cost? His inquiries seemed conclusive against the project. How many ships, he inquired, had been wrecked or injured in the Sound? So far as he couid learn, never any but one vessel of war up to that time: this vessel was a frigate, and its loss had been occasioned by the greatest carelessness on board. The ports had been left open in a gale of wind; she filled and sank. After such a result of his inquiries the eligibility of any such breakwater at Plymouth Sound seemed too extravagant for him to venture on its recommendation.

Notwithstanding his utmost endeavours to draw up the abstract of the proposed report which Lord Spencer had desired, he found it impossible to do so without entering into the subject of changes that would be necessary in the constitution of the Navy Board and of the other departments under the Admiralty. His chief endeavour, therefore, was to obtain at Plymouth many details respecting the superior management of the Navy Board, which might enable him not only to frame a plan for its improvement, but to support it by facts against objections, as he had been enabled to do in regard to the new regulations for the dockyards. Such information could be better collected at Plymouth than at other ports, not only because he had here free access to all books, but because the Resident Commissioner, and the heads of departments, civil and military, were both intelligent and communicative.

Having collected a vast mass of information as to malpractices on the spot, and of the many improprieties resulting from Board management, he returned to town.

On the 9th November, both Mr. Nepean and Lord Spencer devoted themselves to a consideration of the report; he read it over "from beginning to end "with Lord Spencer, who thought the salaries low. He had been disinclined to allow fuel to the dockyard officers, but on representation of the absolute impossibility of preventing a servant from picking up a few shavings and the cover which this would afford to real abuse, the privilege of being provided with fuel was consented to. The allowance which the report proposed of the sixth of an officer's salary as pension to the widow Lord Spencer-thought " very proper," as also that proposed for children to the age of fourteen, but thought that to girls it should continue to the age of twenty-one.

A new opponent to the reform of management now came forward in the person of Admiral Young, one of the Lords of the Admiralty. It was said of him, that he was " laborious in the minor duties of the office, and well-meaning, and not knowing exactly whom to get who would work so hard as he does, he is allowed to have more influence than he would be at all entitled to on any other account." The Inspector-Greneral found that the objections made by the Admiral had been written by him in red ink on the fair copy of the report itself. They were answered as those of the Comptroller had been. This produced further delay of the abbreviated report–when Charles Abbot, as Chairman of the Committee on Finance, who had from the first taken great interest in the proposed reform, now threatened to make some motion on the subject in Parliament. The Inspector-Gfeneral was deputed to see Mr. Abbot "with a view to persuade him not to make any motion in the House respecting the report. Abbot says he has a character to support, and that if nothing is done by Monday sennight he must speak." On the 21st December, the Inspector-Greneral called on Mr. Nepean, by his desire, to inform him of this. It appears that Mr. Abbot did speak, for on the 30th it is noted that " Bentham called on Nepean to justify himself as not having had any hand in making Abbot say what he did in the House yesterday. Nepean has not yet heard the report mentioned in any way by Lord Spencer, but in the Board-room to-day Sir Philip Stephens asked why it was not brought forward."

It was now determined that a report on the dockyards should be drawn up, but it had not been presented for the sanction of the King in Council, when a change of administration took place, and the Earl of St. Vincent succeeded Earl Spencer as First Lord of the Admiralty.

The new Admiralty, having taken this report into consideration, adopted it immediately, that part of the preamble inclusively, which stated " that some progress was already made in the preparation of a new system of management, founded on general principles of acknowledged efficacy;" and the whole was sanctioned by the King in Council, 21st May 1801.

At this time Lord Spencer was frequently so much engaged that he could not give up so much time to the Inspector-Greneral as had been customary, but he was particularly friendly in regard to his private interests. No allowance had been given him for travelling expenses, on account of difficulties that had been made by the Navy Board. On the 7th February, Lord Spencer had said that it was highly expedient that he should now go to Portsmouth, and " that nothing would be done till he went there." There was, on that same day, a report of a change of administration, and on the 8th he learnt its truth from Mr. Nepean, who desired him not to set out for Portsmouth the next day as was intended. On the 9th, Lord Spencer told him that Lord St. Vincent would probably succeed him, and added, "You will losa nothing by the change; Lord St. A r incent has it in his power, and will do more for you than it was ever in my power to do." Yet the journal expresses much regret at the change, Lord Spencer having always been on such friendly terms and so pleasant to do business with.

Lord St. Vincent, on becoming the First Lord, appointed the Inspector-General to go to him on the 16th, at half-past seven o'clock in the morning, thus continuing the early habits of shipboard now that he was in town. The principal subject discussed in this interview was one of the first importance in naval armaments. The Inspector-Greneral ventured to urge his own ideas on a subject on which it might be thought that so experienced and successful an admiral would hardly bear to be lectured by an inferior officer: he pointed out that " the force of a ship consists in the weight of shot she can throw in a given time." This was exhibiting the matter in a new light, but in the course of conversation his Lordship admitted that it was so, but i(did not think that carronades throw far enough." The discussion ended in a permission that the Inspector-Greneral should submit his observations on the subject in writing: this was accordingly done by letter 22nd February 1801.

This communication, together with others on the same subject, both before and subsequently, have doubtless been very useful in increasing the force of our naval armaments so immensely of late years.

But his recommendations of conclusive experiments remain yet to be carried into effect. Experiments have frequently been made as to some one kind of projectile, or of one sort of gun, against some one other kind, but no such series of experiments as he had in view has ever been attempted. He urged that " the most advantageous weight of ordnance for sea service on board different classes of ships, the quantity of powder, and the species of shot best adapted to the several purposes, cannot be ascertained without a course of experiments instituted expressly for this purpose."

He then proposed expedients by which the naval force of the country might be immediately increased without adding to the number of vessels of war, and which, so far from requiring more men, would diminish the number then employed; as, for example, in the instance of a 74-gun ship, the men required in the proposed mode would be less by forty-four than in the old one, though the force of the ship would be more than doubled.

The Earl of St. Vincent at the head of the Admiralty continued the same man that he had been at the head of the fleet. He was as desirous as ever of introducing the Inspector-General's plan of reform in the dockyards; accordingly from the day of the very first interview he indicated his intention of adopting the report that had been signed by Earl Spencer, and even already seemed to consider that no one could be so well acquainted as the Inspector-General with the merits of persons already dockyard officers, or of those whom it might be desirable to introduce. It was not, however, on every point that his opinions and practice coincided with those of his predecessor. During the morning's conversation he said that " Lord Spencer had made an extraordinary number of officers" (naval officers); " that there are a great number unemployed; and added that he would for himself make a vow not to make any one a commander, unless for specific actions, until all the deserving ones of those already made should be employed." It was on this very day, and under this determination, that his Lordship made Lieutenant Matthew Smith a commander, but it was in reward for his brilliant action in the Millbrook with the Bellone.

Dinner on that day was a pleasurable meal, which Captain Smith partook of at the Inspector-General's, when he entered into the particulars which led him to think so highly of the Millbrook, and of her non-recoil armament.

Lord St. Vincent continued his early habits the same as ever. On the 6th he by appointment received the Inspector-G-eneral at breakfast at seven o'clock; he was punctual to the time, and found the tea ready made. His Lordship

"showed him some papers from Mr. Pitt and Dundas respecting a project now in contemplation for the destruction of Archangel." " Spoke of Lord Spencer's jealousy of him (Lord St. Vincent), that no woman could be more jealous; that Pitt had told him that Lord S. would rather that any other man should have succeeded him than Lord St. Vincent." This seemed remarkable, for no symptom of such a feeling had ever manifested itself in the frequent and confidential intercourse which the Inspector-General had had w T ith Lord Spencer; at any rate it was a highly estimable point in Lord St. Vincent's character, that believing this, he should notwithstanding adopt the plans and the persons that had been brought forward by his predecessor. He was pleased with the plan already made out for new bed-places in Greenwich Hospital, regretted that notice had not been taken of the officers' apartments– but the office of Inspector-General was invidious enough, without his meddling uselessly with private interests. His Lordship and the Inspector-General set out together from Mortimer Street to walk to the Admiralty; they met Lord Berkeley, who was on his way, he said, to breakfast with his Lordship–" Not at this time of day; I am up at five o'clock every morning," said Lord St. Viucent. Eentham asked when he would have a little time. " "Why I have no time, but if you will dine with me on Sunday, I will turn people away after dinner." And thus the friendly way in which he received the Inspector-General continued to the end of that administration.

In speaking of what ships should first be brought forward, Lord St. Vincent observed that " without some specific and apparent reason, I am desirous not to alter any of Lord Spencer's arrangements,"–a determination which, if it had been adopted by subsequent Boards of Admiralty, might have saved the expenditure of even millions of money by this time. His Lordship observed too that the inferior Board were " all in fear and trembling;" " that the great plan of alterations in the dockyards conld not be brought forward till peace, but that would not be long first."

The partial regulations for the dockyards having received the sanction of the King in council, he endeavoured to ascertain what persons would be most competent to fill the new office of timber-master. His Lordship disclaimed all patronage whatsoever, saying that " the fittest man, be he who he will, shall be appointed to every situation in the dockyards which he has the filling of." The habit of waste in the instance of the costly article timber had been so great in the royal dockyards, that the Inspector-General proposed taking men who, though brought up in them, had left the service for want of encouragement, and had since been employed in private yards, where the value of that store is known, and every piece of timber turned to good account. This measure was approved of; but it turned out that the emoluments in private business so much exceeded the pay allowed by Government, that most of the persons applied to declined accepting the proffered places. The mistaken notion always has been, and is still entertained, that the civil officers in the Navy Department are overpaid, whereas the fact is that the pay is not sufficient to retain men in the service, generally speaking, whose abilities are of a superior stamp.

On the 4th July, the Inspector-General showed his Lordship a paper which he had prepared of appointments and removals of dockyard officers. He determined to adopt them all. As one of the officers, from his superiority of talents, was supposed to be a favourite with Bentham, he spoke of putting him at a more desirable yard than the one specified for him; this was opposed as not being "for the good of the service," to use the cant term; and Lord St. Vincent was gratified by such forbearance of patronage. Traits of character such as many of the above have not appeared in the Life of the Earl of St. Vincent by Mr. Tucker, and their omission may furnish an apology for introducing so many of them here.

In June of this year, the Inspector-Greneral's commiseration was excited by the intended treatment of some convicts who had been sent to assist in various works in Portsmouth dockyard. The term of punishment of some of the most deserving of these men was to expire within a year, yet they were now ordered for transportation to New South Wales. He had been applied to in their favour by officers who had witnessed their good behaviour. When by means of a confidential person he had made further inquiries respecting them, he felt justified in making application to the Minister on whom their fate depended, to have this order annulled; but not having been fortunate enough to find Mr. Pelham at home, he enclosed to him a list of the deserving men in question, acquainting him that " most, if not all, of these men have been found so trustworthy as not only to be suffered to work without irons or any particular inspection, but have also been stationed to assist the guards in taking care of the rest of the convicts." After specifying other particulars, he added: " The transporting men of this description, besides being evidently unjust, and productive of unnecessary expense, seems also particularly objectionable on account of its tendency to diminish very materially the inducement for good behaviour in all other convicts, who cannot fail to observe that the most meritorious conduct has only served to single these men out for transportation, whilst numbers of the most profligate and disorderly are suffered to remain in the country till their terms have expired." He was much gratified by a ready compliance with his request; and it is believed that these men by their future good conduct left him no cause to regret his exertions iu their behalf. Other convicts were afterwards employed under his management, both at Portsmouth and Sheerness, and he had thus an opportunity of seeing the opinion confirmed which he had long entertained, that, without other pecuniary sacrifice than that of very small rewards for industry, the most beneficial results would be obtained from constant regular employment of such men in useful works, secluding them as much as possible from public gaze without depriving them of intercourse with fellow-men, and by habitually affording encouragement by an increase of kindly treatment according to desert, as well as a separation of the meritorious from the refractory.

It may be well conceived that acquiescence in his views of improvement and reform on the part of the new Naval Administration was to him a source of extreme satisfaction, more especially on account of the First Lord's intimate acquaintance with the civil concerns of the nav, acquired in a long career, during which his discerning and comprehensive mind had scrutinised many of the defects of the civil no less than of the military branch of the service. The report that had been sanctioned by the King in Council did not, it is true, include any other part of the projected general reform than that for the better management of timber and the abolition of the perquisite of chips; but Lord St. Vincent was determined that the new regulations in these respects should be introduced and carried into execution with the fullest force, and therefore directed the Inspector-General to devote his attention principally to this business. He in consequence repaired to the dockyard affording the greatest amount of information, Portsmouth, where there happened at that time to be several officers of great ability; so that by examination of the books, and of the practice as to timber, as well as by discussions with those officers, he might, in addition to his former knowledge on the subject, be well prepared to draw up the details of management in regard to this store. He accordingly submitted to the Admiralty, on the 26th of December, a sketch of the instructions which he proposed should be given to the several officers concerned in the management of timber, from its first receipt to its appropriation to use, as also a set of regulations in regard to it, and forms for the accounts to be kept. These were all of them approved and ordered to be carried into effect, and the superintendence of the new mode of management was committed to him individually for a term of three months.

By these regulations " it was made the sole business of one officer, under the title of timber-master, to direct the converting, stowing, and sawing of the whole of the timber, braces, planks, andc, in each dockyard, that he may stand individually responsible for the due execution of this trust; and that consequently he may have the credit or blame that may result from the comparative view of his management with that of the other dockyards."

The accounts which he framed for this department, traced every piece of timber from its first conversion to its final application to use. Heretofore there had been the formality of many signatures of superior officers; but they were fallacious, because those officers could but rarely know the uses to which specific pieces had been appropriated; and the reports were made at periods too distant to be of use when they reached the Navy Office. By the new mode no other signatures could be of real avail than that of the person who authorised the employment of any given piece of timber, and that of the person who received it for use. At the same time it was provided that the controlling authority, the Navy Board, should be informed daily, instead of at very distant periods, of all transactions in the dockyards relative to this store. This was effected at little cost of time or money, as the copies sent up to town were taken by a copying press from the accounts as kept in the dockyards.

The saving of time in account-keeping was, however, frustrated by the Navy Board. They sent an order to the dockyards that, besides the new accounts, others should be

kept in the old forms, and be sent to them in the usual manner. Seeing the disregard in which pressed copies were held by the Board, the clerks became careless in preparing them, so that instead of those copies being of all others the most faithful, they soon became imperfect, scarcely legible, and consequently, useless.

In this business, as in all the Inspector-General's proposed reforms of management, he looked as much on the advantage of bringing merit to light as to that which could arise from discovering the reverse. In point of fact, a decree of emulation was excited in the timber-masters of the time which fully justified his expectations on that score, though unfortunately it was followed by no rewards; but he had the satisfaction of receiving assurances that by his means most important savings of timber were effected, and still continued to be so, as long as he had opportunities of witnessing conversion. Of late years the stringency of his regulations has been gradually done away with. Kespon-sibility, instead of being individual, has been divided amongst several new officers; and those parts of the evidence given to the Select Committee of the House of Commons on Navy Estimates, 1848, indicate that extravagance again prevails, both in the conversion of timber and in its application to use.

The plan of introducing a clerk chosen by some uncertain mode to witness the receipt of timber was looked upon as a fanciful expedient; but the fact was, that however conscientious superior officers (such as storekeepers and clerks of the survey) might be, yet the storekeeper was often charged with stores without any previous survey of them, and when deficiencies were discovered the facility with which it was customary to discharge him of them was notorious. The Inspector-General, in one of his official statements, said, "In point of fact, that there are abuses in the receipt of stores I am well assured. I have heard that timber or plank to the value of some thousand pounds has been paid for as if received in a dockyard, although articles to so great an amount never appeared but on paper. I am confident that such a practice has existed." Of these assertions no denial was ever attempted, either by the Comptroller of the Navy, the Navy Board, or the dockyard officers, yet all these officers had objected to the Inspector-General's representations of the need of correcting mismanagement and abuse, and were still ready to object to all his suggestions of improvement. He was accused of putting leading questions to underlings, so as to obtain false information from them. On the 19th December 1801, for instance, the Comptroller particularly said that the Inspector-General " got the underlings about him without the knowledge of their superiors." This was on the occasion of his acquainting the Comptroller that in Deptford yard it was the practice to receive mast sticks for 20-inch masts as sticks for 21-inch masts, and thereby to authorise a proportionately higher price for them. The Comptroller said that " when this information was obtained the master shipwright should have been there." The Inspector-General replied, "The master shipwright was there, the storekeeper was there, the clerk of the cheque was there, two assistants were there, the treasurer was there, and the clerk of the cheque's clerks and the storekeeper's clerks were there–is that enough, or should any more have been present? " The Comptroller bit his lips, and said, "When the Inspector-General had given forms for keeping accounts, he hoped he would tell them where to buy timber."

The Admiralty Board consisted at this time partly of old members and partly of new Lords, these being such as Lord St. Vincent had selected from amongst the naval officers in whom he had confidence. Mr. Nepean on one occasion told the Inspector-General that the Board thought him "wrong, very wrong– except, indeed, the new ones; these were Trowbridge, and Markham, and Tucker 3

and Lord St. Vincent; it might please them, it was true; but the Board thought it wrong." This was in reference to letters of the Inspector-General pointing out instances of mismanagement, particularly on the contract made by the Navy Board for the carriage of beech timber to Portsmouth dockyard. The Inspector-General replied that "it was his business to find fault–it was what his situation had been instituted for; but if Mr. Nepean would tell him how he should write, he would do so accordingly." Mr. Nepean was indeed placed in circumstances of difficulty. He had been all along strenuous in his endeavours to introduce all of the improvements suggested by the Inspector-General; he had adopted all which related to management; but during Earl Spencer's administration the endeavour had been to introduce them without injury to the civil servants of the department, particularly so as not to imply any want of probity, or otherwise to implicate their moral conduct. Now the sea Lords, with what was called quarter-deck habits, were too much inclined to impute all imperfections to interested motives rather than to a vicious system, and to punish with all the severity of naval discipline.

One of the letters that had been especially objected to by the old members of the Admiralty Board was that of the 30th August 1801, in which he had said that in the course of his investigations respecting the management of timber, he had found that the Navy Board, by virtue of several Acts of Parliament, were empowered to superintend the preservation of growing timber in some of his Majesty's forests, but that " this salutary interference on their part has fallen almost wholly into disuse; so much so, indeed, that on inquiry at the Navy Office for a certain Act of Parliament mentioned by one of the purveyors as forming the basis of his duty, the very existence of the Act did not seem to be known at the Navy Office;" and particularising various other sources of information, he added, that e serious evils are said to arise to his Majesty's naval service from the present neglected state of his Majesty's forests"–"that by a more careful attention to the existing laws and orders respecting the forests in question, a much more abundant supply of timber for naval purposes might be obtained from them, so much so, that in future they might be made to afford three-fourths of the total quantity actually consumed in all of his Majesty's dockyards; and having reason to believe that even immediately the New Forest might afford as much beech timber as the service of this dockyard requires, as also an additional quantity of oak." It does not appear in what respect this letter could have been deemed offensive– unless, indeed, members of the Navy Board should have so keenly felt their neglect of the royal forests as to regard the mere asking for Acts of Parliament as a reproach to them. The Inspector-General's object was to concert with competent persons some means by which those forests might be for the future so managed as to afford the supply of which they are capable; but it would seem that although more recently Sir W. Symonds has pointed out various particulars that might practically be of good effect, yet of late years the management in regard to them has been even worse than it was when the Inspector-General requested this information.

Having had occasion to notice, verbally, some of the improprieties in the mode of providing this costly article of store, as well as in the management of it, Lord St. Vincent requested the Inspector-General to draw up a written statement of the most prominent objections to the current practice; this was done accordingly in February 1802. This paper not having been officially sent to the Board is not on record in the Admiralty books; it points out inattentions which have at all times been but too prevalent, in regard to the provision of naval stores of every description as well as of timber.

p 3

Flattering as was the dependence which the First Lord placed in the Inspector-General, and great as was the support afforded him, yet it was with extreme difficulty that he could regulate his conduct in such a manner as that, whilst indicating instances of mismanagement, he should avoid imputing blame to individuals. By some old members of the Admiralty, and by the whole of the Navy Board, he was looked upon as acting in a spirit hostile to them personally; whilst by his moderation he often incurred the displeasure of his superiors.

The letter on beech timber, addressed privately to Lord St. Vincent, as being a recent instance of the frequent oversights in making contracts and providing stores, was returned to the Inspector-General with the command to address it officially to the Secretary of the Admiralty, because he was desirous that instances of mismanagement should stand on official record. The letter, when addressed to Lord St. Vincent, had been prefaced with a request that it might be " understood that it is not my intention to impute blame to any particular individuals who may happen to have had a part in the direction of the business in question, persuaded as I am that however injurious to the public service may be the instances of abuse and mismanagement I shall have to bring forward, it would appear, on a full investigation, that they had been the natural consequences of defects in the system of management, rather than of any specific misconduct on the part of the persons employed, and that there is every reason to be assured that,–by making such changes in the system of management as that the scrutiny of all commercial as well as operative transactions shall be committed to the charge of persons distinct from those to whom the execution is intrusted, that the due execution of every business shall be committed to the stimulatidg influence of individual responsibility, and the accounts of all transactions kept in such manner as to bring their comparative economy under observation,–all such abuses would in future cease of course."

But Lord St. Vincent was impeded continually by the opposition of the inferior Board, particularly by the Comptroller of the Navy, who really w as of opinion that the authorities as then constituted were competent to a due and economical management of naval business. There have been many changes since his time, but they have all of them deviated further from the rules by which good management might be expected. There is not, at this moment, any scrutiny as to either commercial or manufacturing concerns, no individual responsibility, no accounts that bring comparative economy under observation. Much has of late been brought before the public as to abuses in the naval department, but abuse is a misnomer; extravagances there are, but of all that have been exhibited there is not one of them that had not been previously specified by Sir Samuel Bentham, accompanied by proposals for remedying the evils; and, to take the words of the King in Council, as they were " founded on principles of acknowledged efficacy," there is good reason to conclude that if they had been adopted, they would by this time have been the means of saving many millions of the public money.

In January 1802, the Inspector-General requested permission to obtain certain kinds of information direct from the dockyard officers. The Comptroller attacked him on this score, saying that he wanted to correspond with the dockyard officers without the knowledge of the Navy Board. To repudiate this accusation, he induced

the Comptroller to read the letter itself–the Comptroller then said he had been told so. Thus was every act of the Inspector-General misrepresented. He replied to the Comptroller, " that his object in asking to correspond with the dockyard officers was to save the time and trouble of a circuitous communication. Was he, when at a dockyard,
P 4 and wanting information from an officer on the spot, to have it sent first to the Navy Board and then to the Admiralty before it could reach him? Was this the readiest way of doing business?"

On this day (22nd January) Sir Thomas Trowbridge came into the Admiralty, where were some of the Lords, the Comptroller, and the Inspector-General. Sir Thomas declared that " all the master shipwrights ought to be hanged, every one of them, without exception." This exclamation had been in consequence of some particulars respecting job-notes at Sheerness. It is true that in this respect the abuses were enormous. The Inspector-Greneral had officially pointed them out, and the remedy for the evil was amongst the improvements that were in progress of establishment by the new regulations. Surely the preventing the possibility of abuse by doing away with fictitious job-notes altogether, as the Inspector-Greneral had proposed, was likely to be a more efficacious remedy than the hanging of all the half-dozen master shipwrights.

About this time great abuses came to light in regard to extra time set down to men of Plymouth dockyard; and in consequence some members of the Navy Board were going to that port with " a determination to turn out" some of the officers and clerks. In conversation with Mr. Tucker on the 29th, the Inspector-General could not help observing that if they punished inferiors, they ought to go further; there was not a single officer in that yard, or at the Navy Board unimplicated, "Eesident Commissioner, Navy Board, all of them." But it appeared " that the do not like to go higher than dockyard officers."

On the 18th May the Inspector-Greneral learnt that an order had been given " for discharging shipwrights in dockyards, and first by superannuating those who are past their labour." A list of no more than twelve came from Plymouth yard, being those only who had (ied for superannuation. To make up the number of dismissals, the Navy Board intended to discharge the last entered;– of course, the young men. The Comptroller showed this list to Lord St. Vincent. (i What," said his Lordship, " are there no more than twelve old men in Plymouth yard? " " No, my lord." " Then Ill go to Plymouth myself." His Lordship then said he should take an Admiralty Board with him, that a Navy Board should also go, and he supposed the Comptroller would go himself. The next day Mr. Tucker told the Inspector-Greneral that Lord St. Vincent had determined to have a commission to examine into the abuses and mismanagement: that when he visited the dockyards he would not enter into abuses, but merely look about him. Thus originated the Commission of Naval Inquiry, a commission which, in its several reports, brought such enormous abuses to light.

A letter had been written to the Inspector-Greneral on the 28th of August of the preceding year, and then signed by the Secretary of the Admiralty; but it was not forwarded to him till the 14th of March of the year 1802. It directed him to reply to the observations of the Navy Board on the subject of his letter concerning the extravagance resulting from carriage of beech timber. The Navy Board charged him with having " endeavoured to prejudice the minds of the Lords Commissioners of the

Admiralty, by laying before them a partial representation of a transaction calculated to make an unfavourable impression, without having made the least previous inquiry into the real circumstances of the case;" adding further that "had he done so, he would have found that his whole statement originated in error?

In relation to this accusation, the Inspector-Greneral, on the 15th April, informed their Lordships that he had made many inquiries, and had obtained much information in consequence. This letter afforded convincing proof, that the transaction had been minutely investigated previously to his first statement of it, and that his statement had originated, not in error, but in facts officially recorded.

Observations necessarily introduced in this communication exhibited other instances of improvidence of that Board as a body; but the Inspector-General added, " that had the blame appeared to him really to attach to any one, either at the dockyard or at the Navy Office, as it certainly is not my duty to be the censor of any one in either of those situations, I should not have presumed to take up their Lordships' time with any observations on this point;" but that " whatever be the management, the duties of the persons concerned are so ill defined, and their instructions so insufficient, that there is no one individual on whom the blame can be fixed."

It may seem irrelevant to the memoirs of Sir Samuel Bentham to enter into the particulars of this transaction; but it must be considered that down to this very moment, (for want of some such system of management and of accounts as that he advocated,) not, as he said, " hundreds of thousands," but " millions " are imperceptibly lost annually in the civil branch of the naval service, so that his endeavours to produce a salutary reform of management become a very prominent and important feature of the services which he rendered. The ill-will necessarily resulting to him from a variety of persons, in consequence of his bringing such malpractices to view, would have deterred men less conscientious and less persevering. Indeed, much as he possessed these desirable qualities, it has been seen that during Lord Spencer's administration he sometimes would have sunk under opposition, but for his support; and now Lord St. Vincent's confidential secretary, Mr. Tucker, was employed to assure him of the support of the superior Board.

In October the service sustained what proved to be an irreparable loss in the death of Mr. Bunce, architect in the Inspector-General's office. Previously to the establishment of the office he had been employed by Sir Samuel in the year 1794 in drawing some of his machinery, and in that part of the designs for a Panopticon prison which required the practical skill and experience of an architect. Mr. Bunce's knowledge of the details of his profession, his taste, the information which he had acquired in Italy, his indefatigable industry and high character, led General Bentham to wish for his assistance; and fortunately Mr. Bunce, from personal regard to the General, was induced to accept the office of architect. From first to last he had been most conscientious in the discharge of his public duty, and his death was occasioned by his zeal. He had attended at the different naval establishments during the whole of the visitation which was this year held by the Lords of the Admiralty, and his strength was already exhausted when he undertook the examination of the Isle of Grain. It was the most unhealthy season of the year; he caught fever, and when recovering, as it was hoped, an unguarded expression in his presence, " that the service was suffering from his absence," brought on a relapse, under which he sank.

As the Inspector-General's plan for affording a fitting education to qualify young men for services in a naval arsenal had not yet been carried into effect, he devised a plan for bringing up working apprentices which should be less objectionable than the existing mode. In his proposal of it, on the 22nd November, he recommended it only as a provisional measure. His proposal was adopted, having proved, as he said, " less costly than the then existing mode, considerably more advantageous to the public service, and more generally beneficial to the deserving artificers."

See before, p. 163.

CHAP. X.

Tour to visit Cordage Manufactories, January 1803–Report, and Adoption of his Proposals–Treatment of Workpeople in Factories– Services of Mr. Brunei in the Introduction of Block Machinery– Method of rewarding Inventors– Advantages of Non-recoil Guns– Abuses in Job Payments– Proposals for a Government Ropery, 1804– Contracts for Timber– Opposition of the Navy Board– Arming of the Mercantile Marine– Timber Coynes– Dockyard Machinery at Portsmouth– Mission to build Ships in Russia, 1805–Arrival at Cronstadt– Difficulties of his Task– Opposition of the Emperor– Illness– His Proposals rejected by the Emperor– Importation of Copper for Sheathing– Detention at St. Petersburg during the Winter– Panopticon of Ochta– Departure from St. Petersburg– Revel– Carlscrona– Return to England– The Office of Inspector-General of Naval Works merged in the Navy Board.

In the course of the visitation of the dockyards, the Earl of St. Vincent and the other Lords of the Admiralty became fully convinced of the expediency of introducing machinery worked by inanimate force to a great extent, as pointed out by the Inspector-General. As he had already overcome opposition to the introduction of steam-engines for working wood and metal, and now contemplated the still more important measure of manufacturing sailcloth and cordage on government account, he obtained permission (January 1803) to visit manufactories in the north, particularly of cordage.

He was fortunate in already possessing the friendship of some of the greatest manufacturers of the kingdom, and by their means obtained introductions to ever manufactory which it seemed desirable to visit. He was much indebted to many with whom he thus made acquaintance for the readiness with which they afforded him means of examining every detail of their business, frequently giving him access even to their account-books, and requiring their subordinates to furnish every required information. He thus visited Birmingham and the manufactories in its vicinity, including Soho; also Liverpool, Warrington, Manchester, Stockport, Leeds, Sunderland, Newcastle, Castle Eden, Sheffield and Rotherham, Derby, Warrington, Liverpool, Shrewsbury, Colebrook Dale, Coventry, and many other manufacturing towns. The seven weeks that he employed in his inquiries, though in the depth of winter, were fully occupied from daylight in the morning till nine or ten o'clock in the evening. For a part of this tour he invited Mr. Brunei to accompany him, in order to give him an insight into such management as Sir Samuel wished to introduce at Portsmouth. Mr. Brunei, not only at the time, but nve-and-thirty years afterwards, expressed in writing his obligation for this favour. Mr. Goodrich, the mechanist, also accompanied him during the whole of the tour.

On the 18th of February, Sir Samuel, in an official letter to the Secretary of the Admiralty, informed their Lordships that he had visited different establishments where cordage was manufactured by machinery, the result of which was that he had " seen reason to be entirely convinced that cordage of all descriptions, from the smallest twine to the largest cable, may be advantageously manufactured by means of machinery, such as may be set in motion by inanimate force; and this, with regard to all the operations requisite, from the first preparation of the raw material to the completion of the article for use." He stated that the principal advantages of such a manufactory would be a saving of half the expense of manufacturing, that the inconvenience then experienced of obtaining a sufficiency of ropemakers would be done away with, that the quantity of cordage might be variable according to the demand, but above all, that an uniform superiority of cordage would be insured.

He endeavoured to prevail on various manufacturers to attempt the weaving canvas entirely without starch or other dressing, but failed in every instance excepting in that of Mr. Scarth, at Castle Eden. In this factory Mr. Scarth had introduced an arrangement of the warp which placed it in the loom so that the roughness of the yarn was laid in one and the same direction, whereby great facility was obtained in beating up the fabric. This peculiarity was at once seen to favour the weaving without starch, and Mr. Scarth undertook to attempt making some webs of canvas without the use of any stiffening whatever.

In the course of this tour many opportunities occurred of comparing the influence of management on the well-being of the workpeople. As an instance of care towards apprentices lodged, clothed, and fed by the master, the flax-spinning mills of Mr. Bage, at Shrewsbury, maybe honourably cited. The 125 apprentice girls were strong, and in fact healthy, perhaps beyond example in any employ or rank of life, though their business of tending the machines kept them in a quick walk the whole of the working time. The extraordinary healthiness and apparent happiness of these girls induced particular inquiry respecting them. The women who had the care and direction of them when not at work, afforded every information requested, the dietary regulations, the account-book of actual expenses, andc. Without this minute examination it could not have been credited that these hard-working, growing girls, from fifteen to eighteen or nineteen years of age, could have been fed at an average of 6d. a day, having meat thrice a week. In the same establishment a few girls were likewise employed in light work at day pay. The contrast was striking; these latter were dirty, ragged, sickly-looking. Both at Messrs. Strutt's and Mr. Bage's, requisite means were taken to afford school instruction.

Sir Samuel's object in acquainting himself with actual good management of apprentices was preparatory to entering: into the details of naval seminaries on a large scale, still intended by Government, in conformity to his former proposal, and to which his attention was soon afterwards particularly called by Lord St. Vincent.

In April, Mr. Brunei having solicited the Admiralty to grant him remuneration for the labour and expense which he had incurred in the invention and perfecting machinery for making blocks, their Lordships commanded the In-spector-Greneral to consider and report what might be proper to be done on the subject of that application.

He was aware that few instances were on record in which remuneration had been given expressly for improvement, although, in point of fact, unperceived reward was habitually afforded, to a very great amount, concealed by a contract for the supply of improved articles. This mode of remuneration was, in his opinion, highly objectionable, as being nowise proportioned to benefit derived to the service. He had long had in view a mode of reward sufficient to the inventor, yet not beyond its value to the public.

It appeared from the Secretary's letter that no doubt was entertained of the expediency of allowing some compensation to Mr. Brunei, and that it was only as to its amount, and the most eligible mode, that Sir Samuel's opinion was required. On this supposition he devised the details of such a mode as should prove satisfactory on that occasion, " but which should also be calculated to afford encouragement to persons of ability in general for the production of other inventions tending to the diminution of dockyard expenses, while at the same time such remuneration should not hold up a precedent whereon claims for compensation could be founded, in any case where the reality of the advantages had not been previously ascertained." This new mode was that the amount of compensation should be proportioned to the amount of benefit derived from the use of the invention, namely, a sum equal to the savings made by Government for some specific period, and which he ventured to propose.

In favour of such a mode of compensation, he observed " that the greater the sum it might be found eventually to amount to, the greater in the same proportion will be the advantage which the service will derive from the inven-tion;" and that the compensation, however great, would be no neiv expense, but only the continuation, for a short and limited time, of an habitual expense, which would hereafter be saved to the public.

It has been, and continues to be, supposed that the whole of the machinery employed for making blocks was the invention of Mr. Brunei. The machines for shaping the shells were indeed so, though they had already been clearly described in Bentham's specification of 1793, but several official documents prove that most of the operations were from the first performed by machines of the Inspector-General's invention, in many instances by machines which he had had at work previously to his appointment to office. Amongst them were those of which he submitted drawings on the 1st of June 1802, as "forming part of the machinery for working in wood." In the same letter he proposed " that these engines should be set up in Plymouth dockyard immediately, to be worked by the steam-engine," particularly specifying that, independently of other uses, " they are, as it were, necessary for the cutting out the wood to the proper scantlings and lengths for shell of blocks" So also it appears from various documents that other machines were Sir Samuel's, such as that for forming wooden pins, an apparatus for sawing timber, turning lathes, a circular saw contrived to cut at pleasure to different angles, and which was employed in the wood mills for cutting off the angles from blocks previously to shaping them. In regard to this and other machinery being then the Inspector-General's private property, it was arranged with the Admiralty that their value should be estimated, and that they should be charged by Mr. Lloyd, and paid for to a millwright, who had been trained by the Inspector-General and employed by him in making them. They were thus furnished to Government at a price much below what they had really cost, to the pecuniary loss of the Inspector-General; while he has also been deprived of the credit of their invention. Continued naval successes by degrees brought conviction to the Lords of the Admiralty of the superiority of the principle of non-recoil for mounting carronades. At Copenhagen, Lord Nelson placed the Arrow and the Dart opposite the Crown Batter, of fifty-two guns, believed to be the most formidable of the defensive works of the town. " He " (Lord Nelson) " said to me that he considered them to be of more effective force than the 90-gun ships." It is evident that he did so, as he placed them against those very formidable batteries. The Lieutenant of the Dart, on being questioned, in July of this year (1803), affirmed that " ohe guns stood well– no breeching was broke– that he could continue to fire twice or three times as quick as other guns, and was two hours and a half in action with the guns all perfect." The Admiralty had also at this time received details of the ordnance fixed on this principle which had effected such pre-eminent service at the siege of Acre. That Sir Sidney Smith considered the success of this ordnance as consequent on Sir Samuel's introduction of non-recoil, is evident from his letter of 7th March 1803. It says, "My dear Sir–I have felt it incumbent on me to recommend Mr. E. Spurring, late our builder at Constantinople, and Mr. James Bray, to

Lord St. Vincent, for promotion in their line; at the same time I feel it due to you to let that recommendation pass through you. I have therefore given the letter in their favour to Mr. Spurring (who has the advantage of being known, and I hope approved of by you), under a flying seal, for your perusal, previous to its delivery." Sir Samuel learnt from them all particulars of the fitting the Tiger's carronades on his principle, and the great benefit derived from it in mounting ordnance for the defence of Acre.

In August of this year the Commission of Naval Inquiry requested the Inspector-General to state to them any " irregularities, frauds, or abuses in any of the Naval departments at Plymouth during the last ten years." He did accordingly communicate information of the nature. required, for which, on the 13th September, he received the thanks of their Chairman (Mr. Nicholls), who, at the end of November, had an interview with the Inspector-Greneral for the purpose of obtaining further particulars. In regard to the pay of workmen, the Inspector-General foresaw that the new establishments for working in wood and metal by machinery would afford opportunity of introducing the improvements which he projected without disturbing the general business of an arsenal.

Bespecting pay by job, he furnished to the Commission much information as an example of the thoughtless extravagance so frequently observable in Navy Board orders. He informed the Commission that in the repairing of boats–a thirty-four foot launch, for example–the Navy Board regulation required that for the smallest repair of such a boat no less a sum was to be set down in the books than 5. 2s.; if that sum should be found inadequate, the repair was to be denominated a middling repair, and 11. Is. was the exact sum to be set down, neither more nor less. Again, if that sum were insufficient, the repair was to be denominated a large repair, and although the value of the work done should have ex-ceeded the 117. Is. only by a few shillings,, the expense was to have appeared in the accounts to have been doubled, and set down at 227. 2s. The building a new boat of the same size and description amounted, he informed them, to no more than 217. 12s. 6d.

Such a regulation appeared to the Commissioners so absurd, that they entertained, and expressed in writing, doubts of the Inspector-General's accuracy. He therefore obtained and communicated to them copies of official documents establishing the fact, and job work was in consequence abolished.

The first important proposal of the year 1804 was the detailing his plan for a ropery. Many of the members of the Board of Admiralty, in the course of their sea-service, had witnessed the frequent imperfections of cordage, both in quality of material and in manufacture, and felt assured that they were not likely to be corrected otherwise than by the establishment of such a manufactory as he proposed. His proposal was therefore approved by the Admiralty, and on their application to the Lords of the Privy Council, the erection of this ropery was sanctioned by the King in Council, and ordered to be carried into immediate execution.

The strictness required by the New Regulations in the receipt of timber, that it should be in conformity to contract, had been greatly adverse to the interest of contractors. They had been habitually permitted to deliver more or less of timber in quantity, and of a value far inferior to that specified in contracts. Discontinuance of these abuses of course occasioned discussions between contractors and the new timber-masters, and often ill-will towards them. Complaints were made to the Navy Board, who thought proper to make in consequence an advance of no less than twenty-five per cent, on the contract prices, and other alterations in favour of con-

tractors. The Board also, on the part of the timber merchants, addressed complaints to the Admiralty, supporting the merchants against the timber-masters. The Admiralty were not deceived, but extracts from Mr. Mars-den's letter to the Navy Board, 13th May 1804, written by their Lordships 1 express command, will best exhibit the opposition of that Board to this very important improvement in management, and the light in which that opposition was viewed by them. Mr. Marsden's letter begins by stating that the Navy Board had not transmitted certain papers which their Lordships had called for, and goes on to say: " The replies, however, which their Lordships have received from the master shipwrights and timber-masters of the several yards, give the most satisfactory as well as positive denial and refutation of the assertions of the timber merchants that rigour or (vexatious strictness and severity is exercised on the receipt of timber, or that they feel the responsibility of their situations in the manner you describe, far less the smallest apprehension of losing their places; and, moreover, their replies fully prove that the root of the evil does not lie in the minds of either the timber-masters or master shipwrights, as you state, but in those ivho encourage a recurrence to the former system of receiving timber, which, however beneficial to the contractors, ivas ominous to the public; and with this true state of the case before their Lordships, it is with astonishment they reperuse the unfounded calumny against the master shipwrights and timber-masters (who naturally have a claim to your protection in the just execution of their duty), which you have thought proper to transmit to their Lordships, to which no other construction can be given than that of your having also the desire that the former system of receiving timber should be again resorted to, under which the receiving officers, on the part of the Crown, were, in fact, the agents of the timber merchants." Their Lordships

CENSURE OP THE NAVY BOAED. 229 then go on to state what they consider as proofs " of the present disposition of the Navy Board," favourable to contractors, but injurious to the Crown, saying that " their Lordships can be no longer at a loss to account for the backwardness of the timber merchants in furnishing supplies, when they are permitted to entertain the hope that the yards will be again abandoned to their undue influence, and the officers be calumniated for the honest discharge of their duty to the public."

Mr. Marsden terminates his letter thus: " Their Lordships command me to conclude by observing that you would not have presumed to use the language with which you have thought proper to close your said letter, had you not confided in that forbearance which you have experienced on the exposure of the negligence, fallacy, and fraud which have pervaded and been fostered by the department under your direction, both at home and abroad, by which the public has suffered immensely, and which would not have passed so long without receiving all the notice it merited, had not their Lordships been impressed with the belief that the consequence which must result from the impartial judgment of the legislature on the facts that have been and will be laid before them, would operate more to the benefit of the public, and be a more useful lesson to future members of the Navy Board, than any measures which their Lordships might have pursued to mark their disapprobation."

The Inspector-Greneral had not been informed that such a letter had been in contemplation, but a copy of it was afterwards furnished him, attested by Mr. Nelson of the Navy Office. It may be said to have been unfortunate for the service as well as to himself. It greatly increased the rancour of the Navy Board, as a Board, towards himself, for it was well known that most of the facts that had been, or were intended to be laid before the legislature, had been either furnished by him, or that he had pointed

Q 3 out to their Lordships and to the Commission of Naval Inquiry, the quarters from which such facts were to be obtained. It was further known that he had for years, with the approbation and at the desire of two successive Administrations, been collecting data, on which to remodel the Navy Board itself, so as to render it a really efficient and responsible Board, by clearly defining its duties and rendering them practicable, by freeing it from those members who could not be supposed competent, by simplifying the mode of keeping accounts, and especially by introducing to a great extent individual responsibility.

On the appointment of the new Ministry, the Inspector-Greneral had the satisfaction to find that the success which had attended every improvement he had proposed, had impressed the new Board of Admiralty with a most gratifying sense of the services which he had rendered. One of the new members, Admiral Grambier, who had himself had opportunities of witnessing those improvements, received Sir Samuel soon after his appointment, in an official private conference. On this occasion the Admiral expressed himself desirous of doing everything to forward any business which the Inspector-Greneral might have to recommend. He replied that " he should attack their Lordships on the armament of small vessels, adding that his plans in regard to them had nothing new in them noiv— they had been put to the test of experience already."

This assertion arose from the protection which had lately been afforded to trade, at his suggestion, by arming coasting vessels with non-recoil carronades, those vessels, notwithstanding, still carrying on their usual traffic.

The Channel and the sea off the east coast had, at the beginning of this century, been infested with numbers of well-appointed French privateers, that took our trading vessels when venturing to sea without powerful convoy, whilst at the same time the naval military force of the country was not sufficient to afford convoy equal to the demands of the mercantile marine. These circumstances had imparted a peculiar interest to General Bentham's plan of giving to trading vessels themselves a powerful armament. It happened that several of the Berwick smacks which had been armed under the former administration as he had proposed, were now lying off St. Catharine's; amongst others, was the Queen Charlotte packet. This vessel, as appears by a letter the original of which had been enclosed to the Admiralty, had had off Cromer an engagement, on the 27th January, with a brig privateer of fourteen guns, direct from port and full of men, in which encounter the Queen had been victorious. She had but six carronades, 18-pounders, but they were fixed non-recoil, and two long 4-pounders. The master of the packet, Mr. Nelson, affirmed that " he now considers his vessel as superior to any of the gunboats– that he actually gives protection to other trading vessels. He has now six carronades on board, and would willingly take four more if he could but have secure protections for eight men; for that, although he has protections for thirteen men, yet he has always some pressed away from him."

For some time back one of the Inspector-Greneral's important inventions, that of coynes for connecting timber, had been ordered for general use in the dockyards, and an intelligent shipwright officer, Mr. Helby, had at his suggestion been sent to the several dockyards for the purpose of exhibiting the uses of these coynes, and the manner of employing them. To the credit of officers of all ranks in the dockyards, instead of reluctance to be taught by one of an inferior grade, they all manifested the greatest-goodwill, ordering bowsprits, masts, andc. for large ships to be prepared according to Mr. Helby's wish. In fact, dockyard officers in general were no longer averse to the introduction of his improvements. Their opportunities of witnessing the success of those already in use, led to conviction in their minds that the adoption of his measures would be advantageous.

The scarcity of oak for shipbuilding had ilduce 1 the Admiralty to order ten frigates to be built of fir by the same designs, two at each of the five dockyards. The Inspector-Greneral, on hearing of this order, learnt that little had yet been done to those in some of the dockyards, and considering this a favourable opportunity for exhibiting the advantages of the innovations in regard to strength, made in his experimental vessels, he, 4th August, submitted to the Admiralty the expediency of adopting some of the improvements in regard to the arrangement and mechanical combination of the parts, such " as were introduced in the construction of the several vessels built under his direction, and of which the efficacy in regard to strength had been proved by more than seven years' experience." This was indeed an extraordinarily favourable opportunity of putting those expedients to severe test, as these fir frigates, being of inferior materials, were expected to be of short duration. He proposed that at each dockyard one of the frigates should be constructed as usual; the other as he should propose, whereby the comparative duration of the two modes of structure would be fairly tested. His proposal was adopted; but on inquiry it was found that too much had already been done in the way of preparation to admit of his improvements being introduced excepting in the dockyards of Deptford and Woolwich.

Ever since his appointment he had been investigating the means by which success in private manufactories is obtained, and whether similar good management could be introduced in that great manufactory, a naval arsenal. Fully aware too that the manufactories which he had established could never attain the perfection in point of economy that he had aspired to give them, unless they were assimilated to private concerns, he had, from the first use of his machinery in Portsmouth yard, by degrees introduced many regulations differing materially from dockyard practice. A good deal of work had for some time been done there by bis machinery and by that of which Mr. Brunei had the charge; but it was not till the 19th February 1805, that he was enabled to acquaint the Admiralty that the whole of the machinery ordered according to his proposals was so nearly ready as to render it necessary that master workmen, and others for the management and use of it should be provided. He therefore requested that he might be authorised to select and engage, in addition to the few hands already employed, such artificers and others as might appear necessary for setting the whole of the machinery to work, and proposed to spend some time at Portsmouth for the purpose of having immediate communication with the master workmen and others engaged in these businesses.

This proposal having been referred to the Navy Board, the Comptroller and a committee of it, then on a visitation to Portsmouth yard, stated in their minute, 27th February, that they had consulted the master shipwright, who professed himself unacquainted with the nature of the works to be carried on by means of the machinery. The committee did not see the possibility of the Board's complying with their Lordships' directions, and they saw no alternative but to adopt the proposition of General Bentham. This having been communicated by the Board to the Admiralty, their Lordships transmitted their report to the Inspector-Greneral, who in rep y acquainted their Lordships that he should " hold himself responsible for not engaging or retaining a greater number" (of artificers and others) than would from time to time become really necessary for carrying " on the work with the greatest economy," andc. In consequence of which their Lordships, on the 30th March, gave their orders to place the three establishments under his management in conformity to the Navy Board's suggestions.

Thus he became individually responsible for the whole direction and management of these establishments, not less than if they had been private concerns of his own and on his own private account.

These establishments were watched from first to last with jealous eyes by a Board that had shown itself all along adverse to the measures which the Inspector-General had proposed; they were watched too by the several con- tractors whose interests were invaded by the introduction of these establishments. In consequence of his experience, and of his extreme care in the formation of his plans, they all of them proved as perfect in execution as he had professed they would be. And as to his management in the outlay of money for wages or otherwise, although about a million sterling passed uncontrolled through his hands in relation to these three establishments, it never was in any instance surmised that he had misapplied a single sixpence, or had abused the confidence reposed in him.

The use of the coynes of his invention was now becoming general; and in the course of his walks in the dockyard, his attention was particularly called by the master mastmaker to the perfection which they enabled him to give to the work in his department–indeed the success of the great variety of improvements which he had introduced here, cheered him and encouraged perseverance in regard to his other plans, retarded as they were by the customary opposition of the Navy Board.

Having at length fairly set the manufactories at Portsmouth at work, he proceeded in June to Plymouth.

His intention was, as that of the Admiralty had been, when he left town, that he should apply himself to the improvement of that dockyard. Immense sums had been lavished upon it, but unfortunately in conformity to plans framed more with a view to splendour than to use. Thus in many instances the new erections had rather impeded than facilitated the business of the port. Scarcely had he arrived when he was attacked by a fever caused by exces- sive exertion. On the 20th, orders were sent from the Admiralty, through their secretary, desiring his immediate return to town, and also the First Lord's private secretary te signified his Lordship's desire that" he " should return to town with as much expedition as possible." But he was too ill to attend to any business, and the letters were opened by his wife. On being made acquainted with the circumstance, they expressed their regret at the state of his health, and added that it would not be requisite for him to pursue his journey, until he should be so far recovered as not to endanger a relapse. The evident desire for his speedy return induced him to set out for town on the very day he first left his bed.

On his arrival in town, he immediately waited on Lord Barham, who announced that the duty on which it was wished to send him, was that of building ships of war in Russia for the service of this country, his Lordship and Mr. Pitt both considering him (the Inspector-General) as the most eligible person. In case of his acceptance of this service, it was wished that he should set out in a fortnight, and his answer was required on the following day. He was at the same time told that permission had already been received for building the ships in question, but that it would remain for him to treat with the persons in that country with whom it would be necessary to have intercourse, whether the Eussian Ministry or the merchants who might be found willing to contract, and that he would have to see that the ships were properly built. In the course of this conversation, Lord Barham mentioned of himself his supposition that he would be desirous of taking his wife.

It happened at this particular time that a variety of circumstances could not but render him desirous of remaining at home, especially the reluctance of his wife, added to his own, on account of the interruption which it would occasion in the education of his children. However, on his next interview, he expressed his willingness to undertake the mission, provided he were permitted to take his wife and family, and that an allowance were made sufficient to cover all his expenses. This was acceded to without the least hesitation, whilst in the course of conversation many nattering expressions fell from his Lordship of his conviction that no other man was competent to this service; but that in him were combined professional knowledge in naval architecture, scientific skill, personal acquaintance with the resources of Eussia, as well as with distinguished Russians; while he was also regarded in the most favourable light by the Emperor himself. Archangel was the port which the Admiralty considered most suitable for the business in question, and the Inspector-General was directed to consider what persons would be required as assistants.

The appropriate knowledge, probity, and other estimable qualities of Mr. Helby, then a quartermaster in Portsmouth dockyard, induced him to recommend this officer as his principal assistant, which was immediately acceded to.

On the 2nd August he sailed in the Isabella, and, on his arrival at Cronstadt, was received with the most flattering marks of friendly distinction by the Commander of the Fleet and Port. He proceeded immediately to St. Petersburg, where he was greeted by old friends, high in power. But, to his astonishment and dismay, he learnt that what by the English Ministry had been considered as a cordial and full acquiescence in their wish to build ships in Russia, had been nothing more than a civil diplomatic reply to their application, and which he found had in fact been very far from a specific request. Under these circumstances, his task was one of extreme difficulty. He however determined to avail himself of all the personal interest which he possessed at St. Petersburg, in an endeavour to obtain for the Ministry of his own country the object of their wishes. Fortunately he had been directed to conciliate the Russian Court, and if possible to render himself useful to the Russian Government, so that he had no hesitation in complying with the condition upon which the Minister of the Marine, Admiral Tchitchagoft, at length gave his consent to the building of the ships. This condition was, that for every vessel laid down for the English Government, a similar one should be commenced for Russia; that the Inspector-General should equally supervise the one as the other during their construction, and that all of his improvements in naval construction should be introduced and exemplified in the ships for Russia–a condition highly flattering to him personally. In his first report to the Admiralty, he gave an account of his progress, of the difficulties which he had to surmount, and of the facilities at length afforded to him by the Admiral.

In conformity with this arrangement, Admiral Tchitchagoft, in October 1805, prepared a paper for the Emperor, in which the above-mentioned particulars were stated, and the Admiral certainly exerted his best endeavours to obtain the confirmation of them. Unfortunately, his reluctance to acquiesce in the wishes of the British Government became but too apparent–yet at the same time he manifested his personal regard for Bentham, his conviction of his superior knowledge and abilities, his desire that many of the inventions and improvements of General Bentham should be introduced into the Russian service. Amongst other improvements the establishment of a manufactory of cordage and sail cloth similar to that for which the Inspector-General had prepared plans in England, was early an object of Imperial solicitude, so that in December 1805, the Minister of the Marine expressed a "wish to have a factory that would do from 100,000 poods' to 300,000 per annum."

The Inspector-General continued strenuous in his endeavours to obtain the Imperial authority which would sanction the favourable proposal of the Minister of the Marine, but all without avail; and this, although several others of the ministers concurred with

Admiral Tchitcha-goft in the eligibility of the measure. At length, having understood that, on the 13th March 1806, the question had come before a Committee of the Ministers of the Crown, the Inspector-General went early to the Admiral on the following morning, for the purpose of learning the decision of that Committee. He found that " it had been determined against allowing vessels for the English service to be built at St. Petersburg; that twelve Ministers were present at the Committee, that they were unanimous in favour of the measure, but that the Emperor himself (also present) had overruled them all, on the ground of the want of timber for their own use; that, however, the Emperor, as well as the several Ministers, had expressed the greatest willingness to forward any plans of General Bentham for his private emolument in the introduction of improvements into their country; particularly they were anxious for a ropery, andc. andc."

He went immediately to communicate this information to the Secretary of Legation, Mr. Stuart (afterwards Lord Stuart de Eothsay). It happened that the then Governor-General of the Crimea, General Fanshaw, was at this time at St. Petersburg, and frequently with the Emperor. As General Fanshaw was an old friend and companion in arms of General Bentham, frequent conversations had taken place between them on the subject of this mission, and to Mr. Stuart's knowledge the Governor-General had regretted that the construction of the contemplated ships had not been proposed from the first to have been in the Crimea, where timber of superior quality might be obtained in abundance and at a low price, from the opposite shores of the Black Sea. Mr. Stuart, in this interview with the Inspector-General, observed that the same objection could not hold good at Cafta as at Peters- burg, and requested the Inspector-General to go immediately to General Fanshaw, and learn what he had to say on the subject. He immediately did so, when the Governor-General said as before, that he was exceedingly desirous of the measure, and that he would give every facility for its execution. He, as every other person in power spoken to on the subject, said he could not conceive what the real ground of the Emperor's objection could have been. The Inspector-General endeavoured, but in vain, to learn what that real ground might have been. Count Kouman-goff could not give any further information.

On the 16th Sir Samuel was advised both by the Ambassador, Lord Gower, and by Mr. Stuart, to obtain leave to go to Caffa to build ships and purchase masts, andc, and to ask General Fanshaw officially whether he would permit ships to be built there, and what encouragement he would give. Mr. Stuart advised farther that, supposing leave should be obtained, Bentham should set out immediately, without losing the time requisite for obtaining an answer from the Admiralty at home. The question was put the same day to General Fanshaw. He replied that " he did not know of the peculiar circumstances in which the Inspector-General was placed here, and of what had already passed as to the refusal of building at St. Petersburg; he should immediately give him the requisite permission, and afford him every assistance in his power; but that under existing circumstances he should think it necessary to take the opinion of Ministers, notwithstanding his own conviction of the eligibility of the measure, and the advantages that would result from it to Russia."

Vexation at the failure of the English scheme of building ships, after all his exertions and hopes, brought on severe illness. He, however, suffered it not to prevent a continuance of his endeavours; even in his bed, receiving General Fanshaw. On this occasion the Governor-General informed him that Count Eoumangoff had said " he sup- posed the refusal to the proposal for building ships for the English Government to be political." The General advised the Inspector-General to see Tchitchagoft again, and obtain from him a decisive answer respecting what steps he would take either for or against the building ships in the Black Sea.

On the 21st the Inspector-General, though still ill, went to the Minister of Marine so early that he was not yet up, sat with him during his breakfast, and at last had a conference with him in private. In this the Inspector-General desired particularly "to be told whether the objection to building ships at St. Petersburg arose from political motives, or from any dislike or objection to him personally. That in either of those cases, it would be folly to contend against such considerations or prejudices, and that accordingly, if either of these be the reason, he should give up all further thoughts of doing anything in any part of Russia." On this the Admiral assured the Inspector-General " that there was nothing political in the objection; and that as to personal dislike to him, so far from it, the Emperor had commanded him (the Admiral) to communicate with Inspector-General Bentham, and to treat with him respecting the introduction of a ropery, or any establishments in which he could assist for the improvement of this country, several of which the Emperor was very desirous of seeing established; and that he (the Minister) considered himself as authorised to proceed with those that related to his department." In reply, Bentham said that " if these were the Imperial sentiments, he should now turn his thoughts to building ships in the Black Sea, with timber brought from Anadolia, sending them to England loaded with stores– would he, the Minister, have any objection? Would he wish any proposals of this nature to go through him, or through what channel? " The Minister answered, " that Caffa not being considered as a naval port, he had nothing to do with business carried on there; that it was in Count Komanzoft's department, and that Bentham should apply to him." The Inspector-General observed that it would probably be more desirable for him to introduce improvements in the south of Eussia than at St. Petersburg; and afterwards in consultation with a friend (General Hitroff), it was decided that he should address a letter immediately to the Emperor, proposing to build ships in the Black Sea. By the 23rd it was written, and proved satisfactory to that prince; next day when General Fanshawe called to read it, he advised the omission of a sentence respecting ships of luar. Sir Samuel afterwards took the letter to the Ambassador; Lord Gower and Mr. Stuart each of them examined it separately, and approved of it, but both agreed that the sentence to which General Fanshawe objected should be retained. As there seemed to be reasons why this letter should not pass through the hands of the Minister of the Marine, the Inspector-General determined, if possible, to present it through his friend General Hitroff. This nobleman had been the companion of the Emperor in childhood and early life, from which arose a mutual affection; but he had never sought emplo3 r ment or distinction on that account, and was therefore looked upon as a sincere and disinterested friend. He happened at that time to be absent; but as the Emperor had dispatched a courier desiring him to return, it was deemed best for the success of the proposal, that it should await his arrival This took place on the 27th, and on the same day the Inspector-General took the letter to his friend, who willingly consented to present it, and caused a translation of it to be made into French, professedly for his own use, but from his anxiety that it should be well done, and from the many verbal alterations which he made, it seemed that he had in view the further object of tendering it in the language most familiar to the Emperor, although His Majesty understood English well. General Hitroff was ill at the time, and continued too much indisposed to go to Court, so that on the 31st March, he sent the letter to the Emperor, accompanied by one of his own, in which he said that Brigadier-Greneral Bentham was not at all willing to re-enter into the Eussian service, but that as an individual he found him ready to do any thing in his power for the advantage of Eussia, whilst he remained, and he advised the Emperor to consent to the building of ships in the Black Sea. Greneral Hitroff having dined with His Majesty, on the 8th of April Bentham went to learn the determination as to Cafta. His Imperial Majesty had told him that the answer in regard to ship building would be given through Prince Tsartorinsky, while in other matters he should commission Tchitchagoff to communicate with Greneral Bentham on the following day. From this he concluded that a refusal would be given to the building.

He lost no time in communicating to the Admiralty the unfavourable result of his endeavours, and on the 9th he acquainted their Lordships that although no answer whatever had as yet been given by the Eussian Grovernment to the repeated applications made by Lord Gower respecting the object of his mission, he "had now reason to believe that the Emperor will not at last consent to the building of any ships for our Navy." He added that luckily, although his instructions had extended to the making preparations for building ten ships of the line and ten frigates, he had abstained from engaging for more timber than was necessary for two ships of the line and two frigates, which he had hoped would have been ready in the course of that summer, and that if a decided negative should be given to this business, he should think it his duty to send home by the first opportunity the persons who accompanied him; although the disposal of the timber, and the need of further instructions from their Lordships, might render it necessary that he should himself remain some little time longer in Eussia.

In reply to his letter, he was directed to obtain, through Lord Grower, a categorical answer, and in case of refusal to send the persons who accompanied him home, as he had proposed; but to remain himself till the materials, tools, andc, belonging to Government should be disposed of.

His endeavour now was to obtain leave for the timber which he had purchased to be sent to England duty free, arguing with Admiral Tchitchagoff that it would be only analogous to what England had done for Russia, andc.

He was answered that this would be permitted, and duty free. This was a far greater boon than would appear at first sight, for not only the duty saved amounted from ten to fifteen thousand pounds, but the great scarcity of this store in England rendered this additional supply of importance in the Koyal Docks.

Although the Inspector-General had had no part whatever in projecting this mission, and had accepted it only as a duty which he owed to his country,– militating as it did against his wishes and private convenience, as also against the prosecution of the various and great improvements at home which he had so much at heart,–yet his mortification at the result was extreme. Untoward as circumstances had appeared on his arrival, the evident appreciation of his talents not only by the Minister of Marine but by the Emperor himself, and the facilities that had in consequence been afforded him in making preparations for building ships for the British Navy, together with many other circumstances that had occurred in private communications, had given him ground to hope that at last he should be permitted to accomplish the purpose for which he had been sent from home. Now these hopes were at an end, and he could only look forward to the odium which, however unmerited, generally falls on a man charged with any mission of which the object fails; still this made no change in his determination to devote himself to the service of his own country.

R 2

For some time back business of a different nature had occupied him a good deal. The demand in England for copper, an article so indispensable to the navy, had caused the great holders of it to combine together for raising its price to an exorbitant amount. Here then was an opportunity of realising one of the benefits which he had indicated in his first proposal for manufacturing that article, namely, that " under circumstances when it may be found more beneficial to use the copper of other countries, it might be imported as a partial supply for the use of her Majesty's Navy, without interference with any general commercial privileges or arrangements." Messrs. Bailey, of St. Petersburgh, had proposed to furnish the Navy Board with a certain quantity of copper at a rate much below the English price. The Board recommended reference to the Inspector-General. Samples of it were therefore analysed at the metal mills at Portsmouth, and the expenses attendant on bringing it to a state for those mills ascertained, so that the Navy Board authorised Messrs. Bailey to furnish 1000 tons, if sanctioned by General Bentham, and if at a price not exceeding 150. per ton. He did authorise the sending a quantity, and he obtained it at 145. lis. 5(7. per ton. This supply, together with the operation of the metal mills, caused the market price of copper to fall as much as 5d. per pound within the twelvemonth following. Independently of other savings made by the manufacture of sheathing on Government account, by that fall alone it amounted to above 38,000. a year.

At length it was communicated officially to our Government that no vessels of war could be allowed to be constructed in Russia for British use.

The Inspector-General, on the communication of this note, wrote to inform the Admiralty that, having been well assured that the answer to Lord G. L. Gower's note would be to that effect, he had been anxious to put an end as soon as possible to the current expenses attendant on his mission, and previously to the receipt of their Lordships' orders of the 11th May, had taken the earliest opportunity of sending home the persons he had brought with him, with the exception of Joseph Helby, who would remain until the timber was shipped.

On the 8th of October the Secretary of the Admiralty wrote, that he had "their Lordships' commands to acquaint you that they approve of what you have done."

On receipt of these letters, the season being too far advanced to admit of his return to England, or of shipping the timber, he necessarily was detained for the winter at St. Petersburgh, yet not without anxiety, as no formal notice had been received of acquiescence in the Imperial desire of obtaining for him a temporary leave of absence. But with the sanction of our ambassador, and in obedience to the instructions he had received to do everything in his power that might be agreeable to the Emperor, he had consented to introduce some of his inventions and improvements.

On the 17th March, 1807, he heard from a private friend that the Admiralty, not having received from the Russian Government any application for his stay at St. Petersburgh, had commanded his return by the 24th June. But a long correspondence and much trouble ensued before he was informed by the Secretary to the Admiralty, that in consequence of the desire expressed by the Emperor, his leave of absence had been extended to September 29, 1807.

This mission affords a striking example of the mischiefs arising from want of precision in diplomatic communications, especially verbal ones. The sending an officer of high trust, and the expenses incurred so uselessly in regard to the artificers who attended him, solely on the authority of a courteous reply from Russia to a vague request from England, but above all the disappointment of obtaining twelve ships of the line and as many frigates in a time of war, might

E 3 have afforded good grounds to an opposition party in Parliament for inquiries respecting the measure. But there happened at this period to have been so many changes in the Administration, that this mission passed unheeded.

The only establishment which he was enabled to commence in Eussia was the Panopticon at Ochta. For the sake of expedition it was built of wood. The progress made in it during the few short months of summer was so great, that its efficacy in affording perfect inspection of all its parts from the centre was manifest-He obtained freight in June for two cargoes of timber, but finding it impossible to procure any means of conveyance for the whole, he wrote to Admiral Gambier to induce him to send transports from England for the remaining 4000 loads.

The Enssian Admiralty having expressed a wish to purchase the copper bolts sent from England, and particularly the tools and engines of his invention, he disposed of them, as well as all the implements, andc, provided for building- the above-mentioned four vessels. Having; completed these arrangements, he took leave of the Emperor, so as to be home by the time indicated, but the Imperial alliance with Bonaparte having already taken place, no passport could be obtained in the usual mode. This delayed his departure to the middle of September, when the Emperor assigned one of his corvettes to convey the General and his party from Eevel to Sweden.

No greater proof can be given of the Emperor's confidence in his honour than that, notwithstanding the war with England, he was not only permitted to examine the important port of Eevel, but allowed to take notes, with the view of ascertaining the best means of improving it. This was the more remarkable, as it was evident that devotion to his own country was the sole cause of his return home. The flattering distinction with which he had been received at St. Petersburg by official men and others, as well as by the Emperor himself, had had no charms in competition with service at home. Pecuniary considerations had been of no avail; for the Emperor had assigned him an allowance, paid monthly in advance, exceeding that of any of his Ministers.

His stay at St. Petersburg had been so unexpectedly protracted, that nightly frosts had already commenced when he and his family left that capital in the middle of September. On their arrival at Revel, two days' rest were allowed them whilst he examined the port. It was intended that the corvette should convey him to Stockholm, in order that he might obtain the King's permission to inspect the naval arsenal at Carlscrona. It proved to be a voyage of alarms and danger, for the commander of the vessel and his officers appeared little competent to manage her, and the sails were so set that often she was carried aback instead of forward. One stormy day she was about to be run ashore on a Danish island, when he at last ventured to interfere. The commander, to his credit, admitted the truth of his observations, and put the vessel under his direction; the sails were altered to his wish, and the corvette escaped. As English, they had unusual dread of any Danish port, exasperated as the Danes were at that time by the late slaughter at Copenhagen. But he and his children spoke Russ as natives, and would have passed as Russians; while his wife's few words of Russ would have sufficed, ill and confined to her cot as she was. At length he thought it prudent to steer for Carlscrona, the nearest port friendly to England, instead of Stockholm, the commander having had orders to land him at any place in Sweden which he might select. Great indeed was his relief when a pilot from that port was once on board. Before going on shore, the Governor had been informed of his arrival, and sent his carriage to receive him on his landing.

s 4 It was not in the power, however, of any of the authorities to admit any one to the arsenal without special permission from the King. This was immediately applied for in favour of Bentham, and accorded in due course of time. He had already acquainted the Admiralty at home that he intended visiting Carlscrona in his way, in order to examine the great works there, especially as the route across Sweden at that time of year, and during the state of war, was the only one that afforded a chance of his timely arrival in England.

This port was the only naval establishment in the Baltic which General Bentham had not previously visited. Its splendour and the utility of its arrangements are well known; but he had opportunity of learning what were the real advantages derived from these works. The Governor of Carlscrona, Admiral Puka, and the Principal Officer of the Naval Arsenal, Major Kilgren, most kindly afforded him every information.

The many anxieties and fatigues which Greneral Bentham had undergone of late had produced an illness that needed rest; yet when he had inspected the works of the arsenal, he immediately set out on his return. His kind acquaintances at Carlscrona had given him letters of introduction to the landed proprietors whose estates were situated on his route. This was fortunate; for. when half way between that town and Gothenburg, his travelling coach, an English one, broke down. He learnt that he was within half a dozen miles of Engeltofta, the residence of a proprietor, Major Schamsward, where there was an establishment of English workmen, for the works needed on the estate. He and his family walked on to Engeltofta, where he was cordially welcomed. His carriage was well repaired; and during the three days requisite for the work, they were entertained in the most hospitable and friendly manner by the Major. On his estate, a few miles north of Helsingborg, amongst the tender fruit-trees were olives, which bore fruit, and a keg of them preserved as in France, had been sent as a present to that country.

On reaching the coast, they had to wait some days for the sailing of a packet before they embarked for England. After a long and dangerous passage, they landed at Harwich, where he received letters from his office, The first which he opened informed him that the office of In-spector-Greneral of Navy Works was abolished, and that, in consequence of a recommendation of the Commission of Naval Revision, it was to be incorporated with the Navy Board, of which he was to be appointed one of the Commissioners.

CHAP. XL

Changes of Administration at the Admiralty– Influences at rork during his absence in Kussia– Acceptance of Office in the Navy Board– Letter from General Fanshawe– Compensation to Mr. Brunei for Sayings on Blocks– Proposal for a Canal from Portsmouth Harbour to Stokes Bay– Mixture of Copper and Tin–Faulty method of Shipbuilding– Covered Docks– Modes of Seasoning Timber– Seasoning Houses– Sheerness Dockyard– Northfleet and the Isle of Grain– Breakwater at Plymouth.

To account for this unexpected change, the different dispositions of the several Admiralty Naval Administrations under which Sir Samuel had been employed must be reverted to. Enough has been already said to prove that, whilst the many glorious achievements of the navy proved the wisdom of Earl Spencer's military measures– he was alive to the want of improvement in the civil branch of the service. His own perception of the value of General Ben-tham's suggestions led his Lordship to induce him to undertake a visit to the dockyards, and then to enter permanently in H. M."s service; yet even from the first his Lordship manifested the ruling spirit of his administration– that of conciliation of the existing interests. Through-out the many years of his presiding at the Admiralty, whilst he listened with the greatest interest to General Bentham's suggestions, and eagerly solicited him to point out abuses and mismanagement, he perceived that it was the system itself, and very rarely this or that individual that was at fault; it was, therefore, a reform of the system itself which Lord Spencer aimed at, as the only effectual remedy. It appeared to him that the Inspector-General's peculiar situation, together with the insight he had had from a boy into the business of a dockyard, rendered him especially competent to contrive a mode of management that should be effectual; but though his talents were acknowledged and appreciated, the Secretary of the Admiralty was associated with him in the business, in order to conciliate inferiors, and he wished the whole to be framed in a manner to injure as little as possible the existing servants of the Crown.

When the Earl of St. Vincent came to preside at the Admiralty, the widely different spirit of the new Administration was immediately evident. This may be accounted for by the mismanagement and abuses habitual in the dockyards, which frequently occasioned delays, disappointments, and useless expenses on board the ships and fleets that his Lordship had commanded, sometimes even sufficient to have put in jeopardy the success of an expedition. His Lordship and his Board had experienced the value of military discipline in bringing seamen to a strict performance of their duty, and it appeared to them that similar means might be adopted with equal efficacy in the civil branch of the navy. His Lordship, moreover, was continually urged to extreme measures by some of the sea Lords in the Board of Admiralty. That abuses did exist sufficient to excite the wrath of a conscientious Board, the few examples adduced in these pages would alone suffice to prove; but the correction of them was not likely to be effected by the frequent habitual use of such intemperate expressions as that the " master shipwrights ought all of them to be hanged." The specific abuse which gave rise to the Commission of Inquiry (namely, the retaining infirm men when past their work, in the dockyards, at the pay of the young and efficient artificers), was an abuse as well known to the Navy Board and to the Comptroller himself as it was to the master shipwrights. But it was in fact neither attributable to the dockyards, to the Navy Board, nor to the Comptroller; but it sprung from the system of management, for that system made no provision whatever for different rates of pa, so that a man after having spent his best years in the service, when at length his strength failed, would necessarily either be altogether discharged, or retained at the same pay as when in his full vigour. It could not be expected that the dockyards or the Navy Board should be so wanting in humanity as to dismiss a deserving artificer so long as he could, on any pretence, be continued on the books.

Of Lord St. Vincent's never ceasing endeavours for the real benefit of the service, the Inspector-General had frequent and convincing proofs. His Lordship's relinquishment of patronage evinced itself frequently, particularly in the appointments at the dockyards, and the introduction of the new regulations for timber. On that occasion neither his Lordship nor any of his Board patronised a single favourite; the best men were sought for and appointed, whether taken from private yards or already engaged in the royal ones.

The succeeding administration of Lord Melville was no less favourable to the Inspector-General than the preceding ones had been; and his various plans of improvement in ship building, manufacturing establishments, and engineering improvements in the dockyards, all were progressing satisfactorily, when the Tenth Eeport of the Committee of Inquiry appeared. The excitement which it produced occasioned a most unfortunate change, ending in defalcations from the measures that had been pursued for improvement and reform through three successive Naval Administrations. Lord Barham, now First Lord of the Admiralty, was known to be unfriendly to the Committee of Inquiry, and Lord Sidmouth has said (Life, vol. ii. p. 362) that " Lord Barnaul's opinions are adverse to those we have upheld."

The Board of Naval Eevision instituted at this time seems to have been decided on with a view to prevent such disclosures as had been elicited by the Committee of Enquiry, to veil abuses from the public eye, and to enable the civil service of the navy to "glide smoothly on in the beaten track which it had worn for itself."

There seems every reason to suppose that if General Bentham had been in this country at that time, and had had opportunity of stating facts to disprove unfounded allegations, no decision could have been come to which could have caused the abolition of his office. Indeed, from the first mention of the mission to Eussia, he could not but suppose that some covert motive in regard to himself personally had been in view. In a letter to Earl Spencer whilst a member of the administration, he says, "I cannot but sometimes suspect, considering the precipitation with which I was sent here, before the Emperor's leave was asked, that an anxious desire of removing me out of the way contributed not a little to heighten the advantages expected from my services at Archangel. I was somewhat confirmed in this suspicion b the expression of a man whose influence at the Admiralty was yery great, when with a most cordial shake of the hand, it came out, as it were unawares that 6 for his part, though he had the highest opinion of my talents and zeal, yet he would give his voice for allowing me at least six thousand a year if by that means he could be assured I w r ould never return again."

Besides the annoyance which the Navy Board felt at having been obliged to give reasons for what they recommended or objected to, there seems to have been very powerful private interest operating during his absence. It had become evident that in Bentham's office most important works had originated and were perfected without extraneous aid, so that the interests of the private engineer no less than of the contractor, w T ere materially affected. Advantage was taken of his absence to attack the metal mills; and as to engineering works, a plan had been brought forward during that time for the creation of a Naval Arsenal at Northfleet, similar to, and in place of that proposed by him in the Isle of Grain. By the adoption of the Northfleet plan, the private engineer and manufacturer of millwright's work could not have failed to derive immense pecuniary advantages. These interests, operating simultaneously and at a time when there were very frequent changes in the Naval Administration, may well account for the abolition of the Inspector-General's office recommended by the Committee of Inquiry.

On Bentham's return he was ignorant of the Grounds on which the Committee of Revision had based their recommendation as to his office, but in an interview with Lord Mulgrave, then presiding at the Admiralty, to use the words of General Bentham's letter to his Lordship 9th March, 1808, he "understood that the intention of abolishing my present office had not arisen from any doubts of the efficacy of it, but merely from the expectation that by incorporating me with the Navy Board, I should be able to continue my former pursuits with less opposition, and, therefore, with more advantage to the public service. This did not appear to me so certain." He, therefore, had requested to submit to his Lordship what appeared objectionable in the measure. General Bentham had then only seen the Fourth Eeport without its appendix– the only one of the Eeports that had been published without such an addition– but having obtained from the navy office the appendix also, to use again the words of that letter, "I saw that the abolition of my office was grounded altogether on the extract of a Eeport from the Navy Board, in which it w represented that the establishment of the office of Inspector-General of Navy Works had not produced any benefit to the service equivalent to the expense of it that he i(saw blame imputed either to me for having in-

REMARKS OX THE SUPPRESSION OF HIS OFFICE. 255 terfered in the business of the Navy Board " or to the Admiralty Board for having made use of me as their instrument in the investigation of business which it was their Lordships' duty to control, and when at the same time it did not appear that any one on the part of the Admiralty had been called upon to produce any documents, or even to give any opinion relative to the utility of this appendage to their own office." He observed in the same communication, that he felt it incumbent on him to make a statement on the subject more in detail than he had conceived would have been needed, when he first obtained permission to draw up such a paper; and added that necessary attention to the current business of his office, together with illness, had prevented his completing it; but having heard accidentally that the patent for the change was making out, he sent a part of his observations and requested some little delay for the remainder. They were accordingly submitted to the Admiralty on the 9th of March and 6th of June.

In these observations the services rendered by the Inspector-Greneral of Navy Works were noticed under their several heads, showing how impossible it would have been to have effected them, as a member of the Navy Board. He farther spoke of the improvements which he had introduced in naval architecture, and of the decided opposition he had had to encounter from the Dockyards and Navy Board, till at length experience had proved their efficiency. He also represented the strict individual responsibility under which the Inspector-Greneral of Navy Works proposed any measure, and brought to notice that by the Third Eeport of the Commissioners of Revision, it had not been intended to abolish the office of Inspector-Greneral of Navy Works, which, therefore, must have been an afterthought, perhaps on a supposition that he was not likely to return from Russia. He urged that of all branches of duty, that of a civil architect was the one for which his previous education and habits were least likely to have rendered him fit; whilst on the contrary he was to be altogether excluded from that duty, to which he had principal ty devoted himself from the period when his classical education was finished, and to which his studies had been particularly directed. No notice was ever taken of these papers, though on one occasion he was taunted by a Lord of the Admiralty with having had the education of a gentleman, previously to his having devoted himself to that of a shipwright.

But the abolition of the office had been determined on.

General Bentham for some time hesitated to accept the proffered seat at the Navy Board. He requested an interview with Lord Mulgrave, to ascertain what would be the pecuniary consequences to himself if he should refuse, and learnt that the retiring allowance intended to be granted would not be sufficient for the decent support of his family. He consulted his friend the Speaker; and having by his advice decided, though reluctantly, to accept a commis-sionership of the navy, on the 29th of August he communicated this determination by letter to Lord Mulgrave.

He accordingly took his seat. The members of the Board were individually friendly, whilst by the Board itself he was subjected to many petty annoyances. So far as these regarded himself, he would not suffer them to stand in competition with the public service; but he soon found that persons belonging to the office of the Inspector-Greneral of Navy Works, now transferred to the Navy Pay Office, were to be injured in their interests: and, in order to retain their assistance, he was under the necessity of remonstrating against the hardship under which his senior draughtsman, Mr. Heard, laboured, he being, by Admiralty order, to be placed as an assistant draughtsman, whilst his junior, Mr. Millar, was to be placed over his head.

General Bentham's time had been in great part engaged in investigating vexatious attacks on the manufacturing esta- blishments in Portsmouth dockyard. On the 6th January, in reply to Messrs. Taylor's assertion that they were fully satisfied that the block machinery would not do what was expected of it, General Bentham informed the Navy Board that, with the exception of a very few trifling obstacles before specified, the wood mills were able to furnish all the articles specified in the blockmaker's contract. So, on the 30th January, in answer to a statement "that the sheathing now manufactured at Portsmouth was of inferior quality to what had before been made there," he wrote to the Board that, on inquiry, he saw no reason for supposing it to be inferior to what it had been before, or that too much labour, as was asserted, had been required from the workmen; but added that if the Board would point out from what particular circumstances their apprehensions arose, he would make further inquiries. On the 9th of April he gave the Board a detailed account of the works completed for the supply of fresh water throughout Portsmouth yard and to the fleet, as also of the works for extinguishing fire.

The new navy patent, in which General Bentham's name was included, was not read at the Navy Board till the 7th December. The books of the office of Inspector-General of Navy Works were, by Admiralty order, removed to the Navy Office.

The General had never given a thought to use the title which was authorised by his Majesty's permission, or to wear in his own country the Cross of St. George. He was advised by his friends, particularly Lord St. Helens, to assume it on his removal to the Navy Board. It was at first intended that the First Lord of the Admiralty should present him anew to the King on his appointment, but it so happened that he was put off from time to time, and that it was not till 1809 that he went to Court, where he was received by his Sovereign as Sir Samuel Bentham, K. S. G.

There appear but few documents relative to the business of this year. Severe and long-continued illness of several members of his family prevented his wife from taking copies of official papers, and he had no longer even a single clerk at his disposal. It seems, however, that he was much occupied in considering the further introduction of machinery, and of various extensive plans of improvement of several naval arsenals, especially that of Portsmouth Harbour.

A letter received from his old friend General Fanshawe, acquainted him that the Panopticon at St. Petersburg " stood well, notwithstanding the shafts of envy," and that he had suggested the erection of a similar building for barracks.

The amount of compensation due to Mr. Brunei had engrossed a great portion of Sir Samuel's time. On the face of this business it might appear scarcely to justify the withdrawing so much of his attention from other matters, but collateral circumstances rendered his investigations of real importance, as it afforded proof of many of the oversights, if not abuses, frequent in making naval contracts. The machinery in question having been in full work by the year 1809, Mr. Brunei, on the 5th June, transmitted to the Navy Board calculations which he had made of the savings for one year, amounting to 21,174. 12s. 10d, The Admiralty had directed the Navy Board to consult General Bentham as to the best mode of estimating the savings made by the machinery for making blocks. The papers were referred to him. He put them into the hands of Mr. Rogers, afterwards a clerk in the Secretary's Office, who after office hours went into various elaborate calculations, which made it appear that, supposing the prices for blocks to be those at which they were contracted for with Mr. Dunsterville, the savings would amount to no more than 6691. 7s. 5L, whereas, according to a calculation based upon the prices paid to another contractor, Mr,

Taylor, the savings would amount to 12,742. 8s. 2d. This discrepancy in the results naturally led Sir Samuel to look into particulars, and the more he entered into them the more further investigation appeared essential. He therefore "went into every possible detail of expense that could have been expected in a private manufacturing concern; whereas Mr. Brunei and Mr. Rogers had both of them set down various items at an estimated amount."

There were, however, circumstances attending this case which rendered it a business of peculiar difficulty. It had been pointed out to him that the savings produced by his own machines, taken from Queen-square Place, were considerable, and that as they were of his invention, not of Mr. Brunei's, the savings made by them ought not to be included in his remuneration. But Mr. Brunei had entered so fully into the General's ideas, and seconded him so ably in the selection of workpeople, that he considered him as deserving some remuneration for the trouble he took in forwarding his views in regard to the general management. He determined, therefore, to base his calculation of savings on the ground of what it had cost to provide blocks and blockmakers' wares in the wood mills, compared with what it would have cost Government to have obtained the same quantity of these stores by contract.

As far as related to the outgoings of the manufactory, the accounts kept of them being in form as simple as they were correct in particulars, the amount under each head was easily calculated; but it was far otherwise with the sums for obtaining blocks and wares by contract. There had been two contractors, Taylor and Dunsterville, and the prices allowed to Taylor were nearly double of those allowed to Dunsterville. To complicate the matter, there were percentages one upon another that had been authorised by the Naval Board as additions to the original contract price; whilst in abatement of the contractors' profits, different naval office fees were to be deducted from the

sums paid them. Sir Samuel took the trouble to examine the quantities that had been actually received from each of those contractors, and in calculating savings from the block machinery, reckoned a quantity equal to that taken from Taylor, at Taylor's prices, a quantity equal to that from Dunsterville, at Dunsterville's prices, deducting in both cases fees: thus the result of his calculation was the amount of saving that had really been made by manufacturing blocks on Government account, which was the sum of 16, 6211. 8 s. 10c. for one year.

It was not till the 25th of July that Sir Samuel was enabled to present his Eeport to his Board. He stated that the difference between the 16,621. 8s. 10t., the 21,174. 12s. 10c?. of Mr. Brunei, and of the two sums of Mr. Eogers, 6691. 7s. 4d and 12,742. 8s. 2d, might well be accounted for by the circumstance of his having gone into every possible detail of expense, whereas those gentlemen had both of them set down various items of an estimated amount only.

Mr. Brunei's statement having been for a sum so much exceeding even Sir. Samuel's, it seems but justice to him to insert an article of his journal, 18th March, 1810:–"At work all day on Brunei's accounts; find that he has made out his with every appearance of the fairest, most honourable intentions; he has given lumping sums ajainst himself, but has taken no advantage without stating it. Eogers has made some omissions and wrong charges both for and against Brunei."

Sir Samuel's accounts given to the Board showed that the capital sunk for buildings and machinery had been so far liquidated, that the remaining outstanding debt (exclusive of Mr. Brunei's remuneration) would be paid off by the next October; that including that remuneration, the whole cost of the block manufactory would be liquidated in October of the following year; the principal and interest, and all attendant expenses, having then been paid by the profits of the concern. Besides this liquidation, the sum of 8732. 0s. 9cl. had already accumulated by the reserve of 51. per cent, to compensate for wear and tear and chance of disuse.

The Navy Board transmitted Sir Samuel's statement on the 14th of August to the Admiralty, who, on the 18th instant, ordered that it should be adopted, and Mr. Brunei's remuneration paid to him accordingly.

This matter has been entered into so minutely as exhibiting a variety of particulars rarely attended to, or thought practicable, in Government concerns; whereas, on the contrary, they are such as ought constantly to be kept in view, and rigorously acted on.

These investigations proved that the Navy Board, in this instance, as in so many others, were unobservant of the sums they were giving by contract over what the same articles might have been obtained for from even another of their own contractors; for by far the greater part of Mr. Taylor's blocks and blockmakers' wares were double the price of Mr. Dunsterville's.

As long ago as Nov. 1799, Bentham had proposed and given a rough plan for a canal from Portsmouth Harbour to Stokes Bay, so as to enable ships to come into harbour under whatever wind; which was either to be confined to the width necessary for the passage of a ship of the line of the largest dimensions, that is, 130 feet wide at the surface, and 34 feet at the deepest part; or to be of sufficient width to allow of a first-rate sailing through it. In either case such a canal would have provided for the entrance into the harbour of ships of the very deepest draught of water, whereas now those drawing more than twenty-two feet are of necessity sent for repairs to Plymouth. The estimate for digging the narrower canal was 50,000., for the wider one of double the area 100,000.; but as Sir Samuel had devised a digging apparatus, to be worked by steam, the real cost of this part of the work

S 3 would have been muchbelow the estimate. This apparatus was to have been on a floating vessel, and in many-respects analogous to the steam dredging machine, but so contrived as that it should dig the dry ground before it and make its way as it advanced, floating still onwards and onwards A triple lock was contrived for each end of the canal, the middle lock for ships of the larger classes, a smaller lock on each side of it, one for small vessels, the other for boats. These locks, with pier-heads and walls of masonry, averaging twelve feet in thickness, were estimated each at 50,000. There would thus have been obtained, besides access to the harbour for the largest ships, a basin subservient to use for such petty repairs as are done afloat, instead of sending artificers and stores to Spithead, while the whole would have afforded most desirable means for the embarkation of troops, and in time of peace the means of laying up a fleet. This canal also would have been applicable as an immense sluice which, with turnwaters and other appropriate works, would not have failed to deepen the harbour itself and its entrance. It is true that the later invention and use of steam tugs has diminished the need for such a work; yet the many collateral advantages of it, and especially the great extent of basin afforded by it, seem to render it still an object worthy consideration.

On Nov. 26th, 1811, Bentham recalled to the recollection of the Board that he had several times mentioned, whilst at the dockyards in the summer of 1810, that the building ships on steps as hitherto practised seemed to him altogether objectionable. He now recapitulated his principal reasons for this opinion, such as the exposure of the materials to the weather, the exposure of the artificers, the impossibility of carrying on the work even in the shortest days of winter for any longer time than the few hours of daylight, the expenses of launching, and, finally, the injury done to a ship by the disconnection more or less of its parts, as shown by the breaking of the ship in launching, which has always taken place in a greater or less degree.

He had considered various modes of forming receptacles for building ships, and after examination of those in other countries he was satisfied that the most suitable would be shallow docks, covered over, lighted by proper windows by day, by gaslights, or otherwise, by night, so that work might be carried on in them at all times and seasons, the same as in other well-constructed workshops; and that these same covered docks would also be the most eligible receptacles for the repair of ships.

With assistance which he provided at his own cost, his plans were made out, amongst other important works, for the construction of covered docks and seasoning houses, including convenient arrangements for the performance of all those works subservient to the building or great repairs of ships which should be carried on by their side, and be aided by mechanical contrivance for saving labour and expense.

In regard to expedition, he felt assured that, the timber having been previously duly seasoned, a first-rate vessel might from its first commencement be completed in even less than six months; or supposing a double set of artificers to be employed, in the short space of three months.

He afterwards stated, in 1813, that the merit of this particular species of accommodation had lately been claimed by several persons; that coverings of some kind for docks had in fact been proposed and even used at times at least as far back as the year 1776, but those coverings had been nothing more than sheds, that is, roofs extending over the slips, but not closed, in at the sides or ends, excepting that some of those that had been proposed since his drawings had been sent in, had had the addition of wooden shutters at the sides. These, therefore, even including the covered docks in the magnificent naval arsenal at Carlscrona, s 4 were either open to the weather at the sides, or the light had been excluded in as far as they had been closed, and all of them were open at the stern. Since the time of sending in his plans, the covering of docks and slips had been very extensively recommended by the Naval Board, and he added that he could not entertain a doubt but that, in all essential peculiarities, those plans of his would be adopted, such as perfect protection from the weather, daylight in abundance, means of heating, warming, ventilating, and artificial lighting at pleasure.

As an important appendage to a covered dock, he contrived timber-seasoning houses. It has been seen that the seasoning and treating timber in different ways, with a view to its preservation, had been objects of inquiry and study even from the first of his investigations in Holland, in the year 1797. On the occasion of reference to him of a proposal for seasoning timber by means of lime, he recommended a trial of that expedient. No experiments were however authorised, but at different times he took advantage of such means as opportunities presented to make trials of the sort;– such as at Plymouth through Mr. Jenner, by the impregnation of wood with oil, to protect it from worms; and in 1805, he caused a cellar of the wood mills to be employed as a seasoning-house, where a course of experiments was commenced by drying wood artificially, by steaming it, by impregnating it with the acid from wood shavings whilst burning, andc; but which experiments were put a stop to by his being sent away to Russia. In 1811, when the destruction of ships of war by the dry rot was so prevalent, he brought to view a variety of important facts relative to the ventilation of ships, and to the preservation of the timber of which they are built.

On the 13th September, his minute stated that he had known the progress of dry rot stopped by thoroughly impregnating the infected parts of wood with a solution of sulphate of iron; and that Dr. Hales had long ago recommended a solution of sulphate of copper with a view to preserve timber, and to protect it from worms.

On the 6th March, 1812, he transmitted to the Navy Board his design for a timber-seasoning house, and prefaced his description of it with the best and fullest account that has (it is believed) ever appeared of instances exemplifying the durability of timber, of the circumstances under which it had proved of long duration, and of various means used for its seasoning and preservation. He instanced Westminster Hall and Abbey, and a number of cathedrals, churches, and old mansions, as affording examples where timber used in constructions on land had remained perfect for many centuries, and the Koyal George as an example even of timber in ships lasting for near a century. On the other hand, of late, when dry rot had taken place, there were instances where the woodwork in buildings on land had fallen to pieces in the course of a twelvemonth, and in ships, within a year or two after their construction was completed.

In instances where the duration of timber for centuries has been unquestionable, it is well known that no preparation was used except that it had been cut down long enough for the natural moisture to have been in a great degree dried away. He instanced the means by which this is usually effected, by piling deals and other small pieces in the open air; and in regard to large timber, by leaving it for years with the bark on, when, that having rotted away, the interior parts of the log have been found to become compact, hard, and dry, with little or no cracking of the timber itself. On the contrary, where timber has been sided, that is, some of the outside of the timber cut off, the outside of such pieces has been found more or less cracked before the inside had been sufficiently seasoned.

The best mode hitherto in use for seasoning timber was leaving it, with the bark on, in the open air, whereby the perfectly formed wood has been protected from the immediate action of the sun and air, and the drying away of the juices from the whole has proceeded so gradually and uniformly as not to cause any cracking or separation of the fibres. But this mode requires a greater length of time than the supply of timber to the royal dockyards has provided for, or can be expected in the case of any private builder. From this might well have arisen the short duration of some ships of war of late years, while the different degrees of duration in different ships were likely to have arisen from various causes of greater or less wet in them. He then particularised some of the expedients which had been tried, such as, in warm countries, covering the timber with sand, so that the moisture might dry gradually away.

Artificial heat had, previously, been successfully applied by manufacturers and others for drying boards and other pieces of small scantling. In Russia, boards and wood cut into small scantlings are suspended in workshops always much heated in winter and very little ventilated. From all the opportunities which he had had of examining the state of timber so prepared, the due seasoning without cracking has appeared to depend on the ventilation having happened to be constant, but very slow, joined to such a due regulation of the heat as that the interior of the timber should dry and keep pace with the outer circles in its contraction. The only instance in which he had seen an apparatus constructed purposely for seasoning timber by artificial heat was at the great cotton manufactory of Messrs. Strutt at Belper, whose planks and deals w T ere seasoned without injury, and in a short space of time, by due ventilation and heat. Under some circumstances a heat even greater than that of boiling water can be applied in a close kiln, as in the instance of steaming planks and thickstuff. It was, therefore, on the providing means of applying heat so as to vary it suitably to different kinds of timber, and to the different states and stages of its seasoning, and on the regulation at pleasure of the admission of dry air, that his expectations were grounded, of deriving advantages from the use of the seasoning-houses which he proposed

The estimate for the seasoning-house was 5929. 10s. To set against that expenditure over and above insuring the most perfect seasoning of the timber, would be the interest of the capital lying dead during seasoning of the timber in the common way Supposing only three ears to be required in that common mode, and 45,000. the value of the timber (at a price less than the then current one), the compound interest upon that sum for three years would be upwards of 7186.; whereas, as he had reason to think that the timber would in three months be perfectly seasoned in one of these houses, the interest on the 45,000?. for that time would be 5621. 10s., that on the capital sunk for the seasoning-house, 74. 2s. 4c.; wear and tear upon it at 5 per cent., 74. 2s. 4c.; supposing 500 tons of water to be evaporated, and half a chaldron of coals consumed per ton (a quantity greater than he knew from experiment to be requisite), the value of the coals would, at 52s. per chaldron, be 650. The total greatest expense, therefore, 1360., leaving a balance upon every 3000 loads of timber of 5826.; and supposing the house to be charged only three times in the year, the annual saving by one of these houses would be 17,478., so that the capital sunk for its erection would be refunded in less than half a year, after which a clear annual saving would be effected of 17,000. by one only of these seasoning houses.

Works at Sheerness dockyard have not as yet been noticed, because it appeared desirable to give a connected instead of yearly statement in regard to them. This dockyard is situated, in some respects, advantageously for the repair of ships coming in from the eastward, but certain winds (and those which commonly prevail) are unfavourable to its approach. The works at this arsenal, as they existed at the end of the last century, were on too small a scale to afford means of repairing within the yard any other vessels than those of the smaller classes: those works themselves were fast wearing out. Sir Samuel was satisfied of the incompetency of those to the eastward for the repairs of large ships, for excepting at Chatham there were no means of effecting what are denominated great repairs: so that ships stationed to the eastward, frequent as was their need of small repairs, could not obtain them at a nearer yard than Portsmouth. This port, so distant from their station, was sometimes attained with difficulty and danger, always with delay and consequent needless expense. He therefore so early as 1799 suggested, in letters to Earl Spencer, the expediency of giving up Deptford dockyard, and of providing a new, complete system of naval establishments in the Isle of Grain, including a basin for laying up ships, particularly large ones.

In his conferences with Earls Spencer and St. Vincent, he did not fail to represent the advantages that would result from such an arsenal as conducive to the speedy repair and outfit of our fleets. Lord St. Vincent's own observations as a naval commander convinced him of the correctness of these views, so that he was prepared, on his visitation in 1802 to the eastern yards, to consider the proposal on the spot. On that occasion his Lordship examined with great attention that part of the Isle of Grain which had been pointed out as an eligible site for a new naval arsenal. His opinion, and that of the other Lords of the Admiralty then on visitation, was so favourable to Sir Samuel's proposal, that they caused an account of some of his reasons for forming such an arsenal to be recorded in his very words in the " minutes of visitation."

It happened that during this and the succeeding Naval Administration, General Bentham's occupations were such as to engross the whole of his attention, without reference to the new arsenal, otherwise than in so far as the introduction of extensive machinery for manufacturing purposes was subservient to the improvements which he contemplated for it. As previously noticed, whilst he was actively pursuing improvements in the western yards, he was early in Lord Barham's administration sent to Eussia.

During the few days Sir Samuel was in town previously to his departure, he could not but suspect that some sinister views had led to this measure. Soon after he left England the Commission of Naval Eevision was instituted, to all appearance with a view to stop the inquiries of the Commission of Naval Inquiry. At the same time members of the Naval Board dreaded that the really responsible, and consequently efficient, management which late Admiralty Boards had been disposed to introduce should now be carried into effect. It was notorious that in Earl Spencer's administration Sir Samuel was the man who had had the courage to point out numberless instances of mismanagement, and that he had devised means for the future prevention of it; that his endeavours were likely to succeed, and the Naval Board could not but surmise that their own duties would come to be clearly defined; that each member would be made responsible for the business assigned to each individually, and thus their duty would become real labour.

On Sir Samuel Bentham's return from Eussia nothing further passed to his knowledge either in regard to North-fleet or to Sheerness, until the 19th January, 1808: when the Admiralty directed him to send assistants in his department (still that of Inspector-General of Naval Works) to examine the damages sustained at Sheerness by the high tide and tremendous gale of the 14th. On the 30th he acquainted their Lordships that the injury done to the wharves there did not appear so great as was supposed: but he added that the wharf walls were in a state of general decay, and pointed out various means by which their reparation could be effected. The mischief done to the wharf during the late gale had been occasioned principally by the rolling of the waves over it, and thus washing away the ground from behind. On consulting with the Commissioners of Dockyards, it appeared that an old ship might be advantageously grounded as a breakwater.

Sir Samuel had consulted the Commissioners of Dockyards with several experienced pilots and others, before he had made up his mind as to the effects likely to be produced by sinking the old ship; and all of them had agreed that no mischief would ensue. It can hardly be doubted that Mr. Eennie had the same motives for representing that Sir Samuel would do mischief at Sheerness, as had lately induced him (as afterwards appeared) to give their Lordships to understand that the mischief done at Woolwich by an improper projection of a wharf, had been consequent on the adoption of a plan of Sir Samuel's, when the fact was that he had not had the least concern in that work, or even the slightest knowledge of it.

By their Lordships' letter of 3rd September it seemed evident that Messrs. Eennie and Whidbey had represented the dockyard as being in a state of general dilapidation and inefficiency. No particulars of this report were communicated to Sir Samuel, but he was directed to examine the general condition of the dockyard, to " prepare a plan for making good the general defects thereof, with such alterations and improvements with respect to convenience, but ivithout any extension of the works, as the state of repairs might in his judgment justify."

On the 30th October he submitted his ideas respecting the remedying the defects of the works, and the altera- tions and improvements which the state of them would justify under their Lordships' restrictions. As to the buildings, wharves, and docks, he considered that though there were but few that did not show some tokens of decay, yet there were scarcely any that were not likely to remain for several years as fit for use as they ever had been.

He deprecated the building or great repairs of ships at Sheerness, because that was the only port to the eastward where they could come for repairs which, though small, were essential; but he recommended the increase of the number of dockyards, so that a ship might be taken in for moderate repairsttrt order to employ artificers when there was no press of business.

Their Lordships, without waiting for the report which they had directed Sir Samuel Bentham to furnish, gave their orders to the Naval Board to cause a river wall to be constructed under his superintendence, but according to a line which had been given by Messrs. Eennie and Whidbey.

When the Naval Board, on the 17th December, requested General Bentham to inform them of the particulars of the timber required for the new line of wall, he stated the impossibility of furnishing them until their Lordships should have come to a decision on the kind of material of which the wall was to be composed. The Navy Board, therefore, applied to the Admiralty, and were by them authorised to fix on the materials themselves. On this occasion they were further directed to give Sir Samuel, now of the Navy Board, a full opportunity of considering all that had been written by Messrs. Eennie and Whidbey on this subject, as also the plans and estimates of Mr. Eennie for the improvement of the dockyard at Sheerness; and they were then to come to a decision on the best plan for its improvement, and transmit the same for their Lordships' consideration.

On the 28th the Board decided that the wall should be of stone, and Sir Samuel, on consideration of the badness of the ground in so far as it was known, thought it absolutely necessary that experiments should be instituted to ascertain the weight it would really bear. As the ordinary mode of probing for this purpose did not seem satisfactory, he devised the plan of spreading a considerable surface of timber on the ground and weighting it. The ground was found soft to so great a depth in the line of the intended wall, that in their report they recommended carrying the line back to where the subsoil was trustworthy, and projecting from it a wharf supported on hollow cast-iron piles. As Sir Samuel approved of this, the Navy Board recommended it to the Admiralty, who on the 15th of May ordered it to be carried into execution.

The work was begun at the end where no difficulty existed, and was carried on as far as where the foundation needed to be but two or three feet under low-water mark. At this juncture it appeared that new apparatus would be required for levelling the ground. He had various expedients in view, by means of which he foresaw that he could obviate the difficulties, and still more the enormous expense, of carrying on works in the usual way, where piles of fifty or sixty feet long would have been required; but not having any assistant but Mr. Goodrich who possessed the requisite scientific knowledge, he proposed that a duly qualified person should be engaged to superintend the works at Sheerness. Although this was denied him, and although he had no adequate assistance afforded him even for ordinary business, he resolved to struggle on to the utmost. The Navy Board, on their part, convinced of the inadequacy of his establishment, rendered him some assistance by permitting the engagement of a working mason; and this man, so long as the Sheerness wall had its foundation but little below low-water mark, proved very useful.

As the time approached when the wall must be con- structed in deep water, and where the foundation would be laid on mud and a quicksand to a considerable depth, it was evident that no ordinary mode of construction could be adopted but at an enormous expense. He could not hear of, nor had he seen either in this country or on the Continent, any example of such a work executed otherwise than under cover of a dam, or in caissons of wood. The latter of these modes, besides being costly, was objectionable, on account of the perishable nature of the wooden case. Various expedients presented themselves to his fertile mind. But before finally determining on any mode, he thought it incumbent on him to examine, in as far as time permitted, the most important works that had been executed on the south-east coast. Accordingly, in August 1810, he combined this object with that of examining the capabilities of various places on the south-eastern and southern coast for becoming harbours of refuge; and at the same time he wished to demonstrate the impolicy of sinking any considerable sum on the repairs of Sheerness dockyard, objectionable as it was on account of its situation in regard to prevailing winds and other drawbacks. On this account he proceeded to examine and consider whether it might not be more eligible to adopt the idea of an arsenal at Northfleet, since the Isle of Grain had been so unfortunately rejected.

Northfleet, it is true, appeared to have been already given up by the Admiralty, since in March of that year the Navy Board had orders to let the land which they had purchased there. Sir Samuel having applied for a sight of the plan for the projected arsenal, the Comptroller assured him that the Navy Board had it not; that they knew nothing of it officially. Sir Samuel had perused, with interest, various pamphlets published in regard to it. He had strenuously advocated, as has been seen, the construction of a naval arsenal "somewhere north of the Forelands;" and although he had pointed out the long-thought-

of site, the Isle of Grain, he was not wedded to it, and would certainly as willingly have advocated any other one, if equally eligible in regard to the most important points. On this tour, therefore, his first visit was to Northfleet, where he found that the depth of water was sufficient, and that the place was well protected from wind. But, on the other hand, the valley appeared difficult to fortify, and he had lately received unquestionable information, based on boring operations carried on at both places, that the ground there was quite as bad as that at Sheerness.

On the 5th July Sir Samuel, in conversation with Mr. Yorke, the First Lord of the Admiralty, directed his notice to several of his official papers which proved the expediency of forming a new naval arsenal to the eastward. In a pamphlet, then just published, advocating the construction of that proposed at Northfleet, the author, after adducing the opinions of two former First Lords, the Earl of Egmont and Lord Howe, in favour of a dockyard at the Isle of Grain, introduces supposititious addresses from Earl Spencer and the Earl of St. Vincent, in both of which the very words of Sir Samuel's official letters are made use of in long quotations as arguments in favour of such an establishment, without, indeed, naming him; and the pamphlet led, besides, to the supposition that the question at that period had originated in their Lordships, instead of, as was the fact, with the then Inspector-General. He had never seen reason to depart from the opinions he had stated in regard to all the eastern dockyards, and therefore could not but feel great reluctamv on this occasion in being made an instrument of sinking such vast sums at Sheerness, a place which after all would have the irremediable disadvantage of "being on the wrong side of the harbourwith respect to prevailing winds."

His inspection of Northfleet again led him to revert to the Isle of Grain as a far preferable site. It is not even

Naval Considerations relative to the Const ruction of a New Naval Arsenal at Northfleet Ridgway, 1810.

at this day useless to recall the subject, although many millions of money have been sunk at Sheerness; for in case of war, our fleets acting in the north and east seas would still be subject to all the former inconvenience, expense, and delays from the want of any arsenal nearer than Portsmouth. It may, therefore, be worth while to relate the comparative advantages and disadvantages of the two sites as appear by Sir Samuel's papers.

As the borings at the Isle of Grain showed that the execution of works close to the water's edge would be attended with expense, the Earl of St. Vincent refrained from authorising the work, the financial state of the country (1802) being such as barely to admit of the armament by sea and by land which our political situation as to France urgently required. But this difficulty in regard to soil existed equally by the waterside at Northfleet; whilst at some little distance inward, the soil of Grain is as favourable as could be wished.

The imhealthiness of Grain has been spoken of as decidedly adverse to that site. But the canal which Sir Samuel proposed would, at the same time that it formed an important feature of the new arsenal, have drained the low land effectually. Thus, were it only on the score of giving a large tract of country to agricultural purposes, and health to what would become a numerous population, the canal would have been esteemed a public benefit. In point of fact, Grain in its then state was not more unhealthy than Sheerness and its surrounding marshes. The disfavour brought on the island by Mr. Bunce's death was unfortunate. His predisposition to disease, occasioned by excess of both bodily and mental labour, was never taken into account by those who adduced it as the ground for rejecting Grain. Examples abound of marshland, when drained, becoming healthy.

As to prevailing winds, the Isle of Grain and Northfleet are under precisely the same circumstances; but under

T 2 adverse winds, a vessel could make the Isle of Grain immediately when coming in from sea; whilst it would still have to beat up the Thames for many miles, especially through the long reach of the Hope, before it could make Northfleet.

As to fortification, the high ground in the Isle of Grain would afford a commanding central spot from whence the works of the intended arsenal could be protected; while, on the contrary, Northfleet is commanded by high ground of great extent, and difficult of fortification. The distance from the stronghold of Chatham is about the same for both; but the water communication is greatly in favour of Grain. The military protection most to be depended on for a naval arsenal, may some day come to be looked for by Government as Sir Samuel viewed it, namely, in naval, not land defences, since vessels of war, particularly of light draught of water, duly armed with heavy ordnance, having the great advantage of locomotion, can at any time be brought to any threatened spot. The Isle of Grain could be, as it were, surrounded by a belt of floating fortifications in case of danger.

The Isle of Grain has also the advantage of a double water route for supplies and succour,–by the Medway from the interior of the country, through which that river runs,– by the Thames for communication with the Metropolis; and to this must be added land communication with the interior of the country, and above all the immediate one by sea.

On the 7th and 8th August,1810, Sir Samuel was engaged at Chatham with a Committee of the Navy Board, who had been directed to give their decided opinion on several plans which had been proposed in regard to Sheerness, by Messrs. Kennie and Whidbey and by Sir Samuel respectively. On the 9th this Committee made their report to the Navy Board.

The Committee state that " the line of the river wall in front of the dockyard, following the course of the current, as described in the plan submitted by Sir Samuel Bentham, is that which in our opinion should be adopted." They next state that Messrs. Eennie and Whidbey, on account of the badness of the soil, speak of the limitation of the dockyard to the repair of the largest frigate, or even a 74-gun ship; whilst Sir Samuel Bentham pointed out the expediency of extending the use of the dockyard to the reparation and outfit of ships of the line of the largest dimensions, and that, to effect this purpose, the only additional work which he proposed was to extend the length and breadth of the docks. As to the requisite depth of water, instead of sinking the foundations, he proposed to raise the water in the basin by means of a steam engine, as practised in Portsmouth dockyard. " Considering, therefore, all the circumstances attendant on the two plans, we have no hesitation in recommending the adoption of that proposed by the civil architect and engineer, excepting in the instances hereafter particularised."

On August 30th, the Comptroller acquainted him that the Board had come to a decision in regard to Sheerness. On September 3rd, he received intimation from the Board that the Admiralty had given directions to carry into execution certain of the works proposed, and to consider and report on others of them; that therefore his presence in town was desired to confer with the Board on the subject. He accordingly went to London, returning again shortly to Portsmouth, where he was then occupied in designing machinery for Sheerness yard, intended to be driven by steam and used in crushing stone for Eoman cement.

Sir Samuel continued his investigations as to the different modes for executing works under water in situations and on subsoils of mud analogous to that at Sheerness, from which it appeared that no other mode of construction offered advantages superior to the one which he had devised.

He determined to form the wall of hollow masses of

T 3 brickwork twenty-one feet square: a bottom was formed of old ship timber, and upon this an inverted arch of brick was built, and sides of brick were then built upon the arch, the whole being set in Eoman cement, until a sufficient height was attained to give buoyancy to the hollow mass. The first was built in a dock, but subsequently this accommodation was found needless. Diagonal walls were constructed in the angles to afford strength. The mass, when capable of being floated off, was navigated to its intended place; when there, the walls were heightened, and the lower part added to in thickness, some shingle, set in grout, being thrown into the lower part. "When the whole had been by degrees made to sink till it reached the muddy bottom, and the walls carried up to nearly high water-mark, a loaded vessel was then brought over the mass. As the tide fell, of course the weight rested on the mass, and pressed it down into the mud till it rested on the solid substratum of clay.

In the autumn of 1810 Sir Samuel's minute was given to the Board, stating it to be desirable that the Admiralty should be acquainted with the success which had attended the fresh-water well at Sheerness, which he had designed with appropriate pump and machinery. He stated from precise data that 180 tons of water were raised from it in ten hours. The fleet has been able to obtain all required supplies of water from this well, instead of from boats bringing it from Chatham, as heretofore. On the 21st February he proposed, in order to store a quantity of water for the supply of any casual extra demand, that a reservoir should be formed capable of containing about 1000 tons.

In 1811 Sir Samuel established himself for a time in the neighbourhood of Sheerness, taking with him his family, who rendered him assistance as clerks, and made for him the drawings he required.

Not long afterwards, the Navy Board acquainted him that they had received their Lordships' orders to state what had been done in consequence of their order of the 12th October, as to settling with the Ordnance respecting workshops at Sheerness, and that their Lordships had signified " that they understood in forming the sea-wall at that place it is intended to adopt the plan of sinking caissons, instead of the usual mode of driving piles, and directed us to report to them whether any estimate of the expense, and probable success of the two modes, has been made," In his reply to the Board, he gave a plain answer to each of the questions proposed; but at the same time, roused by the injustice of insinuations that had been made to his prejudice, he adverted to the many successful works which he had caused to be executed as a reason why in this instance he might be trusted. He added, "I cannot therefore but experience on the occasion of this misrepresentation the same sentiments of surprise and regret which, while with the Committee here last summer, in the presence of the Fust Lord of the Admiralty, I expressed to Sir Joseph Yorke, on the occasion when he spoke of the injudicious works in Woolwich yard as being mine; and when, on my assuring him that I had had no part either in the planning or the execution of them, he replied, that at least they were attributed to me, and expressed in consequence his apprehension that I was about c to spoil this dockyard as I had already spoilt that of Woolwich?

The mischief done at Woolwich had been by the injudicious projection of a wall into the Thames, by which the current being obstructed in front of the dockyard, an enormous quantity of mud was deposited in front of it, where the wall occasioned still water.

Sir Samuel then stated that in fact the mode in which he intended to proceed was, to the best of his knowledge, entirely new, and that it was more analogous to the principle on which security is obtained by driving piles, than it is to the building in caissons.

He explained the construction of his hollow masses of t 4 brickwork, showing that each mass could be considered in fact as an immense pile– a pile of twenty-one feet instead of a foot or two– of masonry instead of wood– driven down by weight instead of by percussion.

As to the estimate of the expense of his mode compared to that of driving piles, he trusted that in a fortnight he should be enabled to lay before the Board an estimate grounded on the expenses that shall have been " actually incurred in forming the foundation of one portion of the wall."

In the mean time, to lessen apprehensions in regard to the expense or the probable success of his plans, he requested them to bear in mind that he had already to their knowledge on many occasions caused the usual modes of construction to be departed from, when saving of expense had been always one of the objects which he had had in view, and that in every instance a real saving had been the result.

On the 15th April, 1811, he acquainted the Board that the first mass was completed and ready to be floated to its place, and sent a short description of this new mode of construction, with an estimate of the expense of a wall so formed, and a drawing exemplifying it.

On the 16th he acquainted the Board that the first mass had been the preceding day successfully floated off and in its place. At the same time he noticed that the urgency of the Admiralty for the speedy progress of the works at Sheer-ness had induced him to construct and deposit this first mass under several circumstances adverse to success– circumstances which, however, would only be considered as proof of the eligibility of the invention.

He had flattered himself with the hope of encouragement; instead of which on the 25th he received through the Navy Board a letter from Mr. Barrow communicating their Lordships' displeasure in terms particularly galling. Still he determined to persevere.

It appears that Commissioner Brown, the Resident Commissioner at Sheerness, having waited on Mr. Yorke (the First Lord) about this time, had had discussions with him as to Sir Samuel, and had seen reason to vindicate his conduct forcibly, though ineffectually.

Bentham had remarked in the late Admiralty letter the contemptuous expression, " as he calls it" twice used in speaking of his invention of the hollow masses. The cause of this expression now came to light. His assistant, Mr. Hull, had said at the Navy Office that this was no invention of Sir Samuel's, and that it had been practised by Mr. Rennie at Great Grimsby. The statement was incorrect, as appears from his letter to his superior, 3rd October, 1810, in which he wrote as follows: "Mr. Kingston returned to the office this morning, after having visited the following places, Hull, Grimsby, York, Leeds, and from thence Spalding and Deeping, but he requests me to say he found nothing in any of the ivories ivhich have been carried on at any of these places that is in the least similar to those ivhich are to be carried on at Sheerness, but that the whole have been carried on nearly similar to the London and West India Docks, under cover of deems, and the walls set-on piles or planks."

Sir Samuel, hereupon, with the knowledge and approbation of his Board, directed Mr. Goodrich, the machinist, to proceed to Great Grimsby to examine and report on the manner in which the works there had been erected. In his letter dated from thence, 23rd May, 1811, he says, "In regard to the works of the dock here, there has been nothing in the mode of carrying on the foundations analogous to the mode you are pursuing at Sheerness," and afterwards, " great difficulties and many failures appear to have been experienced in forming the walls and bottom of the dock, with a little wharfage beyond the lock in the basin; but the whole was formed under cover of a dam made across what is now the entrance into the lock, the piles being driven down to a solid foundation of chalk rock."

Various impediments were found to occur in levelling the foundation of the wall by Sir Samuel's dredging machine. But the engine worked well in twenty-six feet water; and Mr. Goodrich, by skilfully employing harpoons, grapnels, and an 8-cwt. anchor with a sharpened fluke, rendered its operation very effective. Experience was being gained also in the navigation of the hollow masses, which were floated by one tide, without the aid of the vessels that were at first used alongside, to a convenient seat for them to rest on, till a subsequent tide should serve for conveying them to their final destination.

The Admiralty, on the 27th September, 1811, having directed the Navy Board to furnish them with various particulars respecting the new wharf wall, Sir Samuel, 8th October, acquainted the Board–that in regard to expense (according to an estimate grounded on the expenditure hitherto actually incurred for materials, workmanship, and contingencies) in carrying up above 100 feet of the wall to low water-mark, at an average depth of 21 feet, it would be 21 l. 7 s. per foot forward; and supposing the part above low water to be 22 feet high, with a moorstone facing, a length of 197 feet was estimated at nearly 5000., so that the whole wall of the average height of 43 feet would be at the rate of 47. per foot forward; whilst according to the estimate of Messrs.

Eennie and Whidbey, the wall proposed was by their estimate at the rate of 19 1. per foot forward. The expense of Sir Samuel's mode was therefore less than a fourth of that of those gentlemen; and this, although their wall for a considerable length had its foundation but little below low-water mark and upon a natural foundation that was unexceptionable, whilst Sir Samuel's was on an average of the whole length no less than 21 feet below low water, the ground under it being everywhere of the worst.

It was at this time, too, that the influence obtained at the Admiralty by Messrs. Eennie and Whidbey became apparent in regard to another work, the pier and breakwater in Plymouth Sound,–a work which from its magnitude, its immense cost, and its imposing appearance, is held high in general estimation– so highly, indeed, that at this day it may seem folly to bring to notice Sir Samuel's official representations in regard to it: but in this, as in other of the transactions of his life, the public will, it may be hoped, eventually give him credit for his endeavours to serve them no less where his representations failed, than in the many others wherein they were attended with success.

In regard to Plymouth Sound, Sir Samuel had for many years back at various times entertained the idea that some kind of breakwater might be constructed to protect it. He had, however, been deterred from prosecuting any such idea in consequence of information obtained at Plymouth, that, so far as he could learn, not any one ship of the line had ever been lost in the Sound, and that none were injured or were even more liable to injury than in any other good roadstead–Spithead for example– although in the Sound the waves are long and deep, whilst at Spithead the sea is short. He learnt, indeed, that one frigate had been lost at anchor in the Sound; but in that instance the ports had been left open down nearly to the water's edge, so that this could not, any more than the loss of the Eoyal Greorge at Portsmouth, be considered as justifying the expenditure of perhaps a couple of millions of the public money, to the exclusion of improvements more imperatively required.

He was convinced, however, not only of the impropriety of expending so large a sum on the breakwater rather than on other more needful works, but that the mode of execution proposed was less eligible and more costly than others that might be devised; yet, perceiving a determination on the part of their Lordships that a breakwater should be executed in Plymouth Sound, his next object was to contrive some mode of construction which should be free from the objections to that one which had been adopted. He therefore on the 4th October presented a minute, in which he stated the principal objections to Messrs. Rennie and Whidbey's breakwater, and proposed hvo new modes for executing such a work,– which in fact were three modes,– namely, by two rows of cylindrical piers, the piers of one row opposite the intervals between the piers of the other row; 2ndly, by a single row of masses, andc.; 3rdly, by a floating breakwater. By any one of these modes the water from the Tamer, and that of the tide, would have liberty to flow between or under either of the breakwaters which he proposed. In his estimate of expenses the grand total of a breakwater of stone, equal in length to Mr. Eennie's, and including contingencies, at 15 per cent., amounted to 2 84,648.; if a floating breakwater, including also contingencies, at 15 per cent., 201,825.

To this proposal the answer of the Board was, that they " considered that there was not at present sufficient information before them, either as to the plan proposed by Messrs. Rennie and Whidbey, or of the amount of the estimate, to enable the Board to act upon the contents of this minute."

Nothing daunted where he felt himself to be advocating a benefit to the public, he further urged against the plan of Messrs. Rennie and Whidbey, that no opinions appear on record as having been given or required from Admirals or other naval officers of Her Majesty's fleets, in regard either to Plymouth Sound or to any of the other roadsteads or harbours on the south-west coast. The only naval

These modes were twice mentioned in papers printed by order of the House of Commons, first in the year 1812, and again in 1842, when they were ordered to be laid on the table.

opinions in support of the work were those of the Masters-Attendant Jackson, Hammans, and Brown, who generally corroborated Messrs. Eennie and Whidbey's statement; yet, instead of the fifty sail of the line at least which they had stated would be sheltered by their breakwater, Mr. Jackson limited the number to thirty-six under favourable circumstances, and under the guidance of an officer specially appointed for the purpose; while Mr. Hammans in his report of the loth October, 1816, said, "I have only further to observe that, during the ten years I was Master-Attendant at Plymouth dockyard, I never heard of any ship getting on her anchor in Plymouth Sound, or any other ships' anchors."

As to the object of the work, Sir Samuel observed that it was nowhere distinctly defined whether the first and most essential point of consideration were the converting Plymouth Sound into a harbour, in which ships might be adjusted in certain preconcerted situations to which they required to be warped, or whether it were the improvement of the Sound as a roadstead, to which a fleet of ships driven by stress of weather might have easy access even in the night, and bring to by their own anchors as in other good roadsteads. On this point he observed that there were already two good harbours, Hamoaze and Catwater, within the Sound, but without it no roadstead or safe anchoring ground, and therefore the improvement of it as a roadstead was of the most importance, whilst the contracting by the breakwater the entrance to about half its extent, and the closing the greater part of the passage between the Panther and Strood rocks, and contracting the passage east of the Strood rocks, would render access to that anchorage far more difficult than at present.

Lastly, he urged that if the protection to be afforded by It was on account of the danger of ships grounding on their anchors that the breakwater had been proposed-
286 LIFE OF SIR SAMUEL BEXTHAji.
floating breakwaters should on due consideration appeal-insufficient, as also if his other mode were deemed useless or injurious, he had nevertheless reason to believe that even a close pier might be formed (including the greater part of the Sound and the whole of Causand Bay), so as to render Plymouth Sound and Causand Bay both of them good roadsteads, into which the passage should be easy, thus affording a safe refuge for twice as many ships as were provided for by Messrs. Rennie and Whidbey, at even half the amount of the estimate of 1806.

Inquiry had been instituted in regard to every important work without exception that Sir Samuel, as Inspector-General of Naval Works, had proposed: his plans had been uniformly referred to the Navy Board, and by them to the officers of the ports to which the proposals related. When objections were made to his plans these objections were in writing, and were referred to him in order that he might show, in writing also, his specific reasons for considering them not well founded; and so their Lordships were enabled, with the statements on both sides before them, to come to such a decision as the reasons thus alleged should appear to justify. Had Sir Samuel.; papers on the breakwater been referred in the same way to Messrs. Eennie and Whidbey, and had they been required to state any arguments which they might have had to bring in favour of their own views, and in opposition to his, it would have been but just to both sides, and at the same time highly expedient in a public point of view, but no such course was in this case taken.

It appears that the Navy Board, perhaps roused to some sense of real economy by Sir Samuel's constant efforts to effect it, proposed to Mr. Whidbey that a quantity of rock and rubble that had accumulated in Plymouth yard should be used for the breakwater; but Mr. Whidbey (September 1st) informed them that it could not be used fur that purpose. On the 30th November Messrs. Ronnie and Whid- bey reported to the Admiralty, that for 2,334,655 feet of limestone rock, the property of the Duke of Bedford, his agent had required the sum of 11,000., that is, at the rate of about 733,. an acre for barren rock, besides other advantages of constructing and leaving a wharf in good order, andc; and as of this quantity it was calculated that when raised only two-thirds of it would be suitable for the work, it was further required on the part of the Duke that the portion unfit for the breakwater should be left for the benefit of his Grace, to be disposed of as he might deem advisable; thus, besides the 11,000., his Grace would have the additional benefit of having for his use a third of the whole quantity raised at the expense of Government.

It appeared useless for Sir Samuel to interfere further; but it is noted on his copy of the above-mentioned proposal, that there was a great mass of stone suitable for the purpose in the upper part of the dockyard, and in various other properties of G- overnment, in situations where it had been deemed advisable to propose pay-in and laro-e sums for the removal of it in order to level its site. This breakwater in Plymouth Sound has been productive of mischievous results, which will be mentioned presently, and which show how unwise it is to adopt the plans of any man, however eminent in his profession, without fully investigating their merits and defects.

The first intimation of the breakwater received either by the Navy Board collectively, or the civil engineer individually, was by a letter, signed by three of the Lords of the Admiralty, acquainting the Board that the Prince Regent had sanctioned the construction of a pier and breakwater in Plymouth Sound, according to a plan prepared by Messrs. Rennie and Whiclbey, and directing the Board to render assistance in furnishing several costly articles. The Board was further recommended to consult with that engineer, and with their Master-Attendant Whidbey.

This order placed Sir Samuel in a most embarrassing position, since among the duties of his office it was expressly stated to be his " peculiar province to examine and suggest alterations and improvements in all plans for new works." He had lately been greatly blamed, on account of some injudicious works at Woolwich, in which he had had no concern, and where he could not be considered as implicated in the mischief that had been done, unless it were supposed that he ought to have interfered so as to have prevented their execution. He had reason to doubt whether the plans of Mr. Eennie– eminent as was this engineer– were at all times the best that might be devised, or that his statements were uniformly correct; and the late inquiry in regard to his works at Great Grrimsby had brought to light, unsought for, considerable failures, and particularly a disregard of economy in the mode of execution.

Sir Samuel could not but feel the more anxiety owing to the thought which he had himself bestowed on the subject of a breakwater in Plymouth Sound; entertaining, conjointly with Lords Spencer and St. Vincent, an opinion that the money required for such a work might be much more advantageously employed elsewhere.

Of the three modes which he suggested as free from the objections which might be urged against Mr. Eennie's, the third,– namely, a floating breakwater, the estimate for which, including contingencies, at 15 per cent., was 201,825.,– was that which he preferred. His preference arose from the efficacy of a similar breakwater which he had seen, on his return from Eussia, at the port of Eevel; and he had lately had one of the same kind, on a small scale, in use at Sheerness. The floats which he designed for Plymouth were each of them prisms of 60 feet long, 30 feet deep: they were to be moored in two rows, each float of the back row behind the interval in the outer row. The great advantages of this mode were that, whilst small

PROPOSAL FOR A FLOATING BREAKWATER. 289 vessels might navigate between the floats, large ships, should they be driven against the breakwater, would receive no injury,– at the worst, the float would be pressed downwards, and the ship be carried over it. Another very great advantage was, that such a breakwater might be moored for experiment in any part of the Sound, and be easily removed to any other part of it, if such removal should be desirable. The objection to floats of wood is the danger of their being destroyed by the worm; but, many years before, Sir Samuel had caused wood steeped in oil to be sunk for experiment in Plymouth dockyard, and it was found to have remained untouched after a long period, though similar pieces of timber, unoiled, were soon destroyed; so that on a moderate calculation of the compound interest on the money to be sunk on the proposed breakwater, compared to that on the floating one, the latter might be occasionally repaired, and eventually renewed, still leaving a great balance in favour of the floating breakwater.

Time has shown that Sir Samuel's apprehensions have been verified. The breakwater which was scarcely needed has been constructed; it has not only covered the best anchoring ground; but Causand Bay, which formerly afforded so much shelter, has been so much disturbed by the current now driven through it, that ships can no longer take refuge there. In bad weather merchant vessels have been driven upon the artificial rock and lost. The Sound is no longer a roadstead for ships seeking refuge in foul weather, since behind the breakwater vessels require to be piloted in, and when there, if numerous, they must be placed by a harbour-master. The long sea slope has proved incapable of. resisting storms, so that ten or twelve thousand a year has been spent upon it for repair; and for the protection of the lighthouse, it has been necessary to have recourse to an upright wall at that part of the long slope.

The breakwater, from its immense cost, from the length of time which its execution has required, and from its imposing appearance, has in public estimation been regarded as an important and beneficial work: but the practical benefit derived from it is far outweighed by the mischief it has caused, and which in a time of war will be still more fully disclosed.

See Report of Dover Harbour Commission, and Appendix.

CHAP. XII.

Designs for Chatham– Improvements in Dredging Machines–Inadequate Assistance in carrying out his Designs– "Works at Portsmouth– Plymouth Breakwater– His Office abolished– Eemuneration and Compensation– Counter-Claims of the Navy Board– Continued Designs– Sheerness– Employment of Women–Anonymous Charges–Departure for France, 1814– Eeturn of Napoleon from Elba– Bemoval to Tours and Paris– Death of his Eldest Son, 1816– Journey to Angouleme– Eeturn to England, 1827–Fate of the Experimental Vessels, Arrow, Net-ley, Eling, andc.– Transport Service– Interest of Money sunk in Public Works– Form of Vessels– Payment of the Navy– Illness and Death.

The previous narrative renders it unnecessary to detail with like fulness the operations or plans in which Bentham was subsequently engaged. It has already brought into view the extent and the nature of his services; it has shown that his calculations were grounded on the soundest science and the truest economy, and has disclosed the many influences which were at work to thwart changes in old practices, or the introduction of new methods which could not fail to secure a vast saving to the nation and increased efficiency in the public service. An amount of neglect or opposition, which would have roused the anger or chilled the energies of weaker men, could not deter him from carrying on his arduous labours in every subject which came within the compass of his duty.

The rejection of his plans did not prevent him from rendering valuable aid in carrying out those which were preferred to his own. When the Admiralty had come to a determination to enlarge the dockyard at Sheerness rather than construct any new naval arsenal to the eastward, he directed his efforts towards rendering Chatham efficiently u 2 subservient to Sheerness. He had known the place well from his boyhood, having there passed the greater part of his apprenticeship, during which he had been, as he said in a letter to Lord Spencer, "a great navigator of the Medway." The outline of his designs is given in a paper entitled i(Improvements proposed for the Port of Chatham." Among these are specified the straightening the course of the river Medway from its mouth up to Rochester bridge–the affording a basin contiguous to the dockyard capable of holding fifty or sixty sail of the line– the affording a similar basin for private trade near the town of Rochester, as well as other basins capable of holding the whole navy–the providing two channels from Sheerness harbour up to Chatham dockyard and the town of Rochester, in which channels of still water vessels may sail when the wind is favourable but the tide in the natural channel adverse, or wherein they may be rowed, towed, or warped when both wind and tide are adverse in the central channel–the affording a great increase of backwater for scouring and deepening the bed of the river up to the capital. By this plan, among other results, the ground dug out of the cut for the secondary river would serve to widen the existing river walls, not only for the roadway, but for habitation or other purposes; and, being situated between the two rivers, would acquire an extraordinary value.

In executing such extensive works, both as regarded security of the works themselves and their economical performance, his well-proved success gave him confidence for the future. His dredging machine was working well in twenty-seven feet water at Sheerness; by degrees improved apparatus had been added to it; and for the formation of new ground, the mud barges which he had proposed in the year 1800 were competent to the delivery of mud or soil at a considerable height above the level of the water in which they floated. To render the steam dredging vessel and its apparatus competent to work in very shallow water, or even on dry land, he further contrived a modification of this vessel by which, when put to clear away high banks of mud, or even to dig and raise solid ground, the vessel with its apparatus would, as it advanced, clear a channel for itself.

There is no doubt but that the public service would have derived much greater benefit from the exercise of Bentham's genius if he had been properly supported. But his department would not supply adequate assistance for carrying on even the usual routine of its business. He therefore proposed that he might be allowed to engage for a short time, at a guinea a day, Mr. Edmund Aikin, who had shown by his publications that he had studied both ancient and modern architecture, and who was willing, and from his practical experience capable, of following up Sir Samuel's ideas of economy. Sir Samuel had grounded this proposal on the fact of his having several important works to plan, and that he (to use his own words) " looked upon it as very desirable, after so much of the design for a public work is determined on as depends on considerations of use, that more attention should be paid than hitherto has been in regard to the works of my department, particularly those relative to the dockyards, to the giving them an appropriate beauty and grandeur of appearance." The Admiralty replied that they were "not aware of any buildings or works ordered to be taken in hand which require any particular beauty or grandeur of appearance, and therefore cannot comply with the request of the civil architect and engineer, who has already sufficient assistance to carry on the duties of his office."

The assistance he asked for being refused, he determined to engage Mr. Aikin at his oivn expense, to receive him in his house and at his table, as well as an additional draughtsman, at the cost of three guineas a day for months–a sum exceeding the amount of the salary he was himself receiving.

His attention at this time was devoted to the completion of his designs for Sheerness. In their fulness of

U 3 minute detail they embrace every want which applies to arsenals in general, while they specially provide for the particular requirements at Sheerness. Soon after these designs were transmitted to the Navy Board, he was called upon to state what service he was employed on at Portsmouth. In reply he mentioned, among many other subjects, the testing of copper sheathing, about which doubts had again been raised; the extension of metal mills, the design for an enlarged millwright's shop, seasoning-houses, covered docks, andc.

Not long afterwards, the Comptroller of the Navy wrote that "Mr. Whitbread has moved for copies of all your minutes in regard to the breakwater in Plymouth Sound;

they have been all sent to the Admiralty, in pursuance of the order of the House of. Commons, but Mr. Whitbread altered his order last night, and contents himself with having those of the 24th September and the 4th October last, with the estimate attached; and they alone were presented by Mr. Croker and ordered to be printed." The day following he learnt from a friend that the rest were withheld, as containing reflections on Mr. Eennie. This fear of laying such "reflections" before the public might, perhaps, be taken as a proof of their justice. Had they been false, their refutation would certainly have followed their examination in the House of Commons. The papers so withheld he forwarded to Mr. Abbot, Speaker of the House of Commons, who in his letter in reply said,– " As to Eennie's credit with the Admiralty Board, and his discredit with the Navy Board, it seems to me that you are called upon by every motive, official and personal, to discuss his plans and proceedings, although it is not improbable that the premature and apparently irregular favour given by the Admiralty to his projects may have made them more angry at the freedom with which his conduct was treated in the paper (22nd August)." Again: " In truth the Board collectively, as well as yourself individually, would make but a sorry figure upon any investigation of this business, if it should appear that all or any of you had, in disregard of antecedent practice, and dereliction of your specific duties, abstained from making every representation upon so important a concern which your official judgment dictated." Many other subjects were discussed in the same long letter. At its end the Speaker adds,–" I will not conclude upon the main subject without adding that I do not regret your not having had your expected audience of Mr. Yorke, for be assured that you do yourself infinitely more justice by delivering yourself in writing, than by any personal conference. Few men surpass you in clearness and strength of statement upon paper of whatever you wish should make a deep and lasting impression; but in audiences and conferences a thousand accidental circumstances may prevent anybody (and you quite as much as anybody I know) from saying all that he intended, or in the way intended; and nothing can insure that a conversation is rightly understood or remembered."

His endeavours to provide a complete naval arsenal to the eastward were followed by the adoption of Mr. Eennie's plans for Sheerness. It is but justice, therefore, to Sir Samuel to give a comparison of the estimated expense of each design, and the accommodations which they respectively afforded,– this comparison having been made at the time, 1812:–

According to According to Sir
Mr. Rennie's plan. Samuel Bentham's plan.
1,000,000
Estimated expense. 1,762,495
Ordinary docks. 3
Completely covered and enclosed docks for the largest ships. None.
Docks for occasional use for the largest ships None.
Docks for frigates. 1.
Wharfage in the interior of a basin whereat ships of the line could lie to fit. 4.
Length of the above wharfage in feet. 1,600
Wharfage towards the river for vessels of different draughts to lie at low as well as at high water. Less than 800. 1,300

U 4 3,900

As to the estimate, Mr. Rennie's was an estimate in the usual way, but it was accompanied with expressions of apprehension that from the badness of the ground unlooked-for sources of expenditure might arise. Sir Samuel's estimate, on the contrary, for the under-water works on the bad soil, was based on prices for which the same contractors offered to contract,– engaging at the same time to run all risks.

Shortly after that, whilst confined at home by illness, but still labouring in his official duty, he received notice that the office he held at the Navy Board was abolished! He had not before had the most distant or slightest hint that such a measure had been in contemplation.

The abolition had been sanctioned by an order in Council, dated the 28th November, 1812, and the fact was communicated to Sir Samuel by the following letter from the First Lord of the Admiralty:–

" Admiralty, December 3rd, 1812. "Sir,– An Order in Council having been issued, directing that a new arrangement of the Navy Board shall take place, w r herebv the civil architect and engineer is no longer to be a member of that Board, and the office is abolished, I would suggest to you the propriety of soliciting from the Prince Regent such remuneration for your services and compensation for the loss of your office as his Royal Highness in Council may be pleased to allow. I shall be happy to render any assistance in my power towards your obtaining such allowance to a proper and reasonable extent; and as you will now be at liberty to offer your professional services to the public at large, I have no doubt but that the Navy Board will be ready to avail themselves of your skill, whenever the work to be performed shall be of such a nature as in their opinion to require your advice and superintendence. " I am, Sir,

" Your most obedient and humble servant,

" Melville."

The latter part of this communication might have been construed as an intended insult, had not the preceding sentences manifested good will. Architecture and civil engineering never could have been considered as Sir Samuel's profession. Naval architecture might have been so termed, but his profession, if any particular one, was military. Astonished and hurt though he certainly was on perusal of this communication, he immediately requested Lord Melville's instructions as to the mode in which he should apply to the Prince Eegent. His Lordship, on the 5th, " recommended his presenting a memorial at the Council Office, founded on the Order in Council. In the usual course of business in that department it would be referred to the Board of Admiralty for their opinion."

The abolition of the office was not communicated to the Navy Board till the 5th December.

He immediately submitted the memorial.

That Lord Melville was sincerely desirous of amply remunerating Sir Samuel for his services there cannot be a doubt. His Lordship took measures to effect this purpose in a manner which seemed most friendly and satisfactory, by desiring to see Sir Samuel's near connection and friend the Speaker, who declined the interview, and stated his reason for so doing.

"Admiralty, December 11, 1812.

" My dear Sir,– My motive for wishing to converse with you on the subject of Commissioner Bentham's situation, was a desire to promote his interest, and remunerate his services to as great an extent as the circumstances of the case would allow. He has, at my suggestion, presented a memorial to Council, praying a compensation for his services; and it was upon the amount of that allowance that I wished to have had the pleasure of seeing you, being desirous that it should, if possible, be equal to the expectations of himself and his friends.

" I have the honour to be, my dear Sir,
" Your very faithful and obedient servant,
"Melville.
" The Right Hon. the Speaker."

But the question of Sir Samuel's compensation and remuneration liugered on, and the Speaker, in a letter to Sir Samuel Kidbrook (3rd January, 1813), says,– "I have not heard one word from Lord Melville, or of course I should have told you."

" Perhaps you will begin to think I was not very wrong in declining the verbal invitation to a conference with the First Lord; for even when solicited in writing, it does not appear to have been very rapid in its productiveness. But silence on all this business is best. Anything more may do harm, and give your opponents a handle which they seem quite ready to lay hold of."

On the 12th February Sir Samuel was informed that the Prince Eegent had referred his memorial for the consideration and opinion of the Admiralty, and that their Lordships desired him to state his age and the time he had been in the service, specifying the different offices in which he had served.

On receipt of this, he was advised at the same time to submit to their Lordships a brief statement of the services he had rendered. This necessarily was a work of some time, as he determined not to mention any one of them without reference to the official written documents in relation to each, so that it was not till the 31st March that he was enabled to comply with their Lordships' commands.

In this paper, after giving full details, he submitted that his was not a case of superannuation. It was not on the score of age, infirmity, or incapacity that compensation had been prayed for, but in consequence of the abolition of the office he held by patent.

He urged that he had pursued the course pointed out by him for the effecting naval improvements at his oivn personal expense, without receiving any salary or pecuniary aid from the public purse,–that he was placed in both the offices he held, without any solicitation of his own; that he had been allowed to expect that a salary of 2000. a year would be assigned to him; and that " it was in the persuasion that I should receive this salary that I relinquished the emoluments and honours that awaited me in the service of a foreign power."

He continued: "As to remuneration for services, I cannot but hope that it will be grounded on a consideration of the benefits which the public has derived from my services. For the purpose, therefore, of enabling their Lordships to take a view of them with the more facility, I have drawn up a statement, which I take the liberty of submitting herewith to their Lordships' consideration."

He added that in this statement he had not noticed any services that could be called in the regular line of his duty, " but have confined myself to such services as originated in myself, and being of a kind for the non-rendering of which no blame could have attached to me."

Sir Samuel put a copy of these papers into the Speaker's hands; but it was not till the 5th May that he returned them, saying, "Unexpectedly I found some hours yesterday which I could employ in reading the enclosed papers. I am highly gratified by their contents.

" Upon the scrap of paper which accompanies this note you will see some typographical queries which, if you can make them out, may be worth your attention." Some recommendations as to particulars of proceedings followed.

The " scrap of paper " noted fifteen different pages from the general title to page 166,—a proof that the Speaker had perused the whole with attention; and at the bottom of that scrap he wrote,–"A noble Monument of Sagacity, Industry, and Perseverance."

The eulogium was gratifying, and showed that the attention which the Speaker paid to Bentham's case was founded upon a personal investigation of its real merits.

Time passed on. Sir Samuel's salary was at an end, and neither compensation nor remuneration was granted; so that on the 19th May he wrote to the Speaker, begging him now to endeavour to ascertain whether the settlement were likely to take place which Lord Melville had promised to bring to a satisfactory and speedy conclusion. The Speaker on the 20th enclosed it to his Lordship, requesting his attention to it,– " As," he said, "I take a very sincere concern in what respects General Bentham's situation and interests, I cannot forbear expressing my earnest hope that your Lordship's favourable intentions towards him may be now carried into effect."

His Lordship the same day wrote in answer,– " I do not wonder at General Bentham's beginning to feel that a very long delay has occurred in bringing his business to a close. A Bill, however, is preparing on which I have had some conversation with Mr. Yansittart, and have desired Mr. Croker to settle with him as to the bringing it forward. There seemed to be a doubt some days ago as to whether it ought to be confined to the Naval Department, or extended to all other branches of the public service where pensions were to be given by order in Council, and afterwards voted annually in the naval estimates. The latter seems a very innocent and safe power to leave in the hands of the Crown; and I can scarcely think it was intended to be taken away."

In a conference which the Speaker had had with Lord Melville, his Lordship said that he considered that the full salary of office should be granted as compensation for its loss. As to remuneration for extra services, when the Speaker enumerated some of the most important of them, Lord Melville exclaimed, on the mention of the metal mills, "There he stands upon a rock."

The next document is a letter from his Lordship to the Speaker (11th June, 1813), in which he says,–"I cannot

This was related to Sir Samuel by the Speaker.

come to the conclusion that I shall be able to propose more for him than the annual allowance which I mentioned to you;" and in reference to remuneration for extra services, after speaking of the need there would be to go to parliament, he adds that, independent of that, "I think we should find it an awkward precedent to deal with." He added, "I am very desirous to have the matter of the pension settled in the first place," and said that Mr. Croker had given notice of the Bill to be brought to amend the Superannuation Act, adding in a postscript,– "I think I formerly mentioned to you that I should not deem it just that his income should be diminished in consequence of the abolition of his office."

The Speaker communicated this letter the same evening to Sir Samuel, who replied on the following noon:–

" It is some consolation to have such an assurance that my income will not be diminished in consequence of the abolition of my office, and I trust that the manner of doing it will make the pension free of all deductions, or make it nominal in amount sufficient to cover them, and that I shall receive this pension from the day when my salary ceased.

"It also gives me much satisfaction to see that Lord Melville seems to admit that my services are not unworthy of distinct remuneration, whatever may be the difficulties to be encountered in the obtaining it. As to the precedent it would afford, considering it in a general point of view, without regard to my particular case, the rewarding any extra and separate services so clearly beyond what are required by the tenor of an official appointment–as documents will show my services to have been– could not but prove highly beneficial to the public, since a public officer would thereby have grounds to hope that by exerting himself beyond the ordinary duties of his situation, he might obtain for his family some provision proportionate to what he might otherwise have realised had he employed the same exertions for his own private emolument"

These opinions Sir Samuel had entertained from a very early period of life; and the greater his insight became into the management of public concerns, the stronger became his conviction that, to induce men of real intelligence to enter or continue in the service of the public, it was essential to hold out to them examples in which extraordinary abilities and extraordinary industry should be specially rewarded. The want of such a prospect has actually driven many able men to quit the public service and embark in private trade. Yet examples are not wanting where Government has accorded remuneration for extraordinary services.

On the 13th the Speaker, addressing Lord Melville, said,– " As to the remuneration General Bentham claims, and the difficulties stated by your Lordship, they seem to be so much balanced, that I do not, for my own part, see what is to be done for the present; and that subject, I should think, must necessarily be reserved for subsequent consideration, although it is impossible for General Bentham to acquiesce in any imputation on his conduct which might result from the abolition of his office, or to allow that he has been an unprofitable servant to the public.

"The impediments, however, to the allowance of his claims for remuneration, and also to the allowance of his other claims for the expenses of his Russian mission (which expenses the Navy Board have not thought themselves at liberty to allow), place General Bentham altogether in a situation of considerable hardship. And I should hope that the very difficulty of recompensing his services, which are not denied to have been meritorious, may induce your Lordship the more willingly to render him every just assistance in obtaining or scrutinising the payment of what he considers to be a strict debt from the public on his Kussian accounts, and for which I understand he has already memorialised the Treasury."

Sir Samuel's claims on account of the Eussian mission arose from the disallowance by the Navy Board of the monthly sum which he had charged, conformably to the promise of ministers on sending him to that country.

His accounts had shown that a sum of 5308. 18s. 3c?. was due to him; but the Navy Board having recommended that his allowance should amount to less than half the sum which, on the faith of ministers, he had depended on, stated, on the contrary, that a balance of 816?. 14s. 2 d. was due from him to the public. They had repeatedly required him to repay that sum, and at length informed him that, if not paid by a certain day, he would be proceeded against legally. But, fully convinced of the justice of his claims, he replied that his reasons for not paying in that sum were that, " having accepted that mission under certain promises which still appear to me to have entitled me to the balance stated in my accounts, I have intended, and still intend, to present a memorial on the subject."

It was not, however, till the 30th December, 1815, that the Navy Board acquainted him that "the Admiralty, having signified to us, by their order dated the 11th ultimo, that they have had under their deliberate consideration the whole of the papers on the subject of the balance claimed by you on your accounts during the time you were employed in Eussia for the purpose of building ships for His Majesty's service,– together with the opinion of the Attorney and Solicitor-General and Counsel for the affairs of the Admiralty, that the reference which was made to Count Woronzoff, with his decision thereon, is binding as to the rate of allowance which tvas to be made to you; and having been pleased to allow your claims to the following extent" (here follow details of accounts) "we have to inform you that, in consequence of these directions, we have caused a bill to be made out to you in payment of 3467?. Ss. 8c?., as shown by the enclosed statement."

This decision of their Lordships disallowed interest on the sum due to Sir Samuel, which, for the many years he had been deprived of the capital, was a very serious pecuniary loss to him. Up to this time (the end of 1815) the interest, reckoned at 5 per cent., amounted to upwards of 1600. Nor was this the only pecuniary loss which he had sustained in consequence of the mission. He had been obliged at the outset to sell about 2000. worth of investments in the public funds to provide the outfit for the mission. This was sold at the low war prices of 1805; its repayment was now at a time of peace, when stocks had risen, so that the repurchase into the public funds of the sum which he had withdrawn for this service was made at a heavy loss.

But this transaction affords another example of the inconceivable disregard which the Naval Department exhibits of the value of the interest on capital,–inconceivable, because so great a portion of the annual sums which Government has to provide is, on the very face of the annual budget, to pay interest on capital borrowed by the State. It has been seen that Sir Samuel repeatedly exhibited, but without avail, the losses habitually sustained by the public from a disregard in the Naval Department of the value of interest on money.

Even his arrears of salary, now a twelvemonth overdue, had not been paid; but, habitually limiting his expenses to the extent of his means, he reduced his establishment to the utmost, and contrived to exist, without debt or encroachment on capital, till at length the Admiralty determined that his pension should be to the amount of what he had hitherto received from Government, namely 1000. a year as Commissioner of the Navy, with the addition of an allowance of 500., but both only nominal sums, subject to considerable deductions.

It might be supposed that this pension even had been granted, not on the merits of the case, but owing to the interest felt and expressed by the Speaker. But the letters above quoted prove that not even the efforts of one so politically situated as the Speaker, and so eminently distinguished for uprightness as a man, could outweigh the hostile efforts of persons whose interests had been unavoidably thwarted by Sir Samuel for the public benefit.

It was notorious that many officers in the Civil Department of the Navy profited more or less by presents, if not by what could properly be denominated bribes. Sir Samuel on various occasions had been proffered emoluments to influence his opinion, and customary percentages from merchants. It, therefore, occurred to him immediately on the abolition of his office, that he would follow the example afforded by Lord Macartney (as stated in Barrow's life of that nobleman, when he left his government at Madras, and again on his giving up his government at the Cape), and make a similar declaration on oath. Accordingly he declared on oath,– " That although in this country and in Russia various proffers have been made me, directly and indirectly, of shares of profits, percentages, and presents from persons, on the eligibilhvy of whose proposals I have had to give opinions, whose bills I have had to check, on the fitness of whose works I have had to judge yet I never have, during the time I have held those offices, directly or indirectly, derived any emolument whatever beyond my public and official salary and allowances."

This declaration made on oath, and duly verified in the customary manner, was sent by Sir Samuel to Lord Melville.

After the first surprise occasioned by the abolition of the office had passed away, and the mortification, it may be added, that eminent services should thus be treated, Sir Samuel occupied himself assiduously in completing his statements in regard to the proposals that had been referred to him.

He also drew up a paper on the employment of females, having observed and lamented the depravity of a large

proportion of the female population at our great seaports; and this was not confined to the very lowest class, but unfortunately, in too many instances, extended upwards to the daughters of workmen in the dockyards, where they were exposed to much temptation. Even the bringing their fathers' dinners to the dockyard was a pernicious practice, as leading them abroad, and unsettling them for steady occupation at their homes. After much reflection, he felt assured that, by affording useful and remunerative employment to young women, many might be kept out of temptation's way, while their earnings would much assist the parents of numerous families. It was a most difficult attempt to make: general opinion was against it, as well as that of some of the persons most devoted to him, who foresaw the opposition to be encountered. He had, however, determined to make the attempt, had his ropery and sail-cloth manufactory been established. There were some parts of the work to be performed quite suitable for female hands and strength. He proposed to place women only as superintendents of those operations, and to have no admixture of boys or men. He had, besides, in view the extension of this manufactory to the making up of such articles as sacks and bags and colours, and, by degrees, to that of slops generally,– articles which are known to be often so ill put together as to require more or less resewing.

With these minutes terminated Sir Samuel's communications with the Navy Board, as required by the duties of his late office. He thus concisely called attention to objects of public interest, though he could no longer have a part in carrying them into effect.

This duty to the public done, his last letter to the Board became a duty, as he said, "I owe to myself," to take his own words from that letter. An anonymous letter on the subject of the works at Sheerness, addressed to the Right Honourable Spencer Percival, and transmitted by the Ad- miralty to the Navy Board, had contained aspersions on his probity. He was absent from town on the receipt of that letter; and on his return it was only accidentally that he heard of it, when, on expressing his intention of making some observations on it to exonerate him, his colleagues assured him that no suspicions to his prejudice could be entertained on the subject, either by the Board or by their Lordships, so that he did not withdraw time from the business of his office for the purpose of answering that attack upon him. " But now, however, on the abolition of the office of Civil Architect and Surveyor, it has become a duty I owe to myself to have a written record, showing the total want of foundation for the unjustifiable assertions contained in the builder's letter."

The accusations brought against him had been that he had connived at and caused a private offer to be made for the carrying on the works at Sheerness; that it operated to the exclusion of all other builders; that he had artfully contrived to get this offer made through the resident Commissioner; that though it was his duty to promote competition, he had prevented it by recommending work to be done by persons (known and responsible), instead of taking the lowest offer by public tender.

In a full and minute reply he showed the impossibility of any artful connivance by a reference to letters and documents; and that, so far from having prevented competition, he had been more successful in regard to those works in obtaining offers for their execution at lower prices a than it is usual to expect from any officer in the public service, or to find effected in regard to public works of this nature."

And further, for' the satisfaction of his friends, he drew up and published a statement of his services, copies of which he forwarded, amongst others, to the Earls Spencer, Liverpool, Grey, and Mulgrave, as well as to Mr. Croker x 2 and Mr. George Eose. From the Eight Honourable Thos. Grenville, who had been First Lord of the Admiralty during his absence in Eussia, he received the following reply:–

" Cleveland Square, 6th Jul, 1813. Dear Sir,– I have this moment received the favour of your note, together with the book which accompanied it, for which I beg to offer my best acknowledgments. Nobody who has been connected in any degree with the details of the naval service in later years can be ignorant of the advantages which it has derived from your exertions. I shall be sorry, for the sake of that service, if the statement which you publish announces a probable close of your labours in it. I should be sorry, for your sake, if I could believe that there was any danger of liberal remuneration being withheld from laborious and meritorious service, such as yours has been."

The fatigue and anxiety attendant on his endeavours to promote the interest of that branch of the service to which he belonged had materially injured his health. When in the following year the King of France was restored, and the continent became open, he was advised to try the effects of a warmer climate, and temporary absence was thought desirable from scenes where his services had merited both reward and consideration, but where of late his best endeavours had been thwarted or repressed. To give his sons an opportunity of seeing France and Italy before the age at which a steady application to their future profession would be requisite, afforded another reason for spending two or three years abroad. In the autumn, therefore, of 1814, he embarked, with all his family, from Portsmouth for Havre.

France at that time appeared in an aspect totally different from what he had seen it under the ancient rqjime, and wholly unlike what in the course of a few years it became. At the time of his landing, the people generally were enthusiastic in their eulogies of the English; officials, as well as others, were anxious to show their good will; so that at the custom-house his baggage, including some plate and other articles, either prohibited or subject to high duties, were passed free. He had intended to remain for a time at Blois; but he heard on the spot that the winters were severe–sometimes cold enough for the river to be frozen over at the bridge; and as he could find nothing suitable at Tours, he went down the Loire, and took a furnished house at an easy distance from Saumur, in which he established himself for the winter, providing good masters for his children, and making acquaintance with several families of the neighbourhood. Towards spring of the following year, signs of some contemplated movement for the restoration of Buonaparte began to appear. Under the pretext of selling needles, petty pedlars insinuated themselves into the cottages of the peasantry and little farmers, vaunting the glory which the nation had acquired under the Emperor. Some of these men were supposed to be able men of a higher class, disguised with a view to influence the opinions of the rural population. Others, probably agents meditating a revolution, sang ballads to the disparagement of Louis XVIII, to render him ridiculous in the eyes of the people; one especially represented the monarch as a potato-eater. Potatoes were not for many years afterwards in common use, and they were despised as an article of food. After a little time tokens of approaching insurrection appeared in higher classes: the Sous-Prefet of Saumur, at a ball during the carnival, had his apartments ornamented with bees in the hangings; this was shortly before the 1st of March. The decoration was applauded, of course, by Buonapartists, but severely commented on by Royalists. A pleasurable agitation was apparent in the one party, anxious dismay in the other. At length, when the landing of the Emperor was known, his adherents were active, and Sir Samuel felt it but prudent to escape from a place which seemed likely x 3 to be a seat of war. He therefore applied for and obtained, through his friend the Count de Segur, a special passport from the Minister of the Interior for his safe and free passage across France to any of the other continental states. By the time it arrived, matters had assumed a warlike aspect in the surrounding country. The discharge of musketry, sometimes of cannon, was occasionally heard in the neighbourhood. Men, evidently from the whiteness and delicacy of their hands gentlemen, but disguised in the peasant's dress, came inquiring the way to some town or village in La Vendee. All boats on the Loire were withdrawn, and the passage of the bridge across it was about to be interdicted, when Sir Samuel and his family took their departure. By this time the influx of English families had been considerable in many parts of France; Tours was particularly chosen by many as a place of temporary residence; and, as might be expected under such circumstances, British subjects easily made acquaintance with each other. On consultation with them, there appeared to be less danger in remaining there than there would be in travelling through the eastern frontiers, which were about to be the seat of war. The whole family remained quietly in a country house near that town.

One night, after the battle of Waterloo, the noise of a carriage passing rapidly over the bridge was loud enough to wake the family, though half a mile distant,– it was so remarkable that it attracted the notice of all. It was Buonaparte himself flying for his freedom and his life. The reinstatement of Louis XVIII. made little change at Tours beyond that of again turning the board, on one side of which was painted " Rue de la Republique," on the other " Rue Royale." All was tranquil and seemed to promise peace, till a part of the Imperial army was sent from the north to Tours. These troops seemed from their first arrival discontented and menacing; a day was fixed for the celebration of a " Te Deum " in the cathedral on the reinstate- ment of the king. In the way to the cathedral, by some back streets, groups of this Annee de la Loire, as it was called, were seen scowling and whispering with each other; and in the sacred building itself, an appearance of general uneasiness rendered it prudent for an Englishman to return home. The next day a kind of domiciliary visit was made by officers of this army to houses suspected to be adverse to them, and altogether matters bore a threatening appearance. Sir Samuel again decamped, going by Le Mans to Paris. At Le Mans all was enthusiasm for the king. He found Paris in the occupation of the allies. His friend Count Michel, now Prince Woronzoff, had a high command in the Eussian army. Sir Samuel had the pleasure of renewing acquaintance with him and many old friends, amongst others the Duke de Richelieu, now at the head of the ministry, the Count de Segur and his sons, Monsieur de la Harpe, Count and Baron de Damas, the Duke de Liancourt. On his first calling on the Duke de Richelieu he would not give his name, from a fancy to see whether some twenty years had so altered him as to prevent his being recognised. They met at first as strangers; but almost instantly the Duke, French fashion, threw his arms round him, exclaiming, "Mon cher Bentham." From this time to his Grace's death an intimate friendly intercourse subsisted between them. The Duke, as a young man, had been remarkable for a soberness of manner, thought, and conduct different from the generality of young Frenchmen. Bentham used to tell him he was the only Frenchman he had ever known to arrive at years of discretion before thirty. Amongst the English with whom he associated, were his old friends Lord and Lady Colchester: he also made acquaintance with the great traveller Baron von Humboldt, and many other scientific men of different nations. The autumn and early part of the winter were spent most agreeably in such society; but a fatal blow was awaiting him. His x 4 eldest son, a most promising youth of sixteen, was seized with a lingering malady, and died in March of the year 1816. The father bore the loss with resignation, but his sufferings were acute. Many a little incident, and many a scrap of an unfinished letter, found after his own death, bear testimony to the depth of his sorrow. When his boy was interred, it was the father who threw the first earth upon the coffin.

All his plans were now disarranged, but his own health seemed to require a warmer climate. The illness of a daughter forbade immediate travelling; but he removed from the scene of his loss to Arcueil, where, lodged in a part of Monsieur Berthollet's chateau, he had opportunity of seeing many scientific friends of that distinguished chemist. Among those of Madame Berthollet was Voltaire's " belle and bonne," who paid a weekly visit of a couple of days. The lady, tall and thin, was still active, and retained the manners of the old regime.

Previously to setting out for the south, the Duke de Eichelieu gave him letters of introduction to the Prefets of all the departments through which he had any chance of passing.

A visit of a few days to Count Chaptal and his family near Amboise was very interesting. He possessed a large fund of scientific knowledge, and communicated it agreeably; and his manufactory of beet-root sugar was in full activity,– its products excellent.

On arriving at Angouleme, autumn was too far advanced for further progress that year; the town afforded agreeable society, into which he was introduced at the Prefet's table. He therefore hired a furnished house half a mile from the town, and took possession of it for winter quarters.

Sir Samuel Eentham remained on the continent till 1827; but his retirement did not cool his ardour for improvements in the department of his predilection– the naval. After an absence of twelve years he returned home, with the determination of publishing some essays which he had in preparation, accompanied by a variety of documents, chiefly selected from his official papers.

His experimental vessels had all of them, with the exception of the Eling, come to their end in actual service. The Arrow in 1805, her complement (including a dozen passengers) being 132 men and boys, was in company with the bomb vessel Acheron in the Mediterranean, and had thirty-two merchantmen from Malta under convoy, when, with the Acheron, she attacked two French frigates, the Hortense and the Incorruptible,–each of forty guns, and with a complement of 640 men. After a close action of an hour and twenty minutes, the Arrow, being much disabled, and compelled to strike, settled on her beam ends, and went down, but not without rendering the French frigates unfit for service. The vessels under convoy were saved by this gallant action; and in consequence the captain of the Arrow was posted as his reward. However brave, no officer in any other sloop, supported only by a bomb vessel, would have ventured to attack two frigates of such force as were the Hortense and Incorruptible.

The Dart, after having been thirteen years in active service, was taken to pieces at the Barbadoes, 1809, for what reason no information could be obtained, but probably from damage received in action.

The Eedbridge was unfortunately wrecked in 1808, but the circumstances are not known.

The Millbrook was said also to have been wrecked, but the vessel to which this accident happened was a merchantman of the same name. It is not known how long she continued in serviee.

The Netley, after ten years' active service, was captured in the West Indies by the French frigate Thetis, accompanied by the brig Sylphe; was afterwards retaken, and employed again in the British service under the name of Unique.

Lastly, the Elingwas broken up at Portsmouth in the year 1814, having been not less than eighteen years in service. As this occurred after the time of the abolition of Sir Samuel's last office, he had no personal opportunity of ascertaining her state and appearances; but, considering how desirable it would have been on this occasion to examine whether the innovations introduced in her construction with a view to strength had been successful, he wrote to the Navy Board, urging the expediency of directing that particular attention should be paid to the state of connection in which the several parts of the vessel might be found. He never received any reply to that letter, or could obtain any official account of her appearances; he therefore endeavoured to obtain particulars from a shipwright officer (Joseph Helby), then residing near Portsmouth; but his answer was, "No one can give me any information concerning her. The only information I can give respecting her is what I had from Sir H. Peake, in London; he was at Portsmouth during her being taken to pieces; he told me that her timbers and bottom were sound and good; the only defects were the bulkheads, which were of fir; and the fir generally was perished in a great measure." " I do not believe she ever had any serious repairs." From this and other sources he understood that this vessel still exhibited proofs of the efficiency of the expedients that had been resorted to in her construction for giving strength; while her apparent defects had arisen from the decay of the fir timber which had been in some parts substituted for oak. The perishable material, fir, had been introduced in consequence of the great and increasing scarcity of oak at the time when she was built; and, in point of fact, that so perishable a material as fir should have been found to last for eighteen years was in itself a beneficial result of the experiment.

On looking over the most authentic accounts of the duration of vessels of war in time of war, it appeared that eight years was the average. The average duration (and always in actual service) of Sir Samuel's experimental vessels was twelve years and a half; that is, half as long again as vessels of the ordinary construction, although these were built of the more durable material– oak, whilst some very essential parts of Sir Samuel's were of fir. Scouted and despised as they were at first, they have fortunately served as models for the introduction of some of the most important improvements that have yet been made in naval architecture: for example, diagonal braces, lined bulk-heads, metallic water tanks, andc. andc.

On the 7th March, 1828, he addressed a letter to Mr. Croker, on the subject of the transport service, in which, among other suggestions, he remarked more particularly that in times of peace, if, instead of having vessels for any transport or packet service, vessels of war were, instead of lying in ordinary, to be employed for services of all kinds, the annual saving would amount to about 200,000?. He subjoined the estimates by which these savings were made manifest, and added a short notice of some of the collateral advantages that would result from the adoption of his proposal. This proposal, grounded as it was on the incontrovertible evidence afforded by the estimates which he furnished, had its effect at the Admiralty; and Government vessels have since then been more or less employed for transport and packet service. As yet, however, it has only been by degrees, and to a limited extent, that the measure has been adopted.

On April 13th he furnished in writing a view of savings that might be effected by manufacturing a great variety of articles on Government account, instead of procuring them in a manufactured state, stating the principal sources from which those savings would arise. Among these sources are command of capital at a less rate of interest than that at which it can be procured by private manufacturers; better insurance against disuse of an article, for procuring which capital has been sunk; and the saving which Grovernment would derive on the breaking out of war from having a skeleton establishment of the best working hands, for which there is always abundant employment in time of peace, and who would be ready, by the help of inferior hands, to carry on works to the extent required in war; security against evasive constructions of the terms of contract,– for instance, in regard to so-called improved copper sheathing, it was stipulated that, should any of it be found to have decayed within a certain period, the contractor was to provide new sheathing in lieu of the defective. In such a case the contractor was expected to have returned a sheet of new for every decayed one; but instead of that, by what might be called a quibble on the words of the contract, he could only be made to return a weight of new equal to the weight of what remained of the corroded sheets.

It happened that the chairman of the committee, Sir Henry Parnell, entertained a most decided opinion that it was impossible for Grovernment to mauufacture any article so cheap as it could be obtained by contract, so that Sir Samuel was not called on to give evidence on this subject,– one on which he, of all other men, was best informed.

He again attempted to draw attention to that great oversight in regard to finance– the taking no account of the value of interest on monies expended in public works– an oversight which Sir Samuel had embraced every opportunity of bringing to notice for above forty years. He had made his representations on the subject in a variety of forms. He now urged in a few short axioms:–

" 1st. That no work should be undertaken that will not produce an advantage equivalent to the expense it occasions."

" 2ndly. That the advantage of a work may in all cases be measured by a yearly value in money, generally arithmetically demonstrable, when otherwise capable of easy estimation."

" 3rdly. That it is not worth while to sink a capital on any public work, unless the yearly value of it, when obtained, be equal to 8 per cent, on the capital sunk,–that is, 5 per cent, for the simple average interest of the money sunk, and 3 per cent, to compensate for wear and tear of the work, together with the chance of its utility being superseded by some of the many circumstances which, at a future time, render works comparatively less perfect or less needful than at the time of their construction." Still his endeavours proved of no avail; and indeed, up to the present moment, this great desideratum in the management of public money remains wholly disregarded.

Sir Samuel's chief occupation for some time had been the preparing for the press the first of his projected naval essays; and he also caused to be published several of his official letters, under the title of " Naval Papers." These publications are now out of print; and the edition was but small. Many copies were distributed to present and former members of Administration; but they have become exceedingly scarce, although they are to be found in the library of the United Service Club, and some other public establishments; and a critique of them appeared in page 306 of the first part of the "United Service Journal" for 1829. The appearance of that critique drew his attention to the " United Service Journal," and observing in it " a biographical sketch of Paul Jones," containing many mis-statements, Sir Samuel furnished the editor with an account of the actions in the Liman, in which Paul Jones had so falsely ascribed to himself the glorious result of the three actions in question.

About this time the question happened to be mooted, how far one of the reasons stated for the abolition of the office of Inspector-General of Navy Works had been well founded, namely, the uncompensated expense it had occasioned? This led to the mention of a variety of services which it had performed, and which were now paid for at a greater amount of cost, and to a calculation and statement of how far that establishment alone went, by the savings it had produced, towards payment of the officers in the Inspector-Greneral of Navy Works' office. It appeared that on the 1st January, 1812, the capital sunk on the metal mills had been all of it, by degrees, paid off by the profits of the mills, together with all interest and compound interest on that capital, as well as all debts of every kind; that there then remained in hand, in money and money's worth, upon the premises to the value of 68,215?., this capital having been created for the public by the Inspector-Greneral of Navy Works. This sum was then taken as if it had been put out to interest from that time to the end of 1827, for the purpose of creating a fund for the re-establishment of that office, when the capital and interest upon it, compounded half-yearly, were found to amount to 1,257,6 5l. The salaries of the Inspector-Greneral of Navy Works and of the officers of that office amounted to 3000?. a year; a perpetual annuity to that amount purchased in the 3 per cent. Consols, at the then price (85 per cent.) would have cost 255,000.; so that the metal mills had not only provided for the re-establishment of that office in perpetuity, but had, besides, created a surplus of above a million.

During the leisure of late years, Sir Samuel had reflected much on the uncertainty that existed as to the form best suited for a navigable vessel. He had, it is true, so far succeeded in that which he devised for his experimental vessels, as to have rendered them in every respect better sea boats than any vessels with which they had been brought into comparison; and he now saw, with satisfaction, that the best steam-boats had been constructed like his vessels in several particulars of form. Still, on considering experiments that had been made on a small scale, it seemed that a variety of influencing circumstances had never been taken into account,–such as friction on the pulleys or other apparatus used in measuring velocity, the effect of wind on the body to be moved, and the weight of the body itself. In regard to experiments on vessels themselves, the difference in speed even, consequent on form alone, remained still unascertained.

It appeared to him that the costliness of experiments made by means of vessels of war must necessarily in future prove a bar, as it had already done, to their being carried to any extent, but that very important results might be obtained by means of models on a small scale. He, therefore, considered various modes of experimenting with this view, and devised a very simple and inexpensive apparatus, by means of which several important particulars as to form might be ascertained. This done, he considered that, without pecuniary loss, the forms that had proved most advantageous in models might be given next to small craft; and so the experience afforded by their means would furnish data to be depended on for improving vessels of the greatest bulk.

Since Sir Samuel's return home, he had the gratification to find that much of former jealousy had worn away. His communications with many members of naval administration had been very flattering, and there appeared much disposition to profit by his suggestions. Place, or pecuniary reward for his exertions, he disclaimed; but when he had devised the means for making the experiments in question, he volunteered to direct the execution of them. To the Navy Board, which seemed at that time to have it most in their power to carry out such a course of experiments, he addressed several papers, which determined them to authorise the commencement, under his direction, of the set of experiments which he had suggested.

A considerable portion of his time was now devoted to the perfecting the details relative to the intended course of experiments, and in contriving a variety of instruments or meters, for measuring accurately on board ship the several circumstances both as influencing and indicating its progressive motion and direction; he also continued to employ himself in writing his second Naval Essay.

On the 7th February he addressed the Admiralty on the subject of the pay of the navy. He observed, that the plan which he now offered for the payment of the military branch of the service was formed on the same principles as that which he had proposed, thirty years before, for the payment of operatives engaged in the naval arsenals; and that the general satisfaction which that mode had given, adopted as it had been for the operatives in the arsenals, led him to flatter himself that a similar plan for paying the military personnel, might be thought worthy of consideration.

On the 21st February, the Secretary of the Admiralty acquainted him that their Lordships had submitted his letter on this subject to the Right Honourable C. Poulett Thomson for his consideration and report. Sir Samuel was delighted at this determination, so conformable to the practice he had advocated of obtaining individual opinions, in a form which led to discussion, and the investigation of any measure, so as to afford just grounds either for its rejection, adoption, or modification.

HIS FINAL EFFORTS. S21

The proposed experiments for ascertaining the best form for navigable vessels afford a striking example of the difficulties that stand in the way of making any course of experiments in naval arsenals. The Admiralty were known to be highly favourable to those which Sir Samuel had proposed. Sir Samuel, therefore, applied to the Comptroller, requesting him to point out the persons to whom, conformably to his and the Surveyor's wishes, he should apply on the subject; the Comptroller, thereupon, informed him that application must be made to the superior authority. Sir Samuel at first intended to request Sir J. Graham to indicate the course which he should now pursue; but although not personally acquainted with Mr. Laing, of Deptford Dockyard, yet, apprised of his zeal, talents, and skill, he sought to induce him to join in his experiments; to which he readily assented. It was then considered whether, in compliance with custom (bad as that custom was), a committee should be formed to carry Sir Samuel's plan into practice,–this committee to consist of Sir Byam Martin, Captain Beaufort, and Mr. Laing. Sir Samuel, however, though he would gladly have intrusted it to any one of these gentlemen, hesitated in giving assent to any joint assemblage of persons for the execution of any specific service, and was himself engaged in making-preparations at Mr. Maudsley's, who kindly offered the use of his manufactory, and incurred some expense in preparing models of the apparatus to be used. But Mr. Maudsley became seriously ill and died. Sir Samuel also began to suffer from the effects of bleeding, which had been necessary after an accident he met with during the preceding autumn, and his death took place on the 31st May, 1831, at his residence, 2 Lower Connaught Place.

Thus ended a career perhaps unexampled in the variety and extent of the improvements which he had devised dur-

insf a Ions and active life as a naval architect, as a civil engineer, as a mechanist, and especially as the contriver of regulations to correct abuses in the civil service of the country.

THE END.
LONDON
KIM HI) BY SloTTISWOODB AND CO.
NEW-STUlieT SQUABB
RETURN TO the circulation desk of any
University of California Library or to the
NORTHERN REGIONAL LIBRARY FACILITY Bldg. 400, Richmond Field Station University of California Richmond, CA 94804-4698

ALL BOOKS MAY BE RECALLED AFTER 7 DAYS 2-month loans may be renewed by calling (415)642-6753 1-year loans may be recharged by bringing books to NRLF Renewals and recharges may be made 4 days prior to due date

DUE AS STAMPED BELOW : n.: s "
IUN I 9-
JAN 0 7 2000
APR 2 2 200 1
SENT ON ILL
JUL 2 5 2005
U. C. BERKELEY